CRATERS OF THE SPIRIT

We are all drawn toward the same craters of the spirit—to know what we are and what we are for, to know our purpose, to seek grace.

—Joseph, in Saul Bellow's *Dangling Man*

Craters of the Spirit

STUDIES IN THE MODERN NOVEL

by

Nathan A. Scott, Jr.

CORPUS BOOKS
Washington—Cleveland

Corpus Instrumentorum, Inc.
1330 Massachusetts Ave., N.W.
Washington, D.C., 20005

First Printing 1968

Library of Congress Catalog Card Number: 68-15782

To
Amos N. Wilder
In affectionate homage

Contents

CRATERS OF THE SPIRIT

Introduction

The opening manifesto in Susan Sontag's spiritedly opinion-
ated book of two years ago, *Against Interpretation,* concludes
with a remarkable sentence—which says: "In place of a
hermeneutics we need an erotics of art."[1] Throughout many of
the essays in this volume Miss Sontag is undertaking in various
ways to define what she speaks of as "the new sensibility." Its
chief representatives, in her analysis of things, are to be found
among such artists as Milton Babbitt and Morton Feldman in
music, Merce Cunningham and James Waring in the dance,
Mark Rothko and Jasper Johns in painting, Jean-Luc Godard
and Michelangelo Antonioni in cinema, and Samuel Beckett
and Alain Robbe-Grillet in literature. For what is characteristic
of their whole period-style is a great refusal—the refusal, that
is, of the artist "to deplete the world—in order to set up a
shadow world of 'meanings.' "[2] It is precisely in such "a flight
from interpretation" that Miss Sontag perspicaciously finds the
main motivating force of art now. So what we need today, she
declares, is not a hermeneutics but an erotics of art.

In the two dozen or more pieces on film-makers and
writers and critics comprising her book, Miss Sontag is prin-

[1] Susan Sontag, *Against Interpretation* (New York: Farrar, Straus
& Giroux, 1966), p. 14.
[2] *Ibid.*, p. 7.

11

cipally concerned to describe a profile of the immediate present in cultural life, and this she does with a most engaging
impudence of partisanship and bravura of style. But though
she introduces little systematic argument about the distance at
which "the new sensibility" stands from traditionalist modernism, the undertones of much that she says make one feel that
she does, nevertheless, regard this distance as being very great
indeed. For, in one way or another, she is saying, over and
over again, that art has undergone a "transformation" in function, that it represents today a new kind of technique and is
undertaking to be "a new kind of instrument . . . for modifying
consciousness. . . ."[3] What is new is the radicalism with which
the artist, whether in cinema or painting or music or literature,
conceives the essential medium of art to be a sensory medium:
what he wants to provoke is a more intense act of *seeing,* or
hearing, or *feeling*: it is "the luminousness of the thing in
itself"[4] that he wants to render. This, as Miss Sontag believes,
is the exquisite propriety of Jack Smith's film, *Flaming Creatures,* or of a painting by Jasper Johns, or of the music of the
Beatles, or of William Burroughs' *Naked Lunch*—that here are
works of art whose surfaces are "so unified and clean, whose
momentum is so rapid, whose address is so direct that the work
can be . . . just what it is"[5]—namely, nothing other than an
"adventure in sensation."

Early on in his novel *The Man Without Qualities* Robert
Musil tells us that "no serious attempt will be made to . . .
enter into competition with reality." And it is something like
such an abdication that Miss Sontag rightly descries as a
hallmark of contemporary sensibility. For the nervousness that
we feel before a film like *Marienbad* or a novel like Robbe-
Grillet's *Le Voyeur* or the "black" paintings of Ad Reinhardt is
a result of the fact that, instead of proposing any "criticism of
life" (in the Arnoldian sense), such works as these want rather

[3] *Ibid.,* p. 296.
[4] *Ibid.,* p. 13.
[5] *Ibid.,* p. 11.

to give rise to "something like an excitation, a phenomenon of commitment, judgment in a state of thralldom or captivation. Which is to say that . . . an experience of the form or style of knowing something, rather than a knowledge of something (like a fact or a moral judgment) in itself"[6] is what the artist is aiming at. So, instead of making "statements," instead of rendering "reality," he tries to challenge and to stretch the sensorium of his reader or spectator or auditor: his principal interest is no longer in our "edification" and in the conceptual "content" of his own production, for his primary purpose has come to be that of creating an art that will have the effect of "confounding and unclosing our senses."[7] Thus the appropriate response of criticism, as it faces the new literature (as well as the new music and painting and cinema), will be an attempt at working through not another hermeneutics but, rather, a new erotics of art.

It is such a verdict that distinguishes the general line that this brilliant young critic was taking in her book of 1966, and she does indeed make us feel that she has perceived more acutely perhaps than anyone else of her immediate generation in American criticism what is decisively characteristic of the new, post-modern scene in artistic life. Apart from the vivaciousness of her intelligence and the solidity of her learning, what gives Miss Sontag's book its special charm is the unembarrassed passion of her advocacy of "the tradition of the new." Yet it is also just this fervency of partisanship which makes, finally, for too great an imbalance in the underlying poetic which constitutes her *tête de ligne*. She likes, for example, "form" rather than "content" in literature—and she is untroubled by the flatly dualistic terms in which she states her preference. She likes a literature which is "motivated by a flight from interpretation" and wants very much to give her suffrage to the current "revolution in contemporary taste [which] . . . represents a turning away from content . . . [and]

[6] *Ibid.*, pp. 21–22.
[7] *Ibid.*, p. 302.

an impatience with what made [traditionalist literary modern-
ism] . . . prey to the zeal of interpreters."[8] Which is to say that
she does not want a "literary equivalent of program music."[9]
Were she to be bitterly confronted by the necessity of making
an absolute choice as between Aristotle and Coleridge, she
would come down not on the side of Aristotelian *mimesis* but
on that of Coleridgean *imagination,* since, for Miss Sontag,
"style" is all. She quotes approvingly the Robbe-Grillet who
says: "If art is anything, it is everything; in which case it must
be self-sufficient, and there can be nothing beyond it." Which
strikes her as an appropriately drastic way of asserting the
autonomy of the work of art, its "distance from the lived reality. . . ."[10]

But though literature, in certain of its modes, does call
forth such an aesthetic, the theorist whose natural inclination is
toward this kind of premise ought not perhaps too hurriedly to
follow Rémy de Gourmont's counsel regarding "le grand
effort," "eriger en lois ses impressions personnelles. . . ." For
literature, in many of its other modes, most intimately com-
mingles poetic and noetic functions, and its distinctively aesthetic quality and power are defined precisely by this com-
mingling. It may well be true, as Lionel Trilling has suggested,
that literary art rarely finds its animating principle in ideas
which have taken the form of "pellets of intellection . . . precise
and completed, and defined by . . . their procedural recom-
mendations. . . ."[11] But, as Mr. Trilling fully understands,
when an idea has in fact taken such a form, it has already
either ceased to be itself a living cultural reality, or it has
become simply an abstract counter in a purely logical operation. For, when they are truly formative powers in the life of
the mind, ideas are not simply "pellets of intellection or crystal-

[8] *Ibid.,* p. 10.
[9] *Ibid.,* p. 11.
[10] *Ibid.,* p. 30.
[11] Lionel Trilling, *The Liberal Imagination* (New York: Viking
Press, 1950), p. 302.

lizations of thought" but are vital forces, "inescapably connected with our wills and desires, [and] . . . susceptible of growth and development. . . ."[12] In this form, they cannot be considered to be so extraneous to the stuff of literature as Susan Sontag imagines.

Miss Sontag maintains that that tradition of criticism which regards the work of art as a "statement" requiring "interpretation" represents "the revenge of the intellect upon the world." For, as she reasons, "to interpret is to impoverish": it is to turn the given actualities of existence into *another* world. But *our* world, the world as already given, "is depleted, impoverished enough": so a plague on "all duplicates of it, until we again experience more immediately what we have."[13] Yet, though Miss Sontag's stringency is occasioned by her desire to advocate that speciality of artistic idiom distinctive of "the new sensibility," she does in effect remind us that it is a kind of stringency which she is by no means the first to express—when she speaks of "the hypertrophy of the intellect at the expense of energy and sensual capability" as the "already classical dilemma" of our culture.[14] For so it is, at least one of our classical dilemmas—or so it has been felt to be since the advent of the Romantic movement. It has in fact been the desire to rescue the literary imagination from the tyrannizing imperialism of the Idea which has recurrently led theorists of art in the modern period to something like the sort of position which Susan Sontag now so ardently embraces. She speaks of "the most recent revolution in contemporary taste" as one which entails a deposition of the legacy of Eliot and a new elevation of the legacy of Pound; and, in certain respects, the ideographic tenuities of the new *avant-garde*, in their reminiscence of Pound's early imagism, would seem to bear her out. But it is not likely to be forgotten that it was T. S. Eliot himself who, more than anyone else, helped to establish as canonical

[12] *Ibid.*, p. 303.
[13] Susan Sontag, *op. cit.*, p. 7.
[14] *Ibid.*

for modern criticism the notion of ideas or rational thought (or what Miss Sontag calls "content") as alien to literary art. For it was in his essay of 1927 on "Shakespeare and the Stoicism of Seneca" that he announced that, though the literary artist may fashion his work out of the materials of systematic thought (as in the case of a Dante, who had Aquinas behind him), he does not himself engage in any sort of activity which could properly be called "thinking." "I can see no reason," said he, "for believing that either Dante or Shakespeare did any thinking on his own. The people who think that Shakespeare thought are always people who are not engaged in writing poetry, but who are engaged in thinking, and we all like to think that great men were like ourselves."[15]

But, if one has not altogether fallen under something like the kind of spell that so charms Miss Sontag in certain recent artistic movements, one cannot help but feel that the pontification in Eliot's spirited pronunciamento of forty years ago is more than slightly tinged with nonsense. He was, of course, no doubt laudably wanting, like Lessing before him, to insist upon a certain limit for poetry and to say that the poet is not only not a painter but also not a philosopher or a sage, simply a poet: yet, in doing that, he allowed his penchant for the donnish joke to get somewhat out of hand. For, if "thinking" be conceived so restrictively as to forbid our assuming it to be an activity engaged in by Dante and Shakespeare, then it must be an operation of the mind whose nature is arcane indeed. As Erich Heller has wisely remarked of Eliot's thought in this very connection,

> To define "thinking" in such a way that the activity which Shakespeare pursued in composing the speeches of Hamlet, or Ulysses, or Lear has to be dismissed as "non-thought," is to let thinking fall into the rationalist trap from which it is likely to emerge as a cripple, full of animosity against that other

[15] T. S. Eliot, "Shakespeare and the Stoicism of Seneca," *Selected Essays: 1917–1932* (New York: Harcourt, Brace and Co., 1932), p. 116.

deformed creature, mutilated in the same operation: the Romantic emotion. If thought, stripped of imaginative feeling, and emotion, stripped of imaginative thought, become the dominant modes both of thinking and feeling, the outcome is the "Leid-Stadt," that insufferable city of sorrows, or the Waste Land, in which the spirits of Nietzsche, as well as of Rilke, as well as Mr. Eliot feel ill at ease.[16]

The untidy fact, in other words, that we face here and that those theorists who have a great anxiety about the "purity" of literature would burke is that an art whose medium is language and whose material is the stuff of human experience is itself something surely not to be thought of as *contaminable* by "ideas." The difficult question that concerns how our total response to a work of art may be colored by the particular ideas that have entered into the poetic economy, especially if they happen to contravene some settled disposition or outlook of our own—this is a question that has sometimes fascinated modern criticism and that must, inevitably, figure in any adequate phenomenology of aesthetic experience. But it is not at issue in this present connection, for all that I am here wanting to assert (Eliot's testimony—and now Miss Sontag's—notwithstanding) is that poets and novelists and playwrights do have ideas, that such artists as Blake and Goethe and Melville and Dostoievski and Ibsen did "think," and that the "content" of their thought so deeply informs their distinctively *poetic* creations that any attempt to treat it as irrelevant to aesthetic appreciation must be simply absurd. It was not a "man of letters" but a philospher, and one of the most formidable thinkers of this century—Alfred North Whitehead—who reminded us that *Paradise Lost* was not written as an experiment in prosody, but was written to "justify the ways of God to men."[17] A similar annotation is to be made with respect to

[16] Erich Heller, *The Disinherited Mind* (Philadelphia: Dufour and Saifer, 1952), p. 121.

[17] Alfred North Whitehead, *Science and the Modern World* (New York: Macmillan Co., 1925), p. 117.

most of the literature that has added something of permanent value to the furniture of the imagination.

We will, of course, do well to keep as clear a view as possible of the many sharp distinctions that are to be drawn between artistic and philosophic modes of thought. Yet these distinctions, important as they are, ought not to make us forgetful of the many significant convergences between the two disciplines in cultural history—as represented, for example, in the response offered a Wagner by a Nietzsche, or in that offered a Hölderlin by a Heidegger. But not only has art often been a fecundating force in philosophic enterprise: it has also very often itself in turn been profoundly influenced by speculative reflection—as in the relationship, say, between Hopkins and Duns Scotus, or between Joyce and Vico, or between Mann and Schopenhauer. And, however rigorous may be the specialists in aesthetic formalism, their various exercises in discrimination between the "non-discursive" modalities of art and the "discursive" modalities of systematic thought can hardly obscure the fact that art and metaphysics (in one or another of its various forms—theology, philosophical anthropology, philosophy of history, etc.) do very often meet and even coalesce.

So what is required of the theorist of literature is that he not allow himself to become so intimidated by the demands for systematic consistency of a particular poetic as to lose any lively sense of the actual democracy which the world of literature embraces. For, though there is doubtless a large area of literary art that is outside the province of doctrine, there is also, as Lionel Trilling reminds us, "much of literature [which] wishes to give the sensations and to win the responses that are given and won by ideas, and it makes use of ideas to gain its effects, considering ideas—like people, sentiments, things, and scenes—to be indispensable elements of human life."[18] To allow a dedication to some critical fundamentalism to keep one from making this acknowledgment is, in effect, to refuse an

[18] Lionel Trilling, *op. cit.*, p. 289.

acknowledgment of the full catholicity of the literary order.
So let us grant, as Mr. Trilling proposes,

> . . . that the province of poetry is one thing and the province
> of intellection another. But keeping the difference well in
> mind, we must yet see that systems of ideas have a particular
> quality which is much coveted as their chief effect—let us
> even say as their chief aesthetic effect—by at least certain
> kinds of literary works. Say what we will as critics and
> teachers trying to defend the province of art from the dogged
> tendency of our time to ideologize all things into grayness,
> say what we will about the "purely" literary, the purely
> aesthetic values, we as readers know that we demand of our
> literature some of the virtues which define a successful work
> of systematic thought. We want it to have—at least when it
> is appropriate for it to have, which is by no means infrequently
> —the authority, the cogency, the completeness, the brilliance,
> the *hardness* of systematic thought.[19]

Now, however much a certain slant and emphasis in much
literature of the immediate present may to some extent call
forth in its warmest partisans the sort of critical position which
Susan Sontag advocates, the kinds of qualifications which I am
proposing for that position will also be called for, I believe,
most especially by the great classic canon of modern literature
and by the contemporary writing which stands in this general
line. For the canon comprised of the work of such writers as
Dostoievski and Hardy, Lawrence and Kafka, Eliot and
Stevens, Camus and Beckett, Faulkner and Bellow is a literature that is drenched in the stuff of ideas and doctrine: nor are
these ideas describable as "pellets of intellection," but, rather,
they are the largest sorts of metaphors and allegories about the
nature of time and politics and sexuality and salvation. Furthermore, they are ideas often so subversive of received traditions and put forward with a polemicism so intense and urgent
that, if one is to have any dealings with them at all, he must

[19] *Ibid.*, pp. 289–290.

himself in turn summon up (as the followers of John Wesley would say) his own "testimony."

Many of the senior people in Anglo-American criticism today were beginning to maintain a generation ago, in ways that were then quite startling, that a literary work, like all other works of art, is characterized by organic unity, by the fact of its having no loose ends, each part being of a piece with every other part and gathering its meaning from its position in the total context established by the whole. So rigorously was this lesson pressed home by men like William Empson and Allen Tate and Cleanth Brooks that their epigones now are often by way of drearily supposing that the appropriate attack on Forster's *Passage to India* or Stevens's *Sunday Morning* or Malraux's *Man's Fate* is one which involves the compiling of a series of notations on how page 57 anticipates page 238 and how both are tied into some sort of knot by page 296, or on how stanza IV "ironically qualifies" stanza II and how the images of linearity in stanza VII balance off or contravene the images of circularity in stanza V. But, though the study of a text no doubt needs in its early stages to have this kind of focus, it ought never to be supposed that the customary versions today of comma-counting do by themselves constitute a truly civilized mode of discourse about a work of literary art, and especially about those great modern masterpieces that are most frequently made the object of this kind of piddling. *The Castle* and *The Waste Land* and *Harmonium* and *The Good Soldier* and *Doctor Faustus* are scaffolded, to be sure, with an enormous intricacy, but they want chiefly not to call attention to the technique by which they were made—important as it may be for us to have the clearest appreciation of this—but, rather, to cross-question us into a deeper understanding of some phase of ourselves. They invite not an exercise in grammar and syntax but a further act of "testimony."

Literary humanists today are, of course, often eager to be amiable toward their philosophical colleagues in the academy and to win as large a measure of their approval as possible. They do not any longer, it is true, face a reigning philosophy so crude as that which prevailed thirty years ago, when an A. J. Ayer or a Rudolf Carnap was declaring in effect that a work of art tells us nothing more about the world than does a man's laughter or a child's scream, that it is simply a form of expressive utterance quite devoid of any genuine cognitive import. But though the contemporary analytic philosopher is less arrogant in his legislations about "the meaning of meaning" than were the early Logical Positivists, the ghosts of Positivism linger on, and Anglo-American philosophy generally assumes that the literary imagination is, in its very nature, too controlled by "subjectivistic caprice"[20] to permit us to expect from it any decisive clarification of the human reality. And literary theorists who crave the security of *certified* doctrine are often prepared now to tuck in their sails and to say that a poem or a novel does not, to be sure, compete in any way with a work of systematic thought, since its whole purpose is simply to give us the "feel" of immediate experience, the sense of the pressure of the concrete given. But we may be certain, I think, that Dostoievski did not write *The Possessed,* or Mann *The Magic Mountain,* or Eliot the *Four Quartets,* or Sartre *La Nausée* merely for the sake of recording some complex of feeling or sensation. And it is not at all from any such standpoint that we do in fact normally approach the great literature of our period.

Indeed, I am often impressed, as are no doubt many others also engaged today in university teaching, by how much the young tend to approach the classic modern canon as though it were, essentially, a body of scripture. They sometimes make one feel that they resemble the Yeats who supposed (as he suggested in his essay on Blake) that we "make our souls" out of the great literature of our period and that we

[20] Carl Michalson, *Worldly Theology* (New York: Charles Scribner's Sons, 1967), p. 48.

are likely only to "make a poorer sort of soul, by listening to
sermons or by doing or by not doing certain things."[21] They
seem to take it for granted that literature trenches upon the
Sacred, that it can be counted upon to save us—and when,
therefore, they gather in a campus auditorium for a lecture by
some distinguished visiting critic, the atmosphere is often very
much like that of an evangelical prayer meeting. "It is a deadly
error," says Jacques Maritain, "to expect poetry to provide the
supersubstantial nourishment of man."[22] Even if it may not be
quite "deadly," it is no doubt indeed an error, nevertheless. But
it is, I suspect, a better sort of error to make than that which is
made by those who tell us that literature simply gives us the
"feel" of immediate experience, or that the literary artist does
not do any "thinking" and that his work does not line itself up
behind any significant "statements." At least, when we have in
view any of the central expressions of the classic modern tradition in literature, it is the former rather than the latter kind of
error which, for all its erroneousness, will permit the deeper
penetration and the more profound act of seizure.

I should hurry on to say, however, that, as a Catholic (of
Anglican allegiance), I do not find in myself any inclination to
suppose that the religious apprehension of reality has somehow
been effectively disposed of by modern science and that we
must, therefore, seek from the poet or the novelist a viable
surrogate for religion. My own sympathy for this whole view
of things that descends in part from Matthew Arnold is very
limited indeed. Nor do I regard the artist as "a kind of super
advertising man—a specialist at arousing sympathetic emotions for the propositions which he elects to present."[23] And I
have no desire to collapse poetics into the dimensions of

[21] William Butler Yeats, "William Blake and the Imagination," in
Essays and Introductions (New York: Macmillan Co., 1961), p. 112.

[22] Jacques Maritain, *Art and Scholasticism,* trans. by J. F. Scanlan
(New York: Charles Scribner's Sons, 1943), p. 101.

[23] Cleanth Brooks, "Metaphor and the Function of Criticism," in
Spiritual Problems in Contemporary Literature, ed. by Stanley Romaine
Hopper (New York: Harper & Bros., 1952), p. 130.

rhetoric. But the studies which make up this book do rest upon a basic presupposition—and it is that that phase of literature represented by my subject-figures is one whose immense distinction is in part a consequence of the brilliance with which an account is given of those complex motions of quest and exploration that are performed by the human spirit in a.time when "the absence of God moves about . . . with the intimacy of a presence."[24] The vision of hazard and prospect expressed in these writers—in Dostoievski, Hardy, Kafka, Camus, Beckett, Greene, and Flannery O'Connor—is not, of course, a unitary vision; but each is a voyager who navigates some of the deepest craters of the modern spirit: and each wants to make (*pace* Miss Sontag) a large kind of statement about how we live now, and how we ought to live. To scan these particular writers is not, to be sure, to have scanned in an even remotely comprehensive way the central tradition in modern fiction. But they happen to be figures whom I have had one or another kind of occasion to write about in the last few years, and they do also happen at least to be suggestive, I believe, of what that tradition entails—most especially in their common sense of the human interior as embracing "cliffs of fall . . . sheer, no-man-fathomed." And, with Hopkins, they say, warningly—"Hold them cheap/May who ne'er hung there."[25]

[24] Gustav Thibon, quoted in Stanley Romaine Hopper's essay, "On the Naming of the Gods in Hölderlin and Rilke," in *Christianity and the Existentialists*, ed. by Carl Michalson (New York: Charles Scribner's Sons, 1956), p. 158.

[25] *Poems of Gerard Manley Hopkins*, ed. by Robert Bridges (London and New York: Oxford University Press, 1937), p. 62.

I

Dostoievski: The Costs of Unbelief in the Major Fiction

Dostoievski is universally regarded today as one of the great directors of the modern conscience. Our conviction of the exact pertinence of his vision to the distempers of our age is a consequence of the clarity that we find in him about an issue by which we are deeply troubled—namely, the brutalization of our natures that is threatened by our captivity to ideas and to the intellect. We live, of course, in a time in which, as W. H. Auden once remarked, the individual must "do deliberately for himself what in previous ages had been done for him by family, custom, Church, and State—namely, the choice of the principles and presuppositions in terms of which he can make sense of his experience." Not only is he thus bent back upon himself by the absence of coherent traditions that furnish guidance with respect to the ultimate issues of existence: he must also engage in the common adventure of life in a period of history in which it is widely supposed that there has been such an erosion of the religious terrain as makes it necessary for a man himself to create the absolute values that the mind requires for its peace and sanity. So to *exist* has, in a way, been to *think*, and the Cartesian formula—*Cogito ergo sum*—has, to a considerable degree, summed up the lone and final certitude of the modern voyager. He has not been able to live out of any deep center or equilibrium of being, beneath the level of the mental or the ideational, for the circumstances of his culture, with all the spiritual disorder that they have involved, have condemned him to the terrible despotism of the mind. "We are the people of the idea," says Mr. Trilling, "and we rightly fear that the intellect will dry up the blood in our veins and wholly check the emotional and creative part of the mind."[1]

It is indeed a profound horror of the absolute sovereignty of the intellect that forms, from Blake and Wordsworth to Melville and to D. H. Lawrence, a major theme of modern culture. But in no writer of the past hundred years does this concern gain so profound an expression as it does in Dostoievski. For he, above all others, was occupied with the modern "tragedy of mind" and perceived that the autonomization of the mind must be, in our time, the necessary consequence of the belief that God is dead. Fishing in the deepest waters, he took hold, in other words, of our distress at its real root, and we can, therefore, in his books find more of what it actually entails than we can in any other source.

Yet to make this claim for Dostoievski may seem only to obfuscate matters. For, if he describes the problem of modern man as one arising out of his atheism, it would not at first appear that this is really *our* problem. Where, we would ask, are the people whose actual sense of the human reality comports with so extreme an analysis of things as Dostoievski put forward? Do our friends go about proclaiming, with Nietzschean passion, the death of God? No, we will say: however much the basic fact of their lives may no longer involve the fact of God, our conversations with them, when they are not punctuated by the confidences of intimacy, are likely to be focused upon the disorders in our collective life, and what we are constantly attempting to do is to take some measure of the

[1] Lionel Trilling, *The Liberal Imagination* (New York: The Viking Press, 1950), p. 286.

contingencies which harass our world today in its public sector. For, again as Mr. Trilling says, we feel that our present "fate, for better or worse, is political,"[2] and this is the character of our present preoccupations. So, if it was some divine abdication that focalized the concern of this nineteenth-century Russian, how, it may be asked, can he be considered to speak to our present condition?

Well, to this query, should it be put, it must be granted that, yes, our immediate and most conscious concern today is not with the death of God but with the death of the City, of what the Greeks called the *polis*: it is with the death of the human community. What we yearn for are the cultural and political instruments by which we might create a stable international order that would make a technical civilization sufferable: what we seek is "a city which hath foundations." But the author of the *Epistle to the Hebrews* tells us that the builder and the maker of that city is God.[3] Indeed, we do perceive, intermittently and anxiously, that our severances from one another may be a reflection of some profounder dislocation and that perhaps the former will not be healed until the latter has been repaired. "We must love one another or die," Mr. Auden told us many years ago;[4] and he might well have added that we can, however, encounter one another in the dimension of *presence* (which is the *event* of love) only if for us the world

[2] *Ibid.*, p. 100.

[3] "By faith Abraham, when he was called to go out into a place which he should after receive for an inheritance, obeyed; and he went out, not knowing whither he went. By faith he sojourned in the land of promise, as in a strange country, dwelling in tabernacles with Isaac and Jacob, the heirs with him of the same promise: For he looked for a city which hath foundations, whose builder and maker is God." *Hebrews* 11:8–10.

[4] W. H. Auden, "September 1, 1939," in *A Little Treasury of Modern Poetry*, ed. by Oscar Williams (New York: Charles Scribner's Sons, 1946), p. 202. (This most famous line of Mr. Auden's poetry belongs to a stanza of the poem "September 1, 1939" that he chose to remove from the version of it appearing in his *Collected Poems*. So the original rendering is today readily accessible only in anthologies.)

does itself appear to offer some ontological guarantee of the possibility of such encounter.[5] Here it is that we are at the real point of juncture between God and the moral order, and it is at this point that we may see that, when Dostoievski attributes the disorientation of modern man to his denial of any transcendent order of "presence," he is really speaking far more directly to our actual condition than might at first be supposed. At any rate, this is the unifying witness of all his writings, and Ralph Harper gives us a true summation of his mind when he tells us that

> For him [Dostoievski] the crisis of civilization was a crisis of presence and absence, encounters and alienations. His great heroes were always alienated men who longed for a presence they had lost touch with or never had long enough to remember clearly. They all understood that the problem of God and the problem of love or friendship or law were inseparable because they both were the problem of presence, seen in different dimensions.[6]

We might say that what Dostoievski exhibits in the concrete, dramatic structures of his novels is the ontology of modern secularism, its version, that is, of the reality that man is up against in this world. The main tenet of that bill of particulars is that ours is a universe without governance or guiding principle and that therefore, in so far as it is truly a *universe*, or a field of reality constituting a unified and meaningful realm, it becomes so as a consequence of a heroic act of the human mind which "furnishes the world and determines the way of life."[7] The limiting condition of man's existence is, in other words, his complete autonomy—which is, of course, a condition involving no limits at all. So he must himself invent the

[5] The term "presence," in its usage above, originates in the writings of the contemporary French philosopher, Gabriel Marcel.

[6] Ralph Harper, *The Sleeping Beauty* (New York: Harper & Brothers, 1955), p. 57.

[7] Laszlo Vatai, *Man and His Tragic Life* (New York: The Philosophical Library, 1954), p. 11.

purposes of life and the modes of action, creating Good and Evil and creating the categorical imperatives of morality. "Every moral action on the part of the autonomous man is a creative act, for, in it, he recreates himself and his own freedom."[8] Indeed, living in such a void as the universe becomes when all limits have been banished, he must recreate himself anew each day, in order to retain any sense of his own identity. Carrying the whole meaning of his existence by himself, he is constantly in the ironical position of having to struggle desperately to retain some sense of his identity, because, since he beholds nothing in the world except his own image, the world seems to afford nothing against which he might really test himself and whereby he might, therefore, be given a deeper sense of himself. So, amid an essentially empty world, he gives himself to first one and then another gratuitous action, by means of which he hopes to gain the assurance that he craves of his own substantial reality. These actions almost always involve violence, either against himself or against others; and they end in futility and defeat, because the autonomous man, refusing to acknowledge the inter-personal character of human existence, with all the metaphysical implications that it involves, can never discover who he really is. He remains trapped within the solipsistic prison of his own ego, and what, as a result of his anguished experiments in self-realization, he finally apprehends is not his own self's integrity but rather the tragic thing that the mind itself is when, suspended in the void of unbelief, it can find no higher reality than itself and is thus doubled back upon itself in the stark desolateness of its vacancy and isolation.

Now it is the world of such desperateness and isolation that Dostoievski made his own, charting its hitherto unexplored recesses with the audaciousness and austerity of the true tragic poet. We should perhaps first of all turn to a little book that he published in 1864 called *Letters from the Underworld*, for it is here that we get one of his earliest and most

[8] *Ibid.*, p. 14.

revealing portraits of the new autonomous man of the modern age who is engaged in "the experiment . . . of replacing the true balance of living by the despotic activity of the independent mind."[9] We still find it difficult to decide how to view this strange document. Is it a *novella,* or is it a diary, or a confession? We are not sure, but, like Rilke's *Notebooks of Malte Laurids Brigge* and Svevo's *Confessions of Zeno* which give rise to similar questions, its impact upon us is unforgettable and permanent.

The *Letters* are divided into two main parts, the second consisting of a long story which, in terms of action, illustrates the character of the hero whose "confessions" form the first part of the book. He is a man of forty years of age who has for a long period held a minor post in the Civil Service—from which, however, he has recently resigned, after receiving from a distant relative a small legacy of six thousand roubles. As his story begins, we find him in his retirement eking out a miserable existence in a shabby room on the outskirts of St. Petersburg. He has had an education of sorts and has read widely: indeed, he considers himself to be a consummately brilliant dialectician and observer of the foibles of men, and, in every way, a real "figure." But he has somehow never had any gift for incontestably bringing his brilliance to bear upon the world, so that it might be known and properly appreciated. In his external aspect he has appeared so ineffectual and ordinary, so blundering and awkward and shy, that he has very nearly succeeded in being the man whom no one notices is there, and he never ceases to be pained by the pathetic contrast between his own sense of his powers and the public estimate of his worth. But he insists that his essential reality is to be found not in the public self but in the secret, "underground" self, and this it is, therefore, that he sets out to reveal in the long monologue which forms the first half of the *Letters.*

Now this "underground" self is a curious admixture of

[9] D. A. Traversi, "Dostoievsky," *The Criterion,* XVI, No. LXV (July, 1937), 602.

tendencies toward sadism and masochism, toward the most excessive forms of pride and of humility. He regards himself as infinitely superior to all the "superficial" people of his acquaintance, but he is constantly given to contemptuous dismissals of himself as a mere "insect." He wants to be liked and admired by everyone, and yet he recalls that, during his days in the Civil Service, "Whenever people approached my office table to ask for information, or what not, I used to grind my teeth at them, and invariably to feel pleased when I had offended their dignity." His dominant emotions are contempt and envy—contempt of "them," of "everybody," and envy of the success with which "they," in their gross normality, are able to get on with the business of living. It is for the sake of commanding from "them" an act of recognition that this bilious and exacerbated little cypher goes into a tavern one evening to pick a quarrel not with anyone in particular but with whomever may first chance to cross his path. But the upshot of this rather nasty adventure is only that he is brusquely pushed aside by a husky young officer who then pursues his own way without taking any further notice of him. Again, he forces himself upon some acquaintances one evening, as they are holding a party for a friend who is about to depart for a new position in the Caucasus—but before the end of the evening, he manages, by his churlishness and bad temper, completely to spoil the celebration. As the others leave in disgust, he is overcome with feelings of frustration and self-loathing.

In such moments it is his habit to escape into debauchery, and so he enters a brothel. There he consorts with Lisa, a pretty little girl from the provinces who has just recently joined the establishment. After he has taken her body, he lectures her on the degradation of her life, painting such a direful picture of what lies at the end of her road that the girl is reduced to tears. He is simply carried away by the force of his own rhetoric and speaks so movingly that she is persuaded that she must indeed attempt a fresh start. So she calls on him at his lodgings a few days later, expecting to be taken in and given assistance. But, instead, he greets her with laughter and scorn, telling her that he had only been playing a game with her, "the game of forcing your tears, your humiliation, your hysterics." When, perceiving how inwardly broken and tormented he is, she embraces him, in a spontaneous gesture of pity and affection, he deliberately misconstrues her intent and offers her money, as though the embrace had been an act of solicitation. At this Lisa throws the money upon a table and leaves, realizing that in this man there is neither goodness nor decency.

Now we may ask who this man of the "underground" is and what is the meaning of the strange ambivalences that form his enigmatic character. When this question is pressed, we must say, as he himself insists, that he is a "man of acute sensibility" and also a man of thought. Indeed, like Paul Valéry's Monsieur Teste, he *exists* in his *thought*—which is perhaps to say that he does not *exist* at all, but only thinks—and, as John Middleton Murry remarked over fifty years ago in his book on Dostoievski, this is a man whose "thought has paralysed his being, until he can only sit down and contemplate the world that is, which he abhors yet can by no means escape."[10] Though the hero of the *Letters* represents an extreme instance of this *malaise*, the condition itself is constantly reflected in most of the central characters in Dostoievski's fiction, for they are people in whom the mind can never know any surcease from its labors, since the only meaning in their world is that which the mind itself is constantly calling into existence. This it is that constitutes, in Dostoievski's view, their modernity, for he sees the unhappy fate of modern man as consisting in the emptiness which his secularism compels him to find in the universe—an emptiness, indeed, so chilling and so exasperating that the mind is stretched to the very end of its tether. The tragic principle, in other words, as he encounters it in the

[10] John Middleton Murry, *Fyodor Dostoevsky: A Critical Study* (New York: Dodd, Mead and Co., 1916), p. 90.

tonalities of nineteenth-century life, is, in his definition of it, the principle of unbelief. And though, in the hero of the *Letters*, the mode of its functioning is not theatricalized in the grandly operatic manner that characterizes the delineation of Raskolnikov and Svidrigailov in *Crime and Punishment* or Pyotr Verhovensky and Stavrogin in *The Possessed* or Ivan Karamazov, we yet find in him a clear kinship with these great personages of Dostoievski's later work, for he, like them, is a captive to the awful solitude that overtakes the human spirit when it finds itself inhabiting a world bereft of the gracious reality of Presence.

The chief difference perhaps between the hero of the *Letters* and the protagonists of the great tragedies (*Crime and Punishment, The Idiot, The Possessed,* and *The Brothers Karamazov*) is that he, unlike Raskolnikov and Verhovensky and Stavrogin and Kirillov and Ivan Karamazov, is almost wholly passive: he only squirms and quavers in the dungeon of his isolation, whereas they hurl themselves into life with an almost consuming energy and violence, in order that their freedom and independence might be proven in the absoluteness of the concrete act. It is, indeed, these great Faustian characters of Dostoievski who illustrate the bitter dialectic that is fundamental to his conception of the tragic predicament— that, when, by an act of negation, man chooses to live in a metaphysical void in which nothing has any meaning and no values can be affirmed, if he is not betrayed into utter inaction (the hero of the *Letters*), he will be betrayed into some form of moral dilettantism (in which case other men will be regarded as mere puppets to be experimented with) or into some form of blatant self-deification whose premise will be that everything is permissible. But whichever of these two alternatives is embraced, it is clear that the apostate radical will be prepared, ultimately, to commit either suicide or murder. For when life is regarded as being essentially and ultimately absurd—which is what it is for the nihilist—then "the dark victory in which heaven and earth are annihilated"[11] is for him the only kind of victory that is really possible. It is, in a way, such a Pyrrhic victory that the tragic hero in the Dostoievskian drama seeks.

Crime and Punishment is the first of the great novels in which these issues are fully dramatized. It deals, on the surface, with a morose and destitute student, Rodion Raskolnikov, who murders an old pawnbrokeress in order to rob her of her hoard and who then plays a cat-and-mouse game with the police until, being overcome with exhaustion and panic, he is finally taken by the clever police investigator Porfiry. But the most cursory examination of the book immediately reveals that what we have here is not merely a "thriller" compounded of crime, detection, and punishment, and it is only on the most superficial level that Raskolnikov appears as a murderer who has killed for money. For he is a half-educated intellectual who has published an article in which he expounds the thesis that there are some men who by reason of their natural superiority to the common herd, are above the law, above all moral standards—and, being convinced that he belongs to this élite, he has murdered the old money-lender Alyona Ivanovna with an axe, simply for the sake of asserting the transcendency of his ·will. She is, he has persuaded himself, a blood-sucking, tight-fisted old usuress who does not deserve to live, a mere "louse." "I wanted to become a Napoleon: I wanted to have the daring . . . and I killed her."

Raskolnikov is, of course, finally persuaded by Sonia, who loves him, of how humanly impertinent are the presuppositions upon the basis of which he has acted, that none can judge another worthless and a "louse" and thus dispose of him. Indeed, he is brought at last to the point of acknowledging that "I am perhaps viler and more loathsome than the louse I killed. . . ." Yet there is evidence that suggests that this is, though, a conclusion at which he arrives only because, in his very re-

[11] Albert Camus, *The Rebel: An Essay on Man in Revolt* (New York: Vintage Books, 1956), p. 7.

morse and contrition, he discovers what is for him the tragic proof of his having been unable to summon the courage demanded by his principles. He realizes finally, in other words, that in himself there was not a sufficient strength really to live in the power of the absurd. We must therefore conclude that the kind of absolute autonomization of the mind and the will that is represented in the curiously sinister figure of Svidrigailov (who pursues Dounia, Raskolnikov's sister) is something that remains perhaps only potential in Raskolnikov. But, however much Raskolnikov's commitment to his principles may ultimately be rendered uncertain by the incompleteness of his "emancipation," he stands as a major embodiment in Dostoievski's novels of that modern nihilist spirit which, in undertaking to reconstruct human life on the basis of some self-willed invention of reason, only succeeds in wrecking it with the destructiveness of its own demonry.

Of the books of Dostoievski, however, that deal with this issue there is perhaps none that is felt to speak more immediately to the condition of our age than *The Possessed*, in which the implications represented by a Raskolnikov or a Svidrigailov are extended into the concrete actualities of the political life. Though everyone will, of course, acknowledge *The Brothers Karamazov as* Dostoievski's masterpiece, it is *The Possessed* that is felt to be the great book *for us*. We have not to cast about at any great length for reasons explaining our common feeling in the matter, for in this book Dostoievski is concerned to explore the moral complications internal to modern radical ideology, and this is, of course, a subject than which there is none that recent history has more fully prepared us to take an interest in. It has, indeed, been the astonishing metamorphosis that has taken place in Soviet Russia of modern Socialism that has been one of the great decisive experiences of our generation and into which we are thrust once again by the complex moral ambiguities represented by the revolutionaries in *The Possessed* who, for the sake of tactical expediency, permit themselves every conceivable duplicity and every performable crime. When today we read this book that was written almost fifty years before the Russian Revolution, we feel, as we are whirled through the vortex-like movement of its intrigues and betrayals and violence, that we already have, in a way, lived it all through, and Dostoievski's evident desire to sound a warning no longer seems the eccentricity that it once represented for a generation whose political radicalism was uninformed by the disenchantment about radical politics that the events of the past thirty years have made accessible to us.

Irving Howe has reminded us that *"The Possessed* is a caricature of radicalism, a grotesque, a slander and a scandal; it would be absurd," he says, "to suppose that the Russia it presents is a reasonable copy of the Russia of Alexander II or that the radicals spawned in Dostoievski's malice are the actual radicals of mid-nineteenth-century Russia."[12] This is doubtless true: surely the criminal Machiavellianism of Pyotr Verhovensky, in whom Dostoievski gives us his most concentrated image of the revolutionary radical of his age, has nothing visibly in common with the humanistic libertarianism of such leaders of Russian radical thought as Herzen and Chernichevsky and Mikhailovsky or with such earlier continental theorists as Fourier and Saint-Simon and Proudhon. But Dostoievski never intended to be the kind of "secretary of society" that Balzac and Flaubert and Zola were holding up as the ideal for the novelist, and his sympathy for the kind of precise sociological documentation that the naturalistic movement generally in nineteenth-century letters tended to advocate was very limited. What he wanted to offer was a large mythic image of the modern secular meliorist whose activity in the collective life is guided by a socialistic bias and whose dedication to some vision of social harmony is so fanatical as to destroy all the ethical scruples that he might otherwise have about the means that may be employed in the implementation of this vision. And though it is true that in an empirical sense

[12] Irving Howe, "The Political Novel," *Tomorrow*, X, No. 9 (May, 1951), p. 54.

Verhovensky does not truly represent the revolutionary movement of Dostoievski's period, is it yet not true that he is a marvelously prescient symbol of the demagogues and careerists and cabalists who have been the heroes of those totalitarian movements of recent decades in which we have seen the declension and the degeneracy of Western socialism? He may, of course, be dismissed as merely a splenetic expression of the malice toward nineteenth-century radical ideology into which Dostoievski was betrayed by his political conservatism, but such a perspective will hardly allow us to draw a full enough circle of definition about his significance.

Dostoievski was, to be sure, profoundly and bitterly at odds with the Socialist movement of his time, and with all that he could see as being then portended by its promotion—but what we must recognize is that this was a theologically principled rejection, and deeply so. He tells us, for example, in *The Brothers*, that if Alyosha had decided that

> God and immortality did not exist he would at once have become an atheist and a socialist. For socialism is not merely the labor question, it is before all things the atheistic question, the question of the form taken by atheism today, the question of the tower of Babel built without God, not to mount to Heaven from earth but to set up Heaven on earth.

Just here we may see that, despite the over-riding political concerns that control *The Possessed*, it has, nevertheless, its relation to the predominantly religious interests that determine the tragic dialectic of *Crime and Punishment* and *The Brothers Karamazov*. For Pyotr Verhovensky and his fellow-conspirators (Shigalov and Kirillov and the others) are presented as type and example of what Dostoievski considered to be the central disorder of the modern spirit. That disorder, in his definition of it, is, as we have seen, essentially a religious disorder: it is the condition in which man finds himself when, to his own satisfaction, having effectively sundered any linkage between himself and a transcendent order of values, he discovers that the resulting emancipation actually brings no real satisfaction at all and, furthermore, imposes upon him the enormous burden of himself bringing into existence whatever meaning life is to have. Since modern man finds himself in this extremity, Dostoievski believed that the strategem which is ultimately to be expected of him is one that will involve some form of resort to the tactics of socialism: that is to say, what he will try to do is to achieve a definitive and an absolute settlement of human destiny in purely historical terms. Ivan Karamazov remarks on one occasion that "Those who don't believe in God discuss socialism and anarchism and the reorganization of mankind on a new pattern, which are the same questions, only tackled from the other way up." This is, in a way, the burden of one whole side of Dostoievski's testimony, for the fact that he perceived and so wonderfully dramatized in his fictions (most memorably perhaps in *The Possessed* and "The Legend of the Grand Inquisitor" in *The Brothers*) is that, once life has been emptied of meaning by the death—or the banishment—of God, the only thing left for men to do is rigorously to *organize* it into some semblance of meaning. And, all things being permissible, there will, of course, be nothing to check the self-will of those self-appointed few who do the organizing—so that in the utopia of social harmony the equality of the multitude will be the equality of slaves. As Shigalov (the theorist of Verhovensky's "cell") confesses: "I am perplexed by my own data and my conclusion is a direct contradiction of the original idea with which I start. Starting from unlimited freedom, I arrive at unlimited despotism." But the rub is that the unlimited freedom is for only one-tenth of the human community, the other nine-tenths becoming a mere herd and, "through boundless submission," attaining "something like a primeval paradise."

So Pyotr Verhovensky and his colleagues in *The Possessed* are devotees of that same modern experiment in autonomy to which Raskolnikov and Svidrigailov are committed, the only difference being that they carry it into the fateful and expensive realm of *Realpolitik*. Although, in the "Byronic" Stavrogin, this audacious adventure achieves a kind of meretricious grandeur, the pathos of it is to be seen in Kirillov, who reasons that, if there is no God and no will greater than his own, then he must himself be a kind of God and his will must itself be omnipotent—a fact, however, which, on "the most vital point," he must express by killing himself, for he wants to assume the burden of a kind of inverted Messianism whose function will be to announce the dawn of a new age in which man, no longer fearing death, no longer seeks belief in God or the reassurances of belief in immortality.

Everything in Dostoievski moves, of course, towards the resounding climax of his entire career which was made by *The Brothers Karamazov*. For this is his masterpiece, and this is the book which alone would have entitled him to admission into that heaven for novelists that embraces the creators of *The Red and the Black* and *Moby Dick* and *War and Peace* and *The Magic Mountain* and *Remembrance of Things Past*. And when it is set beside *Crime and Punishment* (1866) and *The Idiot* (1869) and *The Possessed* (1872), the greatness of *The Brothers* (1880) does indeed appear a consequence of the completeness with which it summarizes the themes that had already been implicit in the great books which preceded it. The strange psychological quirks and ambivalences of Grushenka and Katerina Ivanovna had already been explored in Nastasya Filipovna in *The Idiot* and in Liza in *The Possessed*. The sensualism of Dmitri has its analogue in Rogozhin in *The Idiot*, as Kolya's representation of the precocity of the schoolboy already corrupted by modern intellectualism is also prefigured in *The Idiot* by Ippolit. Alyosha and Father Zossima also put us in mind of Prince Myshkin in *The Idiot* and Father Tihon in *The Possessed*, but, appealing as are these "saintly" figures in *The Brothers*, Dostoievski no more succeeds in making their virtue relevant to the world that is described in his fiction than he does in his handling of the earlier representatives of this category of his characters. Finally, at the incandescent center of *The Brothers* is Ivan Karamazov, who powerfully recapitulates that erring and tragic adventure in negation and rebellion previously exemplified by such figures as the nameless hero of *Letters from the Underworld,* and by Raskolnikov, Svidrigailov, Verhovensky, Kirillov, and Stavrogin.

There is, however, one special thing in Ivan that sets him apart from many of his progenitors in the Dostoievskian drama, for he does not deny the existence of God: on the contrary, he passionately affirms it, and he purposes, like Goethe's Mephistopheles, to talk to him as an equal, to bring him into the dock, and to put him on trial. He does not choose to debate the question of his existence, for, as he says to Alyosha, "I have no faculty for settling such questions, I have a Euclidian earthly mind, and how could I solve problems that are not of this world?" No, on this ultimate issue he will not commit himself to any controversy: indeed, controversy on this question is forsworn by the deepest dispositions of his personality, and what he finds it impossible to accept is not the fact of God but rather the miserable fact of the world which is held to be under his governance. As he says to Alyosha: "It's not that I don't accept God, you must understand, it's the world created by him I don't and cannot accept."

Ivan's problem is the problem of theodicy: how, that is, are the sufferings and the tears of man to be reckoned with— or, rather, do they not demand to be reckoned with in terms of some principle higher than that presumably ordained by the necessities of a providentially structured natural law? Yes, to be sure, conventional religion teaches us that in that ultimate geometry of which God is the mathematician all contradictions will be reconciled and all dissonances will be harmonized. But, says Ivan, "if the sufferings of children go to swell the sum of sufferings which was necessary to pay for truth, then I protest that the truth is not worth such a price." Why should they "pay for the eternal harmony . . . ?" No, he declares, "It's not worth the tears of that one tortured child who beat itself on the breast with its little fist and prayed in its stinking outhouse, with its unexpiated tears to 'dear, kind God'! It's not worth it, because those tears are unatoned for." His point is that such tears *must* be atoned for, not "in some remote infinite time and space, but here on earth"—for, if we suffer (as, indeed, on the most generous construction of things, it appears to him that we do) only in order to "manure the soil of the future harmony for somebody else," then surely we have been thrown into a most outrageous world. "I must have justice"—this is the persistently recurrent note in the tirade which he hurls into the face of God. Indeed, it is the Principle of Justice to which he holds God accountable and against the measure of which he finds him wanting: for Ivan the Kingdom of God is not worth the tears of a single child, and, if this is its price, the price is too high. So he refuses it, becaue it is based upon injustice: "I renounce the higher harmony altogether." And when Alyosha murmurs, "That's rebellion," he replies: "Rebellion? I am sorry you call it that. One can hardly live in rebellion, and I want to live."

But in the name of what does one live, when one has denied that life is ultimately meaningful? If the immediate chaos of existence is not to be understood in the context of an ultimate order, can one then act in the name of, or with the sanction of, anything other than chaos? In this extremity, has virtue any reward—or evil any retribution? These are the bitter issues with which Ivan must wrestle, and he does finally conclude that, yes, all things are indeed permitted: "Everything is lawful."

Here, then, we have the strange irony that Ivan Karamazov incarnates, of the man who, as Camus said, "trembled at the suffering of a child" and who, "from the moment that he rejects divine coherence and tries to discover his own rule of life, recognizes the legitimacy of murder."[13] And, as Camus saw with such clarity, the ironic element here, surprising though at first it may seem, is inescapably a part of the dia-

[13] Albert Camus, *op. cit.*, p. 58.

lectic within which Ivan is caught, for "the bitter end of metaphysical rebellion" is "metaphysical revolution":

> The master of the world, after his legitimacy has been con-
> tested, must be overthrown. Man must occupy his place. . . .
> But what does becoming God mean? It means, in fact, rec-
> ognizing that everything is permitted and refusing to rec-
> ognize any other law but one's own.[14]

This is the dreadful logic to which Ivan is committed: indeed,
this is what he has chosen—to be logical: his determination to
protest against the tears of humanity has committed him to the
denial that goodness has any *effective* sanction in the universal
scheme of things, so that his dilemma, as Camus reminded us,
becomes that of being "virtuous and illogical, or logical and
criminal."[15] The "visitor" who comes to him during the
delirium of his illness is right, in other words, when he tells
him that "You are forever angry, all you care about is intelligence. . . ." This is in fact Ivan's basic orientation: like all
Dostoievski's major representatives of the modern disorder, he
would live out of the self-sufficiency of his own intellect—to do
which, of course, is to become God: and when man has thus
divinized himself, then "everything is lawful," even crime. Ivan
does, indeed, allow his father to be killed. He goes mad afterwards, to be sure, for he cannot retain his sanity betwixt the
horns of the intolerable dilemma (illogical virtue or logical
crime) within which he is caught. But, though he, for special
reasons internal to himself, remains within the private universe
of his own anguish, "The Legend of the Grand Inquisitor" in
The Brothers does not allow us to forget those demonic careerists of *The Possessed* (Verhovensky, for example—or Shigalov). For, as it reminds us, it is inevitable that metaphysical
insurrection should extend itself from the dialogue between
man and God to the relations between a man and his neighbors. Once achieved, in other words, in the sphere of religion,

[14] *Ibid.*, pp. 58–9.
[15] *Ibid.*, p. 58.

it must also be achieved in the human polity, for towards this conclusion its inner dialectic presses inexorably.

This is, indeed, what Dostoievski means when he tells us that socialism is, above all else, a question of atheism. For, in his view, the whole adventure of socialism does, at bottom, entail the effort of the modern secularist to bring the Kingdom of Heaven down to earth, and he perceived that, once this is done, the new administration must inevitably involve for the human community the reign of a caesarism which can, in principle, admit of no bridling at all. It is of this that the old Inquisitor is prophetic, and the logic of the experiment in autonomy is thus brought to its conclusion by this "Legend" that Ivan relates to Alyosha, of Christ's return to earth, of his appearance in Spain during the Inquisition, and of his confrontation by the "Grand" Inquisitor, who imprisons him and who then proceeds pedantically to "correct" him by pointing out to him that the happiness of man is really to be guaranteed only by offering him bread and relieving him of the burdens of freedom. The tragic lesson, in other words, that is here being dramatized and that is adumbrated at many other points in these great books might be formulated in this wise, that Hitler and Stalin dwell in all men who venture really to live upon the premise either that God is dead or that he is hopelessly impotent.

So Dostoievski is, then, our great modern tragedian of unbelief, and, in the imaginative literature of the last hundred years, his marvelous fictions continue to be the most important repository that we have of the data that the Christian consciousness would bring forward in its debate with what is, ultimately, the legacy of the Enlightenment. He is reactionary, unsentimental, illiberal: he makes us ask questions about what is behind the masks that we conventionally wear, and he is never surprised about what is there to be found: before the moral faults and duplicities of men he is always sober and competent. "His gift," as Alfred Kazin says, "has been icy and merciless clarity; an awareness of man, as man, in his social loneliness, his emotional cheating, his fertile and agile hostility, his limited power to love. . . ."[16] "He knows," says Mr. Kazin,

> that men live as they do because they think as they do, and that their thoughts cannot be replaced by other thoughts until they have reached the bottom of their own. He asks: "Do you know who you are?"[17]

And, like Baudelaire and Kierkegaard in the nineteenth century and Eliot and Kafka in our own, he performs a very drastic kind of surgery.

[16] Alfred Kazin, "Dostoevsky and the Age of Anxiety," *The Inmost Leaf* (New York: Harcourt, Brace and Co., 1955), pp. 253–54.
[17] *Ibid.*, p. 256.

II

Hardy and the Victorian
Malaise

It is a happy custom that we have in the academic community of periodically arranging to notice in a formal way some of the great milestones of cultural history. The disaffiliated intellectual who, as a matter of principle, views the institutionalism of academic life as a threat to genuine freedom of the mind will doubtless find a good deal of pious humbug in these liturgical rites and observances—and so, in fact, there may at times be. But very often these are moments in which a carefully performed act of remembrance assists us toward some deeper understanding of ourselves; and when, in 1947, we celebrated the four hundredth birthday of Cervantes or when, two years later, we celebrated the two hundredth birthday of Goethe, it was surely the access that we thereby won to a deeper grasp of the immediate issues of our age that made these occasions notable.

So, at the end of the 'fifties, it was natural that our historical imagination should remind us of the profit there might be in remembering another birthday, the birthday on this occasion not of a man but rather of a book. Just a hundred years had elapsed since the quiet, at first unobtrusive appearance on the British scene of Charles Darwin's *Origin of Species*, and the elaborate memorial observances of this event that my own

university prepared led me to think again not only of Darwin
but also of the whole Victorian crisis of faith, and of this in
relation at once to Darwin and to Thomas Hardy.

Darwin's book was published on the twenty-fourth day of
November, 1859, and on that day the entire first edition of
1,250 copies was exhausted. By the seventh day of the new
year a second edition of 3,000 copies had been issued, and the
career of one of the great classics of modern intellectual history
was well under way.

At the time of his book's first appearance, Darwin was, of
course, a mature and seasoned scholar whose previous scientific
work had won him the respect and friendship of such distinguished men as Sir Joseph Hooker, Alfred Russell Wallace, Sir
Charles Lyell, and T. H. Huxley. So it is not surprising that the
Origin should have been accorded an initially respectful, if
cautious, reception in places like the *Saturday Review* and the
London *Times*. But by the spring of 1860, though the steady
growth of its reputation had become a cultural event of major
proportions, its success was increasingly proving to be a *succès
de scandale*, and the controversy over what the Germans were
to call *Darwinismus* had already, as the *Saturday Review* remarked, "passed beyond the bounds of the study and lecture-
room into the drawing-room and the public street."[1] In jour-
nals like the *British Quarterly* and the *Edinburgh Review* and
Blackwood's Magazine, both scientists and laymen were by
this time resisting with a remarkable animus what they felt to
be a dangerous subversion of the premises of traditional
thought, and the two old ladies who, in speaking of Darwin,
said, "Let's hope it's not true, and if it is, let's hush it up!"[2]
were speaking for a very considerable body of opinion.

There are, of course, those historians who occasionally like
to pretend bemusement by the prestige that the *Origin* so
quickly won and that it has consistently retained throughout

[1] *Saturday Review*, IX (May 5, 1860), 573.
[2] Quoted in H. G. Wood, *Belief and Unbelief Since 1850* (Cambridge: At the University Press, 1955), p. 50.

the last hundred years. They remind us that the idea of evolution was by no means an invention of Darwin but that it had itself been gradually evolving in the course of the previous century, through the researches of such early naturalists as Buffon and Lamarck, and Darwin's grandfather Erasmus and the anatomist Geoffrey Saint-Hillaire, and through the work of his friends Lyell and Wallace; we are also reminded of Darwin's great indebtedness to this whole tradition. Nor can this kind of historical witness easily be gainsaid. But surely what is of the highest importance is that, though Darwin did not represent the kind of absolute originality which, apparently, these historians are alone prepared to honor, it was he who canvassed more thoroughly than had any of his predecessors all the evidence then accessible which pointed to the fact that species have developed in time. And the primary consideration for the intellectual historian is that, during the last century, not a single bit of evidence has been adduced in contradiction of Darwin's central thesis that all living things have developed out of earlier and simpler forms.

So, since it was in the *Origin of Species* that the nineteenth century found the most massive summary of the evidence establishing the fact of organic evolution, it is not surprising that this is the book which both its friends and its foes came to regard as the focal text of the age: in a deep sense, it was felt to have altered the fundamental scene of human life.

For the purposes of this essay, a brief notation of what was spiritually entailed in this revolution will suffice. What ought perhaps first of all to be remarked is that, over and above the metaphysical immanentism that Darwinian biology appeared to require and quite apart from the flat contradiction between this immanentism and the account of the ultimate origins of existence which orthodox Christianity had drawn from the book of Genesis, it was Darwin's apparent subversion of traditional teleology that had the most distressing effect of all upon Victorian intellectuals. For, prior to the middle years of the nineteenth century, had you asked even a typical rationalist or free-thinker of the period what he considered to be the cardinal tenet of whatever he took to be the *philosophia perennis* of the Western tradition, he would doubtless have said something to the effect that he considered it to consist in the notion of a creative intelligence operative behind the phenomenal world, and to which was to be ascribed such order and design as could be empirically observed. Even the great Romantics, for all of their heterodoxy and heresy, had not called this primary tenet into question: on the contrary, they had often wanted to insist upon the presence of a divine spirit in all things, shaping and guiding them toward their destined end. But, with the appearance, first, of Lyell's *Principles of Geology* (1830–33), and then of Chambers' *Vestiges of Creation* (1844), and finally of Darwin's *Origin of Species,* the modern mind was confronted by a plausible and a most cogently elaborated doctrine that pictured nature as a kind of besieged arena in which survival of the processes of "natural selection" was a victory to be won only by those individuals and species that could manage so to deviate from their kind as to win the necessary adaptability to their environment. Indeed, by just the slightest imaginative stretching of the Darwinian scheme it could appear that ours is a universe adrift, without guiding purpose or principle and utterly indifferent to moral values. Or, if the theistic premise were still clung to, it then seemed that one must posit some deep and tragic dissonance between God and the created universe.

Here, for example, is how Tennyson raises the issue in *In Memoriam* (which, though published nine years before the appearance of the *Origin,* yet expresses many of the perplexities that were being aroused by the new geology and biology):

> Are God and Nature then at strife,
>   That Nature lends such evil dreams?
>   So careful of the type she seems,
> So careless of the single life,

That I, considering everywhere
    Her secret meaning in her deeds,
    And finding that of fifty seeds
She often brings but one to bear,

I falter where I firmly trod,
    And falling with my weight of cares
    Upon the world's altar-stairs
That slope thro' darkness up to God,

I stretch lame hands of faith, and grope,
    And gather dust and chaff, and call
    To what I feel is Lord of all,
And faintly trust the larger hope.

And Tennyson wonders if we

    Who trusted God was love indeed
    And love Creation's final law—
    Tho' Nature, red in tooth and claw
    With ravine, shriek'd against his creed—

are destined for some grim and futile end:

    What hope of answer, or redress?
    Behind the veil, behind the veil.

"It is an awful moment," said Frederick Robertson,

when the soul begins to find that the props on which it has blindly rested so long are, many of them, rotten, and begins to suspect them all; when it begins to feel the nothingness of many of the traditionary opinions which have been received with implicit confidence, and in that horrible insecurity begins also to doubt whether there be any thing to believe at all. It is an awful hour—let him who has passed through it say how awful—when this life has lost its meaning, and seems shrivelled into a span; when the grave appears to be the end of all, human goodness nothing but a name, and the sky above this universe a dead expanse, black with the void from which God himself has disappeared.[3]

[3] Stopford Brooke, *Life and Letters of Frederick W. Robertson* (New York: Harper and Brothers, 1870), p. 86.

Robertson was here speaking not only for himself but for all
his contemporaries—for men like Arnold and Clough, Sterling
and Mill, Carlyle and Kingsley. For all these men faced that
"brainless Nature" of which Tennyson spoke—that "brainless
Nature" who, in Darwin's disclosure of her, "knew not/that
which she bore!" Ours is a generation, said W. K. Clifford,
which has seen "the spring sun shine out of an empty heaven, to
light up a soulless earth; we have felt with utter loneliness
that the Great Companion is dead."[4] What had been lost was
the one meaning that gives meaning to all other meanings, and
the anxiety that was felt, as a consequence, was what Paul Tillich calls "the anxiety of emptiness and meaninglessness."[5] Thus
men like Kingsley and Tennyson and Arnold were often driven
to that same abyss of meaninglessness over which the modern
existentialist voyager so often hovers. The difference, however,
between the great Victorians and a contemporary existentialist
like Camus is that they had not perhaps lived long enough
with despair to be able to command what Dr. Tillich calls "the
courage of despair," and so they often simply wriggled in
their unhappiness and, facing "a universe of frozen apathy,"
were chilled into "an apathy of their own."[6]

Pascal says: "The greatness of man is great in that he
knows himself to be miserable. A tree does not know itself to
be miserable. It is then being miserable to know oneself to be
miserable. . . . All these same miseries prove man's greatness.
They are the miseries of a great lord, of a deposed king."[7]
This, I take it, moves somewhat in the direction of the kind of
courage Dr. Tillich is speaking of, but this is a calm, this is a

[4] W. K. Clifford, *Lectures and Essays*, ed. Leslie Stephen and
Frederick Pollock (London: Macmillan and Co., Ltd., 1901), p. 250.
[5] Paul Tillich, *The Courage to Be* (New Haven: Yale University
Press, 1952), chap. v.
[6] Lionel Trilling, *Matthew Arnold* (New York: Columbia University
Press, 1949), p. 82.
[7] Blaise Pascal, *Pensées*, trans. William Finlayson Trotter (New
York: E. P. Dutton and Co., Inc., "Everyman's Library," 1943), Fragments 397 and 398, p. 107.

serenity, that one does not often come upon in Victorian literature. Its great masters did often look into a deep chasm, the
same chasm into which Baudelaire and Nietzsche peered, the
same chasm into which Kafka and Camus looked; but, when
they peered down into it, they were not thrilled or exhilarated:
no, they looked down into it and simply felt debilitated by
their vertigo and then yearned for someone who might com-
miserate with them over the unfortunateness of their condition. In this respect, I suppose, they are not "modern": that is,
they do not have that fierce, reckless bravery, that stern and
uncalculating courage, which has so often been a distinguish-
ing feature of the great heroes of the intellectual and spiritual
life in this century. There is, I suppose, a sense in which John
Stuart Mill would be no match for Heidegger, or Arnold for
the early Eliot, or Hardy for Faulkner. Yet it may well be that,
if we want to understand these heroes of our own time, we had
better, first of all, seek an understanding of the great Victorians: for they were among the first martyrs of our modern
crisis of faith, and, without them, we might not have the more
experienced and competent *directeurs de conscience* who figure so prominently in the literature of this century.

Before turning, however, to a major strategist of the
poetic imagination in the Victorian age and to the expression
that he gives to the temper of the time, it should be remarked
that, when men like Robertson and Clifford spoke of the awful
hour in which the heavens are discovered to be empty and
when Arnold spoke of the recession of the "Sea of Faith" in
"Dover Beach," they were responding to a crisis of which the
Darwinian revolution was not the sole precipitant. Indeed, we
shall fail to take the fullest measure of what was critical and
unsettling in the idea of evolution, if we do not take account of
the respects in which its impact upon the last decades of the
nineteenth century was in part a consequence of the extent to
which it cooperated with still another revolutionary movement
—namely, the new Higher Criticism in the study of the Bible.
We have here, of course, two separate traditions of nineteenth-

century thought, and yet there is at least one important sense
in which they constitute a single development, for the rise of
the modern historical study of the Bible is something that was
closely linked with the predominance of the idea of evolution.
That is to say, not only was the impulse to apply historical
method to biblical study born out of a cultural ethos very
largely shaped by Darwinian thought, but, once this method
was so applied, the results cooperated (or were felt to cooperate) with Darwinian science in the disablement of Christian orthodoxy. For both the new biblical criticism and the
new natural science had the effect of calling into question the
conventional belief that the Scriptures present an infallible
revelation of absolutely reliable truth even in regard to matters
now regarded as falling within the domain of natural science
itself.

Ever since the time of Schleiermacher, radical Continental
scholarship had in various ways been undertaking to make the
literature of the Bible acceptable to what Matthew Arnold
called "the hard-headed modern multitudes." The widely influ-
ential Tübingen school of Baur and Strauss gave the most
effective publicity to the notion that the New Testament narrative is a tissue of myths originating in early Christian communities, "a wreath of adoration woven round the Master's
head by worshipping fancy."[8] Numerous Dutch scholars, from
the 'fifties on, advanced various versions of the Christ-myth
theory[9] which had originated in France, where, of all the
avant-garde mythologues, it was Renan, with his *Vie de Jésus,*
who gained the widest popularity. This whole body of literature, in its Christological reconstruction, in its notation of internal discrepancy and inconsistency in the biblical narrative,
in its questioning of traditional theories of inspiration and

[8] Hugh Ross Mackintosh, *Types of Modern Theology* (New York:
Charles Scribner's Sons, 1939), p. 118.

[9] *Vide* Eldred C. Vanderlaan, *Protestant Modernism in Holland*
(London: Oxford University Press, 1924).

miracle, and in its derogation of the historical authenticity of the biblical record itself, had a most profoundly unhinging impact upon the European religious situation in the latter half of the nineteenth century.

Nor were British theological scholars at all slow in responding to these new developments: indeed, one explosion after another soon occurred, as they began to produce their own versions of the Higher Criticism, and of at least one of these commotions some notice should be taken. It got under way in 1860, after the publication in March of that year of a little book entitled *Essays and Reviews,* written by six clergymen and one layman. The editor of the volume was the classicist and Master of Balliol College, Benjamin Jowett, and his colleagues included such men as Frederick Temple, Headmaster of Rugby and later Archbishop of Canterbury, Mark Pattison, Rector of Lincoln College, and Rowland Williams, Vice-Principal of St. David's College, Lampeter. Their intention was the "free handling, in a becoming spirit, of subjects peculiarly liable to suffer by the repetition of conventional language, and from traditional methods of treatment." Their essays dealt with various issues in apologetics and biblical interpretation, and, of the seven, it was Jowett's "On the Interpretation of Scripture" that was perhaps the most significant and that indicates very well the general tone of the book as a whole. His contention was that,

> although the interpretation of Scripture requires . . . at least a moral and religious interest which is not needed in the study of a Greek poet or philosopher, yet, in what may be termed the externals of interpretation, that is to say, the meaning of words, the connexion of sentences, the settlement of the text, the evidence of facts, the same rules apply to the Old and New Testaments, as to other books.

This was in effect for Jowett to insist that the Bible must be "interpreted" like any other ancient book, with a proper regard

for the original meaning of the texts. He assumed that traditional methods of exegesis, with their woodenheaded theories
of verbal inspiration, rendered such an approach impossible.
He reminded his readers of the variety of literary forms in
Biblical literature—myth, legend, proverb, law, etc.—and he
maintained that to be inattentive to this variousness was to
confuse poetic imagery with statements of historical fact and
to land in a disastrous literalism.

There is not room, even with respect to Jowett's essay, to
recapitulate the argument in any great detail, but enough has
been said to indicate the general line that *Essays and Reviews*
was taking. Judged in terms of its intrinsic merits, it is not a
great book, and it brought forward little, if anything at all,
that scholars might have regarded as fresh or new. Yet it trig-
gered an explosion that is among the fiercest ever detonated in
British cultural life. The authors were denounced in the press
and from the pulpit; they were condemned by the Bishops of
the Church of England; the Court of Arches and the Judicial
Committee of the Privy Council were even called into session,
and the seven contributors were finally anathematized as
"Septem Contra Christum," their book symbolizing to the rank
and file of men everything in the heterodoxy of the age that
was undermining traditional belief.

Now the *Origin of Species* and *Essays and Reviews* are,
perhaps above all others, the two texts, especially when taken
together, which lead us into the very center of what was problematic in the spiritual situation of the English-speaking world
a hundred years ago. Here we encounter the perspectives that
were radically transforming the soulscape of nineteenth-century man, and we might well say that, on the English scene, it
was the influence emanating from the two revolutions in
thought symbolized by these books that led John Ruskin to
declare: "There never yet was a generation of men (savage or
civilized) who . . . so woefully fulfilled the words, 'having no
hope, and without God in the world,' as the present civilized

European race."[10] It was these same influences that led Matthew Arnold to declare:

> There is not a creed which is not shaken, not an accredited dogma which is not shown to be questionable, not a received tradition which does not threaten to dissolve. Our religion has materialized itself in the fact, in the supposed fact; it has attached its emotion to the fact, and now the fact is failing it.[11]

It is no wonder that James Anthony Froude, in looking back upon the middle years of the century, recalled that for himself and his friends "the lights [were]all drifting, the compasses all awry": "All round us," he said, "the intellectual lightships had broken from their moorings...."[12]

So the image of the Victorian eminence that was created by the generation of its students most popularly represented perhaps by Lytton Strachey is an image that is quite false to what the actuality really comprised. What is central in our new grasp of the great Victorians is the realization that they were far from being a people in the grip of a sluggish certitude and complacency. It is, on the contrary, their desperate *uncer*tainty and their grim, black doubt that makes their most sensitive representatives speak so relevantly today to a generation whose sense of reality gains its most characteristic expression in the melancholy existentialist language of anxiety and dread. Many of our most recent researches into the Victorian experience have begun to make us feel this and to be alive to "that inexhaustible discontent, languor, and home-sickness, that endless regret, the chords of which," as Walter Pater said, "ring all

[10] John Ruskin, *Modern Painters*, III (New York: Wiley and Halsted, 1857), chap. xvi, p. 258.

[11] Matthew Arnold, "The Study of Poetry," *Essays in Criticism, Second Series* (London: Macmillan and Co., Ltd., 1896), p. 1.

[12] James Anthony Froude, *Thomas Carlyle: A History of His Life in London, 1834–1881*, I (New York: Charles Scribner's Sons, 1884), chap. xi, p. 248.

through . . . [the] literature [of the period]."[13] Indeed, when we turn to the Carlyle of *Sartor Resartus* and the *Essays,* to the Mill of the *Autobiography,* to the Tennyson of *In Memoriam,* to the poetry of Arnold and Clough, or to the George Eliot of Cross's *Life,* we feel that the impressiveness of these people is in large part a consequence of the extent to which they mirror their age in the modes of their response to what Arnold in his "Memorial Verses" called "this iron time/Of doubts, disputes, distractions, fears." They had known something of what Nietzsche's madman announced in *Die Fröhliche Wissenschaft* —long before he ran through the streets of his town crying out that "God is dead!" It is this that makes them for us a people to understand whom is to understand something essential about the mentality of the modern period.

Now, among all the versions in Victorian literature of the spiritual losses that men had then to endure, the account that most nearly achieves the dimensions of tragic grandeur is that which we get in the writing of Thomas Hardy. In his young manhood, when he came up to London in 1862 from his little provincial town in Dorset to serve as an apprentice in a prominent architectural firm, Hardy had not, of course, the kinds of social connections with Victorian intellectual life that were the privilege of many of his contemporaries in their youth. George Eliot, for example, as an assistant editor of *The Westminster Review* and as a close friend of people like the Hennells and Herbert Spencer, was an *habituée* of many of the most important drawing-rooms and was familiar with much of the most advanced thought of her time. Or, again, Matthew Arnold, as the son of the distinguished Thomas Arnold of Rugby, though he had his own career to make, was on terms of intimacy from childhood with many of the most important intellectuals in English life of his father's generation; and, in his undergraduate years at Balliol College, by way of friendships with such men

---

[13] Walter Pater, "Coleridge," *Appreciations* (London and New York: Macmillan and Co., 1889), pp. 105–106.

as Froude and Clough, he soon became a respected figure among the circle of his own contemporaries who were destined for intellectual and cultural leadership. But Hardy, when he came up to London at the age of twenty-two, was a half-educated provincial, was from a remote corner of southern England, and what Arnold called "the tone of the center" was, therefore, something to which his whole background and early experience of life did not give him easy access. And, though the moral and religious certitudes with which he was early equipped by his High Church upbringing in Dorset were in time corroded by the acids of modern scepticism, he never changed altogether, perhaps even could not have changed, the spiritual tenor of his mind. It is true, of course, that the boy who taught Sunday School in the parish church of Stinsford and who for a time dreamed of taking Orders did, after the London years, develop into a man whose agnosticism was of a piece with the main heterodoxies of his time. But, in the spaciousness of his imaginative scope, in the passion with which he brooded upon the ultimate issues of life and death and eternity, in the whole sweep of his vision, we feel—particularly in the great Wessex novels and in many of the poems—that here is no self-assured, complacent secularism of the sort that we meet, say, in Meredith or, later on, in Shaw and H. G. Wells. In 1915 he wrote to a friend: "You must not think me a hard-headed rationalist for all this. Half my time . . . I 'believe' . . . in spectres, mysterious voices, intuitions, omens. . . ." This confirms, in a way, one of our most abiding impressions of Hardy's fundamental position, that here was a mind divided between two worlds and torn by the kinds of conflicts that made Tennyson and Clough and Arnold and many of the representative figures of the age feel that they were "here as on a darkling plain." It is the primitive simplicity, the stern, valorous passion, the solemn, majestic beauty, with which he dramatizes this plight in books like *The Return of the Native,* *Tess of the d'Urbervilles,* and *Jude the Obscure* that makes him, in many ways, the richest and most resonant exemplar of a time when a full acceptance of the claims of the Christian faith was perhaps more difficult than it has ever been.

In at least one respect, Hardy's experience was very much "of the center," for, as was true in the case of so many other young men in the 'sixties, the two books which played the most decisive role in the shaping of his mind were the *Origin of Species* and *Essays and Reviews*, of whose readers he was among the earliest. Though we know that, in the years following his arrival in London, he became familiar with the work of men like Huxley and Mill and Spencer, we cannot measure with any great precision the effect that the new iconoclasm generally had upon him. But entries in the *Notebooks* and numerous other testimonies which he himself made clearly indicate that it was Charles Darwin and Benjamin Jowett's collaborators who conveyed to him, more effectively than anyone else, the full impact of the period's reconstruction of traditional belief.

In the *Essays* Hardy encountered, for example, by way of Frederick Temple's chapter, the notion that the Bible might be viewed as a kind of history book, merely recording the most significant religious developments that were contemporaneous with the time in which it was written. Or, again, C. W. Goodwin, in his essay, opened up Hardy's mind to the conflict between the Mosaic cosmogony and modern science. Baden-Powell, in his chapter on "Evidences of Christianity," was not only putting forward the argument that miracles must be adjudicated in the light of our best scientific knowledge but was also suggesting that Darwin's researches had rendered untenable the account that is given in the Book of Genesis of the origination of the forms of life. And throughout *Essays and Reviews*, Hardy was exposed to the kind of shock that the new radicalism was administering to the traditionally oriented imagination of the time.

It was, however, his reading of Darwin that most deeply unsettled him. For, far from providing him with any confirma-

tion of his early belief that "love alone had wrought" the web
of life, it did instead suggest a view of the world as caught in
the violent, brutal struggle of individuals and species for survival—a struggle the gratuitousness of whose cruelty allowed
nothing other than absolute anarchy to be the reigning principle of life. He doubtless quickly perceived what was also a
major implication of Darwin's whole position—namely, that by
reference to processes immanent within existence one could
satisfactorily account for whatever a transcendent principle
had previously been invoked to explain. But one suspects that
what most deeply shook Hardy was the strong unlikelihood that
was implied by the new biology, of life's being providentially
ordered by any gracious Deity. Indeed, the law of natural selection seemed actually to indicate that the processes of nature
and the destinies of men were governed ultimately by nothing
but "lawless caprice." So, at the age of twenty-six, we find
Hardy writing in the poem called "Hap":

> Crass Casualty obstructs the sun and rain,
> And dicing Time for gladness casts a moan. . . .
> These purblind Doomsters had as readily strown
> Blisses about my pilgrimage as pain.

It was, then, very probably in the years immediately following his arrival in London—the period extending roughly
from '62 to '66—that, as a result principally of his reading of
Darwin and of the contributors to *Essays and Reviews,* Hardy
lost the last vestiges of the religious faith in which he had been
nurtured. His conclusion seems to have been that, even if the
theistic premise is to be retained, God cannot be assumed to
have any real concern for man's welfare. Hardy's was not a
mind that had any inclination toward systematic formulations,
and this metaphysical pessimism was never deliberately elaborated into any highly coherent world-view. As he remarked in
the Preface to a volume of his poetry that appeared in 1901:
"Unadjusted impressions have their value, and the road to a
true philosophy of life seems to lie in humbly recording diverse

readings of its phenomena as they are forced upon us by chance and change." Indeed, throughout his life he seems to have had this kind of skittishness about committing himself to strict, measured statement on the ultimate quandaries that baffle human thought, and about all he could do was to acknowledge his own inability to see as final anything other than "crass Casualty" and "purblind Doomsters"—which is to say that Hardy would have agreed with Melville, that "Though in many of its aspects this visible world seems formed in love, the invisible spheres were formed in fright."

It is true, of course, as the Norwegian scholar Georg Roppen reminds us, that, increasingly through the 'eighties and 'nineties, Hardy, perhaps under the new influences of Von Hartmann and Schopenhauer, was envisaging a coordinating but unconscious Immanent Will that is operative in and through natural law. This is a tendency that is particularly evident in much of his poetry of this period, and, finally, it gains its consummate expression in the great lumbering epic drama *The Dynasts*, which appeared late in 1914. But even Dr. Roppen, who wants very much to stress this aspect of Hardy's mature and ripened vision (with its tacit reinstatement of a melioristic teleology), has finally to admit that, this notwithstanding, Hardy never managed wholly to resist the impulse "to see human destiny as a 'palpable dilemma,' ruled by inescapable forces, and Nature as a process governed by Chance. Even in *The Dynasts*," he says, "published half a century after the *Origin of Species* appeared, the influence of Darwin is still evident, and the world which Hardy deplores to the end, with the Spirit of the Pities, is one of natural selection, of fortuitous variations, and fierce struggle."[14] A world whose "invisible spheres were formed in fright."

Now this is (in Rudolf Bultmann's phrase) the "sense of existence" that is to be found controlling Hardy's most charac-

[14] Georg Roppen, *Evolution and Poetic Belief: A Study in Some Victorian and Modern Writers* (Oslo: Oslo University Press, 1956), p. 315.

teristic books, and, when it is his role as novelist (rather than his role as poet) that is primarily in view, it is surely *The Return of the Native* that must be held up—above even *Far from the Madding Crowd* or *Jude the Obscure* or *The Mayor of Casterbridge* or *Tess of the d'Urbervilles*—as the central example of his art: here we get what is undoubtedly our richest impression of the spiritual terrain in his major fiction.

Like so many of Hardy's novels, *The Return of the Native* is a tragic love story, and, taken merely at this level, it presents us with an extraordinarily affecting drama. Clym Yeobright has been away from his home on Egdon Heath for several years, and, during this long period, he has been steadily rising to success in the diamond trade in Paris. But, having grown weary of the frivolous easiness of his life there, he has returned to his mother's house and the scene of his early years, hoping to find a way of setting up a school on the Heath and of serving its people as a teacher. Soon after his return he meets and falls in love with Eustacia Vye, a beautiful and tempestuous woman, whose great desire is to get away from her lonely, isolated home on Egdon and to go precisely to that place of imagined elegance and splendor from which Clym has just fled. So she accepts his proposal of marriage, believing, despite his announced intention of remaining on the Heath, that in him she will have a connection with and a way of getting to the larger world of her long cherished dream.

Eustacia has had a secret affair with Damon Wildeve, the husband of Clym's cousin Thomasin, and when, after Clym's eyes are badly damaged as a result of excessive reading in preparation for his teaching mission, he goes out to work on the Heath as a furze-cutter in order not to exhaust his savings, Eustacia feels that perhaps she has chosen badly. This reversal of sentiment in her becomes particularly emphatic after Damon inherits a sizeable legacy that gives him independence; then, indeed, it does appear to Eustacia that it is he, not Clym, who holds for her the chance of a larger life, and, since Damon has never lost his affection for her, they begin to meet again.

Now Mrs. Yeobright, Clym's mother, having always distrusted Eustacia, had never approved of her son's marriage, and it is many months before she can bring herself to call on them at their little cottage on the Heath. But at last she does visit them. Thinking that Clym is absent, Wildeve has just called, but Clym is asleep in the cottage; and, on seeing Mrs. Yeobright through a window, Eustacia takes Wildeve to the garden behind the cottage, confident that Clym will hear a second knock. But Mrs. Yeobright, having detected Eustacia peering through the window, takes her failure to admit her to be a deliberate snub and, feeling that she has been turned away from the house of her son, does not knock again: instead, she turns homeward, and, in the course of the long journey back across the Heath, collapses and dies.

Clym later discovers what transpired on the last day of his mother's life, and his anger at Eustacia results in a separation. Freed at last from her marriage, but to a desperate kind of freedom, she and Wildeve plan to leave the Heath together. But, in the end, Damon is not "great enough for her desire," and, on a dark, rainy November night, unhinged by her despairing unhappiness, she leaps into the black pool of the whirling current that drives the Egdon mill wheel. Damon loses his life in the effort to save her, and Clym, who is very nearly drowned in the same effort, alone survives. But, when we leave him at the close of the action, he has lost the resolution and the energy that he had brought back to Egdon, and, now spent and somehow shattered, he goes about the Heath as a lay preacher, expounding to the bemusement of the Egdon peasantry a simple, Tolstoyan gospel of love for man and for God.

This is, of course, but the merest sketch of the action, and, in hewing close to the central narrative line of the novel, it takes no account of many personages who are memorable elements of Hardy's total design. But unquestionably the freight of its main meaning and power is chiefly borne by Clym and Eustacia. In her we meet a pure instance of that romantic imagination whose history has been so brilliantly analyzed in our time by Denis de Rougemont.[15] "To be loved to madness," says Hardy, "—such was her great desire. Love was to her the one cordial which could drive away the eating loneliness of her days. . . . she seemed to long for the abstraction called passionate love more than for any particular lover." And Clym, who "had reached the stage in a young man's life when the grimness of the general human situation first becomes clear" —Clym is one in whom there is "the ache of modernism":

> In Clym Yeobright's face could be dimly seen the typical countenance of the future. Should there be a classic period to art hereafter, its Pheidias may produce such faces. The view of life as a thing to be put up with, replacing that zest for existence which was so intense in early civilizations, must enter so thoroughly into the constitution of the advanced races that its facial expression will become accepted as a new artistic departure. People already feel that a man who lives without disturbing a curve of feature, or setting a mark of mental concern anywhere upon himself, is too far removed from modern perceptiveness to be a modern type. Physically beautiful men—the glory of the race when it was young— are almost an anachronism now; and we may wonder whether, at some time or other, physically beautifully women may not be an anachronism likewise.

Yet, internally complicated as these two people are, their personal story is, in a way, subdued and subordinated by the world of Egdon Heath itself—whose function in the novel is well defined by Walter Allen as that of describing "the real circumstances in which man lives." Hardy offers the Heath, Mr. Allen suggests, as "an extended image of the nature of which man is part, in which he is caught, which conditions his very being, and which cares nothing for him."[16] Hardy never allows us to dissociate his central characters from the Heath.

[15] *Vide* Denis de Rougemont, *Passion and Society*, trans. Montgomery Belgion (London: Faber and Faber Ltd., 1940).

[16] Walter Allen, *The English Novel: A Short Critical History* (New York: E. P. Dutton and Co., Inc., 1957), p. 293.

The late Joseph Warren Beach suggested many years ago in his fine book on Hardy that it may well have been just for the sake of Eustacia that he took such pains in producing the rich and moving evocation of night upon the Heath in the first book of the novel[17]: she is the "figure against the sky," the "Queen of Night," and never do we lose a sense of a deep affinity between the harsh, craggy magnificence of Egdon and the dark tower of the spirit in which this passionate woman lives with such irresponsible and turbulent independence.

As for Clym, he is "inwoven with the heath"—"permeated with its scenes, with its substance . . . his estimate of life had been coloured by it." It reminds him of "the arena of life": it gives him "a sense of bare equality with, and no superiority to, a single living thing under the sun," and the dead flatness of it sometimes overpowers him.

Indeed, the Heath's dark, gloomy, threatening presence is the dominating force in the novel. Its "Titanic form" seems always to be awaiting something, and it is "full of a watchful intentness": all the significant characters and actions of the novel are held within its compass, and its massive, brooding fixity everywhere emphasizes the insignificance of its human denizens. "Haggard Egdon," says Hardy,

> appealed to a subtler and scarcer instinct, to a more recently learnt emotion, than that which responds to the sort of beauty called charming and fair.
>
> Indeed, it is a question if the exclusive reign of this orthodox beauty is not approaching its last quarter. The new Vale of Tempe may be a gaunt waste in Thule: human souls may find themselves in closer and closer harmony with external things wearing a sombreness distasteful to our race when it was young. The time seems near, if it has not actually arrived, when the chastened sublimity of a moor, a sea, or a mountain will be all of nature that is absolutely in keeping with the moods of the more thinking among mankind.

[17] Joseph Warren Beach, *The Technique of Thomas Hardy* (Chicago: University of Chicago Press, 1922), p. 103.

So, believing a barren waste to be the appropriate image of what life in the modern world is like, Hardy makes this obscure, isolated country of Egdon Heath, in all its "ancient permanence," the scene within whose horizon the entire drama of Clym Yeobright and Eustacia Vye runs its course. He does this because the Heath is intended to be the type of that blind, massive inertia in things whose indifference to all the great aspirations of the human spirit is the proof of the frailty and impotence of man—who, when he appears upon the scene, appears (as we are told in the title of the second chapter of the first book) "hand in hand with trouble."

Nor is the tonal unity established by the Heath in any way broken by the large role that is played in the action by the undesigned and fortuitous, by "crass Casualty." It is a sheer accident that Diggory Venn should misunderstand Mrs. Yeobright's direction as to how the money is to be divided between Clym and Thomasin; and it is out of a situation arising from this accident that the misunderstanding between Eustacia and Mrs. Yeobright develops—which in turn leads to the quarrel between Clym and his mother. Or, again, it is a sheer quirk of fate that, on the occasion of Mrs. Yeobright's visit to Clym's cottage, he should have called out "Mother" in his sleep and that Eustacia, on hearing him, should have supposed that he was awake and was greeting his mother. And how utterly fortuitous that Clym's letter which might have repaired the rupture between himself and Eustacia should by her go unopened and that, believing herself to be cast off by her husband, she should have gone out into the storm on that last fatal night. And so on it goes not only throughout *The Return of the Native* but throughout the whole world of Hardy's fiction, whether one turns to *Tess* or to *Jude* or to *The Mayor of Casterbridge*: the decisive event is always the utterly gratuitous event, and we feel that we are in, as indeed we are, that modern universe of absurdity with which writers like Gide and Kafka and Camus have long since made us familiar. The truly executive powers are "purblind Doomsters" against whom man is without any protection at all—and, given his infirmity and the bleak, wintry emptiness of the heavens that gaze disconsolately down upon him, it is, therefore, simply futile to hope that goodness and mercy, or even justice, will ultimately prevail. The time is out of joint, and the world is incomprehensible. And, though this metaphysic of ambiguity may seem to depart very considerably from the primacy in Darwin's thought of the idea of orderly processes of causation, it is, nevertheless, a characteristic expression of the kind of metaphysical anguish that was suffered by many sensitive men in the late years of the nineteenth century as a result of the profound dislocations following upon the intellectual movement with which Darwinism was affiliated. Nor does it appear, when we read books like Jean-Paul Sartre's *La Nausée* or Albert Camus' *L'Étranger*, that this is a kind of anguish which exists today solely as an object of historical study. Its present vocabulary is, of course, not one which was familiar to the great Victorians, and its immediate irritants in the world of scholarship and culture may to some extent have changed. But, when Camus tells us that in this mute and abandoned universe of ours there is nothing by which we can be nourished but "the wine of the absurd and the bread of indifference,"[18] we are reminded that the world of the modern imagination may still be the world of Hardy's "Hap"—a world, that is (as Bertrand Russell said many years ago), of "secular hurryings through . . . space."[19]

Yet, despite all the brilliance of his little book on the Victorians, surely G. K. Chesterton quite failed deeply to understand Hardy's position, when he disposed of him as merely a "village atheist."[20] In this instance, as in others, Chesterton

[18] Albert Camus, *The Myth of Sisyphus and Other Essays*, trans. by Justin O'Brien (New York: Alfred A. Knopf, 1957), p. 52.

[19] Bertrand Russell, "A Free Man's Worship," *Selected Papers of Bertrand Russell* (New York: The Modern Library, n.d.), p. 3.

[20] G. K. Chesterton, *The Victorian Age in Literature* (New York: Henry Holt and Co., 1913), p. 143.

gave way to what was occasionally for him a great besetting temptation, of a kind of sharp, ungenerous, carping malice— and thus his own self-indulgence in temperament made, in this case, for a failure in critical and theological discrimination. For his epithet connotes a mean, narrow, unimaginative kind of rationalism and "free thought" than which nothing could be further removed from the qualities of mind that we meet in Hardy's major work. Indeed, it was F. A. Hedgcock who brought us very much nearer the fundamental truth about Hardy, when he said: "C'est ce pouvoir de suggérer le mystère métaphysique, si nous pouvons parler ainsi, derrière les actes les plus ordinaires, qui donne aux oeuvres de M. Hardy leur cachet particulier et distingue leur auteur des autres romanciers de son époque."[21] This is precisely it: nor need it be for any other reason than this that we should wince at the heavy condescension of those who follow Henry James in regarding him as "the good little Thomas Hardy."

It is true, of course, that, when he was most acutely perturbed by the pressure of the metaphysical crisis, Hardy tended to reach for a grandness of rhetorical gesture that often tripped him up and led him to write "badly"—as, for example, in the familiar last paragraph of *Tess* in which we are told that "'Justice' was done, and the President of the Immortals [in Aeschylean phrase] had ended his sport with Tess." It is also true that, in his approach to his craft, he never revealed the kind of technical sophistication of which criticism in our time has made so great a fetish: the art of fiction was something that he somehow stumbled into, and he never won the kind of self-conscious *expertise* that was the pride of a James or a Conrad. Yet, with the natural fabulism of the born storyteller, in figures like Tess Durbeyfield and Michael Henchard and Eustacia Vye and Clym Yeobright and Sue Bridehead and Jude Fawley, he created a gallery of characters in whom there is

[21] F. A. Hedgcock, *Thomas Hardy: Penseur et Artiste* (Paris: Librairie Hachette & Cie, 1911), p. 172.

preserved (as Alfred Kazin has observed of the not too dissimilar case of Dreiser's characters)

> a certain wonder, a forgotten, provincial detachment from the brutalities around them, that gives them the quality of contemplatives in a world they no longer hope to master. They have that brooding attachment to strange new forces in life that we find in old sagas. . . . they are like figures in a dream that they are astonished to be weaving around themselves.[22]

The great characters in Hardy's novels live in a world in which, as he says, the "harshnesses of mankind are tenderness itself when compared with the universal harshness out of which they grow." Yet there is no cynicism in the creatures of his imagination: Tess and Jude and Clym have "the sort of worn, deeply engraved dignity that is given to those who know only that they are doomed to face in one direction and never another,"[23] and, though unsupported by any great hope, they face the inexhaustible mystery of the world with a kind of reverential amazement—an amazement that "rushes back at us with a sound primitive, innocent, and grand, like man's first discovery of the nature of his existence."[24]

In Hardy, then, we encounter an extreme instance in Victorian literature of the *maladie du siècle*: he was a martyr of that "iron time/Of doubts, disputes, distractions, fears"—and, in his books, we have an important index of the cost to the spirit that it entailed. And not only does he lead us back into that trauma in the nineteenth century out of which the modern existentialist imagination was born, but he also brings us forward into our own time and to that anxious perplexity for which so many of the great writers of this century (Kafka, the early Eliot, Malraux, Camus, to mention only a few) have been major spokesmen. To re-read his books is to be reminded that, as Paul Tillich says, "the decisive event which underlies

[22] Alfred Kazin, *The Inmost Leaf* (New York: Harcourt, Brace and Co., 1955), p. 239.
[23] *Ibid.*, pp. 239–240.
[24] *Ibid.*, p. 241.

the search for meaning and the despair of it in the twentieth century is the loss of God in the nineteenth century."[25] Yet, though Hardy thought that he had attended God's funeral and that he crept toward the myth's oblivion "Sadlier than those who wept in Babylon,/Whose Zion was a still abiding hope," he was no "village atheist."

In attempting to define what is central in the thought of one of Hardy's not so distant heirs, Ernest Hemingway, Robert Penn Warren suggests that, in *A Farewell to Arms*, the story that lies beneath the story of Frederic Henry and Catherine Barkley is a story of "the quest for meaning and certitude in a world that seems to offer nothing of the sort. It is, in a sense, a religious book; if it does not offer a religious solution it is nevertheless conditioned by the religious problem."[26] It is precisely in the same vein that it must be affirmed against the witness of G. K. Chesterton that the testimony that is formed by the writings of Thomas Hardy—like that of many of his contemporaries who somehow survived such events as the *Origin of Species* and *Essays and Reviews*—is a profoundly religious testimony, even if it does not offer a conventional and "orthodox" solution to the religious problem. Indeed, one suspects that none of the "solutions" to that problem which may be fashioned in our own day will be relevant to the dislocations of the age, if they are uninformed by a deep knowledge of what the world appeared to be like to the author of *The Return of the Native* and *Jude the Obscure*.

[25] Tillich, *op. cit.*, p. 142.
[26] Robert Penn Warren, "Ernest Hemingway," *Selected Essays* (New York: Random House, 1958), p. 107.

III

Kafka's Anguish

Erich Heller, in a recent essay on Friedrich Nietzsche, says:

> Name almost any poet, man of letters, philosopher, who
> wrote in German during the 20th century and attained to
> stature and influence; name Rilke, George, Kafka, Thomas
> Mann, Ernst Jünger, Musil, Benn, Heidegger, or Jaspers—
> and you name at the same time Friedrich Nietzsche. He is to
> them all—whether or not they know and acknowledge it (and
> most of them do)—what St. Thomas Aquinas was to Dante:
> the categorical interpreter of a world which they contemplate
> poetically or philosophically without ever radically upsetting
> its Nietzschean structure.[1]

The range of that literature which Nietzsche interprets "cate-
gorically" might well be extended far beyond the confines of
the German language, to include the Italian tradition of
Moravia and the French tradition of Malraux and Sartre and
the Anglo-American tradition of Hemingway, Durrell, Mal-
colm Lowry, and John Hawkes. For the rumor that drifts
throughout this entire modern "scripture" is that which was first
publicized by Nietzsche, when he announced in his book of
1882, *The Gay Science* (*Die Fröhliche Wissenschaft*), that
"God is dead."

[1] Erich Heller, "The Importance of Nietzsche," *Encounter*, Vol.
XXII, No. 4 (April, 1964), p. 59.

One of the important critical essays of the nineteenth century is Matthew Arnold's inaugural lecture as Professor of Poetry at Oxford—"On the Modern Element in Literature," which he delivered in 1857 and which he published a decade later in *Macmillan's Magazine*. In this, as in so many of his other critical pieces, Arnold was trying to achieve a clear definition of the essential meaning of "modernity" in cultural history. If this essay were now to be rewritten, at a little more than a century's remove from the original version, it would surely have to be said (as Arnold did himself to some extent discern in many of his other essays) that the distinctively "modern" element in modern literature—the thing that gives the period's literature its peculiar form and pressure—is the sense that it almost everywhere evinces of the eclipse and the disappearance of God. "Quietly," says Karl Jaspers, "something enormous has happened in the reality of Western man." This happening which has gradually slouched upon the awareness of the men and women of the twentieth century is one that entails nothing less than the darkening of an old sun, the demise of something that for countless ages had supported and given meaning to human life. The event, as it was defined in the melodramatic language of Nietzsche's *Gay Science,* is nothing less than the death of God—the death, that is, *in* the modern consciousness of a sense of nature and history being animated by any Power or Presence or gracious and providential Spirit. "We need a theme? then let that be our theme," advises Conrad Aiken in one of his finest poems: and this is precisely where much of modern literature has found its basic leverage: "it takes its foothold in the fact that we have no foothold,"[2] and the theme that is explored is that (as Aiken says) we are "poor grovelers between faith and doubt" and that our "heart's weak engine [has] all but stopped."

Now, if Nietzsche is the chief "categorical interpreter" of this modern *malaise,* it is Franz Kafka who is his chief coun-

[2] Stanley Romaine Hopper, *The Crisis of Faith* (New York-Nashville: Abingdon Press, 1944), p. 119.

terpart in the realm of imaginative writing. As a distinguished poet remarked a few years ago, "Had one to name the artist who comes nearest to bearing the same kind of relation to our age that Dante, Shakespeare, Goethe bore to theirs, Kafka is the first we would think of." This is so, because it is from this remarkably gifted Czech Jew (who died in 1924, at the age of forty-one) that we get what is widely acknowledged to be the most archetypal presentation of the modern hero in the literature of this century: he, so to speak, gives the age away—which is to say that, in the haunting fables of his stories and novels, he makes public a secret nightmare that has been dreamt over and over again, on pummeled pillows everywhere. The man whom we encounter at the center of Kafka's fictions is a creature

> . . . lost,
> Each man lost, in some blind lobby, hall, enclave,
> Crank cul-de-sac, couloir, or corridor of Time.
> Of Time. Or self: and in that dark no thread. . . .[3]

"We were fashioned to live in Paradise," says Kafka in one of the notes accompanying the collection of his stories and parables entitled *The Great Wall of China*—"We were fashioned to live in Paradise, and Paradise was destined to serve us. Our destiny has been altered. . . ." And that blunt announcement— "Our destiny has been altered"—summarizes his whole sense of man's condition. For man does not live in Paradise: he is one who has been ousted from that Good Place where it would delight the soul to be, and his condemnation, in Kafka's vision of the human predicament, is to a world in which he is a stranger and in which he can nowhere descry any reassuring landmarks or any promise of his being ultimately accommodated. In this darkness, there is no thread. "There is a goal," as Kafka says, "but no way: what we call the way is only wavering." Everywhere there is mystery—black, impenetrable, men-

[3] Robert Penn Warren, *Brother to Dragons* (New York: Random House, 1953), p. 7.

acing: mystery in the inaccessible interior of a man's own life, mystery in the unbridgeable distances that separate him from his human fellows, mystery in the permanent remoteness of that Castle of Grace the reaching of which would bring joy and healing to the heart's dispeace. So it is a world of fear and trembling—in which (to borrow a figure of Scott Fitzgerald) it is always three o'clock in the morning.

There is an early film of Charlie Chaplin's—*City Lights*—in which the little tramp is picked up by a rich man on a drunken spree and taken back to the man's great mansion, where he is installed as an honored guest. But then, when the man's intoxication has passed, he throws Charlie out of his house. The relation between these two that is so hilariously chronicled by the movie is one that consists of a long series of reunions and rejections: when the rich man is half seas over, he embraces his little friend and takes him home, putting his splendid house at Charlie's disposal: but, once he emerges from his alcoholic stupor, he flings the tramp out, and Charlie is simply overwhelmed with bewilderment by the caprice with which he is buffeted about. Now the arbitrariness which the little tramp of *City Lights* experiences as the governing principle of his life is something like the senseless fatality that Kafka's heroes encounter as the sovereign principle of their own existence. The young protagonist of *Amerika*, for example (Kafka's first novel), is sent away from home after his seduction by a village girl. But, after his arrival in this country and his installment in the New York house of a wealthy uncle, a messenger suddenly hands him one night his uncle's notification of his dismissal: he has been visiting friends of his uncle's, at their country house near New York, and, just as he is preparing to return to the city, he is given the envelope marked "To Karl Rossmann, to be delivered personally. . . ." From there on, young Karl drifts from pillar to post over the United States, being taken in here and ousted there, as though he were the plaything of invisible and maleficent potencies. But this is what the world is like, in the Kafkan perspective: it is a place teeming with insecurity and fortuitousness, asking to be rendered in the slightly askew scrawlings of a Paul Klee—a world so ordered by disorder as to make it not at all unnatural for a young man to wake up of a morning to find himself under sudden arrest for an unspecified crime (Joseph K. in *The Trial*) or to find himself transformed into a gigantic bug (Gregor Samsa in *Metamorphosis*). Things are terribly out of joint—and so one is all the time trying in vain to catch the ear of sinisterly scatterbrained officials, and one's complaints never reach the right office, and one is always detraining and yet never quite reaching journey's end, or one reaches the intended destination but only to find that one is too late. It is all a kind of ghastly comic strip, such as might be invented by some infinitely poised and sober artist miraculously in possession of the gifts at once of Sterne and Picasso and Pascal and Daumier, and the early Walt Disney.

"Our art," says Kafka in one of his Aphorisms, "is a dazzled blindness before the truth. . . ." But the difficult question as to what is the general bent and curvature of this "truth" has furnished the subject of one of the great exegetical controversies of modern criticism. It seems generally to be agreed that, however this truth exactly is to be defined, it is of a character at least as complex as the physics of nuclear fission. Yet, though Einstein is reported to have returned a book of Kafka's to Thomas Mann with the comment that he couldn't read it, that the human mind isn't complicated enough, he is perhaps (as Professor Angel Flores has remarked) the only man who has ever admitted his bafflement by this strange and unexampled art. For nearly everyone who has in any way made his reactions to Kafka a matter of public record seems to be absolutely certain not only that *he* has unlocked the secret of what Kafka "really" means but also that he *alone* has found the proper key.

The fascinating diversity of these various "readings" need not be canvassed on this present occasion, but there is one general line of interpretation which does require to be noticed, if—as this essay proposes—Kafka is to be regarded as an exemplary figure not only in the literary but also in the religious history of our time. For there are many of his interpreters who strenuously deny that his fiction is properly to be viewed as belonging to any sort of religious ambiance. They maintain—as in the case, for example, of Günther Anders and his brilliant little book[4]—that what is remote and mysterious in Kafka's world is not a "figure" of the hiddenness of the divine but is simply an expression of how "infinitely" inaccessible the *actual* world of empirical time and commonplace history had come to be for him. This effort to "naturalize" the meaning of Kafka's fiction springs from a rejection of still other styles of interpretation that are, to be sure, highly dubious. It is motivated, for example, by an impatience with the attempt that was so frequently being made a few years ago to interpret Kafka as a sort of theologian *manqué* who, having misconceived his vocation, adopted a cryptic form of allegorical fiction as his medium and whose meaning is therefore definable only as the allegory is translated into the terms of a kind of "crisis-theology." But this is an approach than which none could be more wrongheaded. To handle the work of one of the great artists of our age in such a way that its explication becomes merely a matter of notating parallels with the Kabbala and the theologies of Sören Kierkegaard and Karl Barth is surely to mishandle it in a stupidly brutal way. For the business of one who undertakes to talk about imaginative literature is not to hurry after its presumable nonliterary sources; and to permit one's eye to glance off the literary object toward extrinsic considerations of one sort or another is to forfeit the chance of saying anything *literarily* relevant about the given work of literature. And, in Kafka studies, this is a wrongheadedness that has frequently prepared the way for still another error—namely, that of regarding Kafka as a modern Bunyan whose fables record an essentially religious pilgrimage, and a journey that

[4] *Vide* Günther Anders, *Franz Kafka*, trans. by A. Steer and A. K. Thorlby (London: Bowes & Bowes Ltd., 1960).

is as decisively Christian as that which is recounted in the *Pilgrim's Progress*. But to approach this tortured martyr of modern agnosticism as a kind of "underground" Christian requires an extraordinary nimbleness of sophistry, and such a tucking away of contradictory evidence as has finally robbed all interpretations in this mode of any truly compelling cogency.

So the opponents of "religious" interpretation are doubtless right in offering resistance to much that they reject. But to grant that a work of literary art is stupidly misconceived if it is approached as an essay in philosophical theology rather than as a work of the poetic imagination and, in this particular case, to grant also that Kafka, far from being any sort of crypto-Christian, is one of the great exponents of what is in many respects a *post*-Christian age—to make these admissions is not to have foreclosed the possibility that, nevertheless, the essential subject of his art has to do with a profoundly religious ordeal. Indeed, to insist, as Günther Anders does, that *The Trial* and *The Castle* concern only a certain curious alienation from the "actual," commonplace, ordinary world of everyday is in fact to blind oneself to the diabolical *irony* with which Kafka occasionally *pretends* that the empirical actuality of the commonplace is the ultimate reality. And it is just in the *ironical* character of the pretense that the religious depth of his scepticism may best be seen.

Stories such as "The Judgment," "The Penal Colony," and "Metamorphosis" and the novels, *Amerika* and *The Trial,* all furnish important evidence of what is centrally characteristic of Kafka's vision, but the really crucial case remains the book which in the general consensus is regarded as his masterpiece, the novel on which he began work in the spring of 1922 and which, though not completely finished at the time of his death, was posthumously published for the first time in 1927 under the title *Das Schloss, The Castle.* Once this remarkably brilliant *tour de force* is in view, what one wants, inevitably, first of all to remark is how strange it is that so profound a sense of mystery should be evoked in us by a novel whose surfaces are so limpidly clear and apparently uncomplicated. The plot is of the slenderest possible sort. A young man—whose name consists of but one letter, "K"—comes into a village. We do not know from whence he comes, or indeed anything at all about his past. He is identified only as a land-surveyor, and as one who believes he has received a professional appointment from the village's executive authorities who govern the community from a great castle situated on a hill overlooking the little hamlet. But no one in the village appears to have been expecting his arrival, and he quickly discovers that there is no prepared place for him. So his task soon becomes that of winning some clear certification from the Castle that he does in fact bear this appointment and that he has his "place." But it is just this "nod of recognition" that proves exasperatingly difficult to attain, for the inner workings of the Castle represent bureaucratism run wild, and establishing any kind of contact with the officials is a matter of almost infinitely complex protocol, involving documents and proofs and dossiers and endless reams of "papers."

So complex is the "method" of the Castle that K. is soon thrown into doubt about his ability ever to secure any unambiguous statement of his position. Indeed, the further he presses his "case" the more does K. find the Castle to be simply one huge question-mark, a world cloaked in the darkest mystery, impenetrable even by the permanent residents of the village who, when they undertake to speak of it, invariably end by contradicting themselves and one another. They do not even agree about which roads lead to the Castle and which do not, so that about all it is possible for K. to conclude is that some roads lead to the Castle and some do not: but, as to which of the roads are used by the officials in traveling between the Castle and the village, it seems impossible to say, for "now one of them is in fashion, and most carriages go by that, now it's another and everything drives pell-mell there. And what governs this change of fashion has never yet been found out." So much at variance with any common-sense view of things is the world of the Castle that it is even impossible to predict what its officials will look like from one day to another; their very physical appearance is constantly changing: Klamm, for example, who is highly placed in the Castle-hierarchy, "after having his beer . . . looks different from what he does before it, when he's awake he's different from when he's asleep, when he's alone he's different from when he's talking to people. . . ." And the inhabitants of the village can never agree about "his height, his bearing, his size and the cut of his beard. . . ."

So this young man who, at the beginning of the novel, seems to come out of nowhere, with no home of his own, with no past, with no memories, is in a dark wood—into which we feel he may have stumbled simply because his life has had no foundations, because he has had no real home and no deep allegiances. But what he wants no longer to do is to continue to live without foundations, and the entire plot of the novel might be regarded as gathering its coherence from K.'s effort to base his life on what he now conceives to be its ultimate Foundation: yet the depressing discovery that he makes is of the remoteness, the distance, of this ultimate Foundation. Having discovered after his arrival in the village that he has no definitely assigned and generally acknowledged place in its scheme of things and that, if he is to prosper there, he must obtain from the Castle a formal certification of the appointment that he believes himself to have received, he never ceases to seek this confirming word. He encounters obstruction upon obstruction and hindrance upon hindrance; and his difficulties are not merely serial, in the sense of following upon each other; they are also interlocked, and they tower upon each other. Each contact that he succeeds in establishing with the Castle—his liaison with the former mistress of an official, an occasional letter received from a minor functionary, a telephone conversation overheard, the two young men who are sent to be his assistants—each contact at first appears to be promising and to hold out the hope that he will finally manage to gain confirmation of his appointment as the village's land-surveyor; but they all prove to be worthless in the end.

Yet K. is incapable of resignation, and he never relaxes in his effort to penetrate to the center of the ultimate mystery and to wring from it a kind of evidence or validation of his right to exist. He keeps his hope that a direct confrontation with the Castle's chief executive is possible, and one that will result in a clarification of his destiny. The possibility that things are ultimately organized upon the basis of a principle of arbitrariness wounds him so deeply that he refuses to accept the notion of it. Yet the fact of it never ceases to stare him in the face. For all his encounters with the representatives of the Castle seem to make a mockery of his striving, and, indeed, from the standpoint of the villagers, they are all figments of his imagination. "You haven't once . . . come into contact with our authorities," they tell him. "All those contacts are merely illusory, but owing to your ignorance of the circumstances you take them to be real."

But, while he is suffering the indignity of employment as the janitor in the village school (a temporary job accepted to "make ends meet"), he receives a letter from Klamm, who tells him: "The surveying work which you have carried out thus far has my recognition. . . . Do not slacken in your efforts! Bring your work to a successful conclusion. Any interruption would displease me. . . . I shall not forget you." From this, it would appear that there is truly some possibility for K. of a direct relationship with the Castle; but it somehow never quite comes off, and he never gets anywhere at all.

The universe, then, that is exhibited in this book is a dreadful phantasmagoria: it is a universe of insecurity and of uncertainty, presided over by an ultimate Authority, but an Authority to the nature of which the Protestant conception of the religious enterprise, at least as it is conventionally understood, is quite irrelevant. For K. cannot be his own priest: he cannot reach this ultimate Authority without benefit of mediation: there is no possibility of the direct and immediate vision.

The Castle is, at every point, surrounded by impenetrable mystery, and this mysteriousness is a sign of the elusiveness of the truth, of the ultimate truth, of the truth that would be a joy and a gladness to the heart could it but be apprehended. So the human situation, as Kafka describes it, is essentially that which Pascal describes in the 72nd Fragment of the *Pensées*, where he says:

> We sail within a vast sphere, ever drifting in uncertainty, driven from end to end. When we think to attach ourselves to any point and to fasten to it, it wavers and leaves us; and if we follow it, it eludes our grasp, slips past us, and vanishes for ever. Nothing stays for us. This is our natural condition, and yet most contrary to our inclination; we burn with desire to find solid ground and an ultimate sure foundation whereon to build a tower reaching to the Infinite. But our whole groundwork cracks, and the earth opens to abysses.

It is the anguish suffered by man as a result of this cracking of his groundwork that constitutes K.'s great burden.

K., then, is alone, utterly alone: he is the foreigner, the outsider, the alienated man, the man pressing his nose against the glass and wanting to come in, yet being perpetually baffled and thwarted and confused as to where is the door that might grant him entrance. Now, to be sure, he lives in a state of alienation from the community of the village, from the world of his human neighbors: there, on that level of things, he is unincluded, unintegrated. But to define his isolation in exclusively infra-human terms—as do many of those critics who deny the presence in Kafka's fiction of any significant religious element—is not only to take an incomplete view of that isolation but it is also to be unable finally to account for it. For K.'s estrangement from the villagers is a consequence of his inability to make contact with the "higher-ups" in the Castle: he cannot win a secure position in the human order—in the world of his mistress Frieda, and Pepi the little chambermaid at the *Herrenhof*, and the landlady of the Inn by the Bridge—until

the Castle grants him a validating guaranty of that position. So
he faces unswervingly towards the Castle—and, for him, it
stands not merely for some possibility *within* the human order
of settling one's secular affairs, one's citizenship and occupation and residence: no, in the logic of the novel's design the
Castle is, for K., the source of the ultimate and absolute truth
about himself and his human condition: it is the source *outside*
the village, *outside* the world, of any capacity that a man may
ever hope to achieve of living satisfactorily *within* the world.
The great fact about the Castle is that it is closed, and inaccessible to the human pilgrim—an infinite perpendicular from the
starless heavens, intersecting the incommensurable plane of
man's life in concrete, historical time. Thus it is, as Erich
Heller says, that "Kafka represents the absolute reversal of
German idealism. If it is Hegel's final belief that in the Absolute truth and existence are one, for Kafka it is precisely
through the Absolute that they are for ever divided. Truth and
existence are mutually exclusive."[5]

So K.—like the hero of *Amerika,* like the hero of *The
Trial,* and of many of Kafka's stories—faces the future always
with misgivings, always with mistrust, and always with infinite
longing. For between the dreary inanity of daily existence and
the Radically Significant there yawns an unbridgeable chasm.
If we try, therefore, to systematize the understanding of reality
that knits Kafka's poetic economy into a coherent whole, it
must be said that the term which renders with technical ac-
curacy the human condition, as he pictures it, is the term *existence* which, in its most literal sense, means "standing-out-
from." For this is indeed what Kafka takes the human situation
to be—a standing-out-from, or away-from, or in-separation-
from, the Ground of reality. It is the lesson that at many points
is enforced upon us by the narrative of *The Castle,* and most
especially by the account that is given of the relation between

    [5] Erich Heller, *The Disinherited Mind: Essays in Modern German
Literature and Thought* (Philadelphia: Dufour and Saifer, 1952), p.
172.

Klamm and the landlady of the Inn by the Bridge. She says to K. in one of their conversations: "Klamm once chose me as his mistress, can I ever lose that honour? . . . Three times [he] sent for me, but he never sent a fourth time, no, never a fourth time!" And she asks K.:

> "Why should he have concerned himself about me, or better, how could he in any case have concerned himself about me? . . . The fact that he had ceased to summon me was a sign that he had forgotten me. When he stops summoning people, he forgets them completely. . . . And it's not mere forgetting, it's something more than that. For anybody one has forgotten can come back to one's memory again, of course. With Klamm, that's impossible. Anybody that he stops summoning he has forgotten completely, not only as far as the past is concerned, but literally for the future as well."

But then she asks: "Where is the man who could hinder me from running to Klamm if Klamm lifted his little finger? Madness," she says, "absolute madness, one begins to feel confused . . . when one plays with such mad ideas."

Now it is clear that, for the landlady—though she was with Klamm only three times, and then the affair was at an end—this remains the most important event of her life. After it was over, she married her husband Hans—but, as it were, half-heartedly, the great experience of her life having now been lived out to its conclusion. Indeed, the sweet memory of it is the only thing that now makes the humdrum monotony of her life endurable. But the fact that the most real event of her life belongs to a brief moment in the past, the fact that now, in the present, she is completely out of contact with Klamm—this bespeaks how great a distance it is at which life has to be lived from that which gives it meaning and significance. "When he stops summoning people, he forgets them completely." And the fact that Klamm "forgets" means that no secure and stable relation with the Castle is possible: to be sure, the woman "surrendered," unlike Amalia, one of the girls in the village,

who angrily refused a sexual proposal of Sortini, one of the
Castle's high officials, and who, in so refusing, called down
upon herself and her whole family the wrath of the Castle and
of the entire village. The landlady "surrendered," but the act of
surrender did not itself make possible any closure of the hiatus
between the divine and the human: it simply rendered it just
barely tolerable.

But it is precisely the impossibility of any closure of this
hiatus that K. cannot accept. So he resists the landlady's testimony. He insists that the idea that Klamm forgets "is a legend,
thought out moreover by the girlish minds of those who happen to have been in Klamm's favour." The landlady's husband
is a dull, stupid man, and, when she thinks of what she has had
with Klamm, she cannot regard the phase of her life that is
formed by her marriage as having any importance at all: in it
surely there is, as she says, "no trace . . . of Klamm"—no trace,
that is, of anything divine. But K. is prepared to imagine that
in some mysterious way Klamm may himself have arranged
the liaison, simply in order that, being married to so unimpres-
sive a man, his former mistress might not be disinclined to
come to him, should on some future occasion he desire to
summon her again. "But," says the landlady, "it's next to madness to imagine that Klamm could have given me such a man
as Hans as a husband simply that I might have no great difficulty in going to him if he should summon me sometime
again." It strikes her as next to madness to imagine such a
thing, for to do so is to suppose that Klamm had really not
forgotten: it is to suppose that there is some possibility of
living with confidence and certainty in a stable relationship
with the Transcendent: but to play with such a notion is, in her
view, utterly absurd and "next to madness"—and it is to be
remembered that she is an initiate, she is one who has "surrendered."

K. will not, however, accede to any doctrine or view of life
that posits nothing other than absolute ambiguity at the heart
of things. He knows, of course, how remote is Klamm, the

Castle's principal. Yet, all the while, he expects that, by reason of having taken as his mistress a girl who was once Klamm's mistress, he will, through his relationship with Frieda, be able to strike some sort of agreement or understanding with Klamm. To the landlady, though, K.'s plan is the sheerest nonsense, and she is careful to remind him that his only chance of getting a "nod of recognition" from the Castle is by way of the protocol of Momus.

Momus—this namesake of that Son of Night whom the Greek gods authorized to find fault with all things—is Klamm's "village secretary." "Herr Momus," as K.'s landlady explains, "is Klamm's secretary in the same sense as any of Klamm's secretaries, but his official province . . . is confined to the village. . . . That's how it's arranged," she says; "all the gentlemen in the Castle have their village secretaries." It is in this official role, as Klamm's secretary and as a writer of depositions, that Momus bids K. to give a report of his activities in the community. He proposes to keep a strict record on K. for Klamm's files—not because the record will ever be read by Klamm, but simply, as he says, "for the sake of order." And yet, though in all likelihood Klamm will never see the file on K. that Momus is preparing, it is the only means by which K. can hope to gain access to Klamm, for, at least, it will be put into Klamm's village register: more than this none can say.

But K. wants something more than this: he does not want to trust his fate to the depositions that Momus is taking, for he cannot bring himself to accept the notion that the ultimate determination of his destiny rests on something so provisional, so uncertain. Yet no less doubtful a prospect is ever offered. So—like the protagonists of Svevo's *The Confessions of Zeno* and Musil's *Man Without Qualities* and the two tramps of Beckett's *Godot* and the Joseph of Saul Bellow's *Dangling Man* and many another modern hero—this poor derelict, finally, can do little other than "wait," and, in his waiting, there is as much of dread as there is of hope. For his residence is in a world where the dominant experience is of the distance and the ab-

sence of God. It may well be just their commitment to such a
world that accounts for why it is that the heroes of Kafka's
novels are today so generally regarded as presenting *the* crucial instances in our literature of the twentieth century's characteristic *malaise*. For ours, as Paul Tillich once remarked, "is a
time of waiting; waiting is its special destiny."[6] Even believers
have fallen under the sway of our period's most powerful myth
—the myth which speaks of the "death" of God, or (put less
melodramatically) of the death in ourselves of any power to
affirm many of the ways of thinking about God which belong
to the received traditions of religious faith in the West. "It is,"
as Heidegger says, "the time of the gods that have fled and of
the god that is coming. It is the time of *need*, because it lies
under a double lack and a double Not: the No-more of the
gods that have fled and the Not-yet of the god that is coming."[7]

Heidegger's way of formulating the matter may, in its
stylistic aspect, be marred by the characteristic heaviness and
turgidity of Teutonic philosophy; yet it has the merit of reminding us that the kind of sensibility that is expressed in so
much of the art and literature of our age is, for all of its
religious negativism, wrongly assessed, if it is simply interpreted as "sheer undialectical atheism."[8] For to assert the absence of God, to assert that God is nowhere to be found among
the phenomena of the world, is really (in a term of Professor
Ronald Gregor Smith's coinage)[9] to "dedivinize" the world. It
may well be that it is only when the world is seen as "sheer
world," as a place distinct from God—it may be that it is only
when the world has thus been radically "dedivinized" that the

    [6] Paul Tillich, *The Shaking of the Foundations* (New York: Charles
Scribner's Sons, 1948), p. 152.

    [7] Martin Heidegger, *Existence and Being*, trans. by Douglas Scott
et al (Chicago: Henry Regnery Co., 1949), p. 313.

    [8] Ronald Gregor Smith, "A Theological Perspective of the Secular,"
The Christian Scholar, Vol. XLIII, No. 1 (March, 1960), p. 22.

    [9] *Ibid.*, p. 21.

question of God can then be truly asked, for this ultimate question concerns "men as having to do with what is not themselves, with what they do not and never can possess at all, as part of their self-equipment or as material for their self-mastery."[10] The question of God, in other words, concerns "what comes to . . . [men] all the time from beyond themselves"[11]; it is the question of the Ground of our ultimate dependence, it is the question of grace—and this is a question that can never be powerfully asked until the profound indigence of the world has been radically faced.

So, because of considerations of this order, it is necessary that we approach, with great care and with great tact, much of the extreme religious negativism in the literature of our period which is so perfectly instanced in the novels and stories of Franz Kafka. A novel like *The Castle* or a play like Beckett's *Godot* does, to be sure, exhibit men as inhabiting a radically profanized world and as "waiting"—waiting perhaps for some great disclosure of meaning and grace that will "redeem the time." But it is to be remembered that, as Paul Tillich says:

> . . . although waiting is *not* having, it is also having. The fact that we wait for something shows that in some way we already possess it. Waiting anticipates that which is not yet real. If we wait in hope and patience, the power of that for which we wait is already effective within us. He who waits in an ultimate sense is not far from that for which he waits. He who waits in absolute seriousness is already grasped by that for which he waits. He who waits passionately is already an active power himself, the greatest power of transformation in personal and historical life. We are stronger when we wait than when we possess. When we possess God, we reduce Him to that small thing we knew and grasped of Him; and we make it an idol. Only in idol worship can one believe in the possession of God.[12]

[10] *Ibid.*, p. 15.
[11] *Ibid.*
[12] Paul Tillich, *op. cit.*, p. 151.

If in this passage Tillich is approaching the real truth of the matter, it may just be that such an artist as Franz Kafka, for all of the wintry bleakness of his landscape, can be for us something like what Heidegger calls a "shepherd of Being"—one, that is, who, by the very resoluteness with which he plunges us into the dark, precipitates us out of our forgetfulness, so that, in a way, our deprivation of the Transcendent brings us into proximity to its mystery, and the distance of the Castle becomes itself a kind of witness to the Indestructible. This is not, of course, in the case of Kafka, to gainsay the testimony of those critics who deny the presence in his work of any sort of genuinely *affirmative* religiousness: for that indeed is hardly to be found. The question is not to what extent his work, by being tucked in here and stretched there, can be made to yield religious meanings of a positive and affirmative kind, for it would seem clear that this kind of adjustment can be accomplished only on the basis of misguided or dishonest interpretation. The question is rather to what extent, after the full stringency of his nihilism has been acknowledged, that nihilism can itself be religiously appropriated as a discipline of purgation —and this is perhaps the most truly serious question that we are asked to face not only by the fiction of Kafka but by much of the most representative literature of our age.

IV

The Modest Optimism of
Albert Camus

There is perhaps no other European writer of our period who has exerted so great a pressure on the imagination and conscience of his generation as has Albert Camus, whose life, at the age of forty-six, abruptly ended in an automobile accident in the south of France, January 4, 1960. His role in contemporary cultural life is one that puts us in mind of how unstable have been the lines of demarcation in our time between literature and philosophy. This is undoubtedly in part a result of the fact that the philosophy of the academies has often been so intimidated by science that it has consented to be deprived of first one and then another of its fields of inquiry, so that, at the last, there is little else left for it to do but to practice the disciplines of logical and linguistic analysis. Thus, for instruction in the unique facts and experiences of human personality, the men of our age have turned to poets and novelists or to thinkers like Heidegger and Jaspers and Marcel who have been converting philosophy itself into a kind of metaphysical poetry or drama.

But, however we choose to account for this tendency today of literary and philosophical categories to coalesce, it must be granted that in a very deep and integral sense the great literature of our age has been by way of becoming "an

instrument of metaphysical consciousness."[1] The art of such
writers, for example, as Pirandello, Gide, and Malraux is of
enormous technical interest, and their work cannot be properly
appropriated if this dimension is ignored. But, when we read
Les Faux Monnayeurs, it is not the experimentalist in "point of
view" but Gide in his role as theorist of the gratuitous act who
interests us most deeply; in the theatre of Pirandello, what we
are perplexed and engaged by most profoundly is not the sheer
pyrotechnics of his eccentric dramaturgy but the bitter existential comedy, say, of *Right You Are;* and, in a novel like *L'Espoir,* the thing that we feel to be of high significance is not
Malraux's adaptation of the techniques of cinematic *montage*
but his tragic humanism, his vision of fraternity, and his *mys-
tique* of action. Indeed, it has been more often true than not
that the major writers of this century—such figures as Kafka,
Lawrence, Mann, Eliot, and Auden—have in some deep sense
been, as the French say, *directeurs de conscience,* and it is the
gravity and the brilliance with which Camus carried this tradition into the present time that in large part accounts for the
great prestige that his name continues to have among us today.
The literature that he produced is a literature drenched in
ideas, and I suspect that he makes so great an impress upon us
in his plays and novels because theirs is a rhetoric that is
vibrant with the central themes of the modern consciousness.

Camus' vision is, in other words, an emphatically modern
vision: in him we behold the style of the age, and this is so
because, for him, the ultimate exigency which man faces in our
time is an exigency arising out of a great abdication, a terrible
collapse, a tragic death, in the City of God himself. What
Camus gives a home to in his work is the characteristically
modern sense that the only anchorage for the human enterprise lies somewhere within itself and that any principles of
meaning by which man's universe is to be ordered he must
himself contrive out of the inventiveness of his own untram-

[1] Gaëtan Picon, *André Malraux* (Paris: Gallimard, 1945), p. 64.

meled creativity. He apprehends the human voyager as utterly alone and without anything to rely upon except the compass of his own mind and heart. Man has no one to look to but himself for the bearing of his own weight, and there is no information agency for the human tourist: he must give himself his own directions: it is up to him, and to him alone, to decide where he shall go. This is the sense of the human condition that forms the core of the drastically truncated Pascalianism to be found in the remarkable texts produced by Camus in the last twenty years or so of his life.

It is, to be sure, a sense of life that gained in lucidity and coherence, as he passed from youth into middle age, but it proved its shaping force as early as his first book, the slim collection of lyrical essays that Edmond Charlot published in Algiers in 1937 under the title *L'Envers et l'endroit*. Most of the studies in this book—indeed, all but one of the five—have it as their function to create a repertory of images that will each incarnate some aspect of the nakedness and vulnerability and solitude and banality that make for man's permanent and irremediable anguish. In, for example, the first of the essays, "L'Ironie"—which, like the others, approaches the form of the short story—we meet an old woman (whose portrait may owe something to the grandmother who, in Camus' boyhood, lived in the impoverished apartment of his widowed mother in Algiers): she represents, says Camus, "la misère de l'homme en Dieu." Which is to say that here is a religion without joy or happiness or indeed any real personal validity at all, its sole function being merely to provide some meager consolation before the frightening imminence of death; and it is suggested that, had she any expectation of recovering from her illness, her rosary and her plaster St. Joseph would quickly fall into disuse. But she is without hope, and so, in her corner of neglect, she despairingly clings to the machinery of her piety and drones out her complaints against the bleak abandonment which is her fate. When the younger members in the family leave her to go out to the cinema in the evening, she clutches her daughter's hand, and a young guest is overborne by a sense of the pathos in the spectacle and the occasion—"an old, crippled woman [whom] they were abandoning to go to the movies." Like the old man whom we also meet in this section of the book, as he futilely attempts to engage some young people in conversation in a café, she is "condemned to silence and solitude"; and, as they both approach the last great emergency of death, "old age comes over [them] . . . like nausea." They are *isolés* who, when they look up, descry only "the vacuous indifferent smile of the sky" and who, when they look back upon themselves, behold only their stark exposure to the hazards of old age and imminent death.

In the second essay, "Entre oui et non," Camus recalls his early years in Algiers and the straitened circumstances in which he and his widowed mother lived together, in poverty and in silence, neither ever managing in any deep way to reach the other or to find in their relationship any relief or release from their fundamental human separateness. Though held together by the primitive power of the filial bond itself, each was a stranger to the other, and neither found in the other such comfort as might have reduced their sense of being strangers in the world.

And in the studies which immediately follow, "La Mort dans l'âme" and "Amour de vivre," this sense of strangeness and alienation becomes, even more emphatically, the central theme. These are essays in which Camus recalls his experience as a traveler, and what he finds to be most characteristic of that experience is the special kind of self-dislocation which is induced by one's passage into new scenes and places that are without familiar signs and landmarks. To face a strange and devious landscape is, he suggests, to be given access to some hitherto unrecognized and unexplored dimension of one's own selfhood, for the kind of unheeding inattentiveness that is induced by a familiar routine and a familiar locale becomes no longer possible. The self is suddenly dispossessed of everything in its environment that customarily permits the conventional illusions of security: "the curtain of habit . . . slowly rises and reveals at last the white face of anguish. Man is face to face with himself." In the world of Prague, for example—which is spoken of in "La Mort dans l'âme"—Camus confesses to the sense of disconnection by which he was overtaken, as he struggled with an alien language and with all the difficulties of finding his way about an unfamiliar city. Nor was this feeling of alienation put off, he tells us, when he moved from Czechoslovakia to Italy: indeed, the very warmth and opulence of the Italian landscape bring a depression of their own, since, by their intensification of one's awareness of the grandeur and beauty of the world, they awaken in us, with a new stab of poignancy, a sense of the tragic brevity of man's life and of the terrible cheat that is ultimately practiced upon us.

In the second travel essay, "Amour de vivre," Camus carries forward this strain of melancholy, as it arose for him, now in the Balearic Islands of Majorca and Ibiza, where, again, the very bounteousness of the landscape's splendor has the effect of reminding the traveler of the bitter fact which it conceals, that ours is a "universe which has no place for us, in which our life makes no sense." Thus, paradoxically, it is the very love of life that brings at last a profound despair about life.

In the final essay, which gives the entire collection its name, Camus makes explicit the duality that underlies the book as a whole and that is alluded to in the *envers* and *endroit* of the title. For, on the one hand, as he says, are "les hommes et leur absurdité," their poverty and dereliction and helplessness before the cruel contingencies of life; and, on the other hand, opposed to the precarious transiency of the human enterprise, there is the indestructible beauty of the sun and the sky and the sea and of all the great enduring places of the earth. So, he contends, given this essential rift in the scheme of existence, in our exulting commitment to the concrete, sensual materiality of the world—despite the absence of all ultimate sanctions—we must " 'Live as if. . . .' ": this, he says, "is the sum of my wisdom" which was spoken to him by "the irony which lies hidden at the heart of things."

Now, despite the sternly reticent and austere tone that was already a noticeable feature of Camus' writing, *L'Envers et l'endroit* is, nevertheless, decidedly the work of a very young man. The essays, taken as a whole, are not unified by any developed and coherent view of the world: the one basic observation that they tenuously record is that of the 90th Psalm, that our years are brought to an end as a tale that is told and that our strength is but labor and sorrow, so soon does it pass away. Yet, for all the disjointedness of the book, it does present a first, inchoate statement of what was to be the guiding axiom of Camus' entire meditation on the human problem, that man is "alone, helpless, naked," in a world whose beauty and splendor only emphasize its unshakable indifference to *la présence humaine*.

2

In one of the letters collected by Eberhard Bethge into the volume *Letters and Papers from Prison*, the distinguished young German theologian, Dietrich Bonhoeffer, who was executed in Hitler's Germany in the spring of 1945, recognized that "we are proceeding towards a time of no religion at all: men as they are now simply cannot be religious any more."[2] There is no other writer of our period who gives us a deeper insight into the condition of this new "religionlessness" than does the late Albert Camus. To contemplate the movement of his thought is to discern anew the causes of the decline of what Bonhoeffer called "the religious premise," and it is also to discern what is most vital and promising in the "religionlessness" that is today so generally a part of our intellectual situation in the Western world.

[2] Dietrich Bonhoeffer, *Letters and Papers from Prison*, ed. by Eberhard Bethge and trans. by Reginald H. Fuller (London: SCM Press Ltd., 1953), p. 122.

One of Camus' most sensitive American critics, R. W. B. Lewis, in discussing his "quarrel with God," has expressed regret that it should have been marked by such "inaccurate firing."[3] Mr. Lewis means that in part Camus' refusal of Christian theism was a refusal of a doctrine of divine transcendence on whose standing or falling the integrity of the Christian faith is not at all really dependent. But, though this is so, it cannot be gainsaid that the apologetic which modern intellectuals have encountered and known about has very often been an apologetic that has spoken about God in the manner of a *terra incognita*, as though he were *a* being or person beside or above other beings or persons, and one whose "existence" was a matter of theoretical knowledge. The kind of spatialization of the divine that has sometimes been implicit in supernaturalist theism is, of course, profoundly at odds with the deepest meanings of biblical faith, and what we have also to grant is that it is a frigid and blasphemous monstrosity which the human reason can accept only by committing suicide. This is a God who, since he is *a* being amongst others, "is bound to the subject-object structure of reality . . . [and is, therefore,] an object for us as subjects. At the same time we are objects for him as a subject. . . . For God as a subject makes me into an object which is nothing more than an object . . . [appearing] as the invincible tyrant, the being in contrast with whom all other beings are without freedom and subjectivity. . . ."[4] This is the God whom Camus knew, and the refusal of whom is at the root of the melancholy that lies just beneath the surface of even his most positive affirmations.

Now, having rejected the ineffectual consolations of an unserviceable supernaturalism and not having envisaged the possibility of a "god above the God of theism,"[5] Camus ad-

[3] R. W. B. Lewis, *The Picaresque Saint: Representative Figures in Contemporary Fiction* (Philadelphia: J. P. Lippincott Co., 1959), p. 78.

[4] Paul Tillich, *The Courage to Be* (New Haven: Yale University Press, 1952), p. 185.

[5] *Ibid.*, p. 186.

dressed himself in his first books to the question as to the basis
on which human life is to be sustained against the immense
indifference of the world. Early in his book of 1942, *Le Mythe
de Sisyphe,* he tells us that "in a universe suddenly divested of
illusions and lights, man feels [himself] an alien, a stranger.
His exile is without remedy since he is deprived of the memory
of a lost home or the hope of a promised land." It was the full
implication of this terrible and absurd forlornness of man's
estate that he proposed to clarify.

In *Le Mythe de Sisyphe,* man's exiled condition is called
"absurd," because it is so completely alien to the mind's deepest desires. For the essential impulse of the human spirit is to
behold the world as its real home, is to be assured of some
basic congruence between its aspirations for intelligibility and
the fundamental constitution of reality. But, in this world, everything is given, and nothing is explained: the mind's hunger
for coherence is countered by the irremediable incoherence of
existence: "all the knowledge on earth will give me nothing to
assure me that this world is mine." Though, in imagination, we
touch the fringes of the eternal, we are but the feeblest reeds
in nature, engulfed within the infinite opacity of the world.
Indeed, the ultimate outrage is the certainty that we will die,
and "the cruel mathematics that command our condition" involve us in a tragic calculus that seems, in the end, to make for
an absolute nullification of every conceivable value. Hence, the
opening sentence of *Le Mythe*—which is one of the most
famous sentences in recent literature: "There is but one truly
serious philosophical problem, and that is suicide."

The bitter despair that is promised by this opening sentence turns out, however, not at all to be the predominant
stress of the book. It is, indeed, Camus' whole purpose in *Le
Mythe* to demonstrate that suicide can be no real solution to
the problem of the Absurd. For, if the Absurd results from the
clash between the human demand for clarity and justice and
"the unreasonable silence of the world," it cannot be resolved
by destroying one term in the polarity which gives rise to the

problem. "If I attempt to solve a problem, at least I must not by that very solution conjure away one of the terms of the problem": this would be to annul it, not really to solve it. What is more, it would be for man to consent to his own defeat, for, in the desperate leap out of the Absurd into the spurious relief of nothingness, he repudiates himself: he consents to his humiliation, himself becomes the agent of it, and, in thus succumbing to his impotence, effectively abdicates his humanity.

So, then, if the ultimate quandary of our existence cannot be resolved by fleeing from existence, our choice must therefore be *for* existence and for the lucidity by which alone we can live in the Absurd with dignity and honor. And not only are we forbidden "the leap" out of the Absurd by self-inflicted annihilation: Camus also castigates any and all other attempts to "leap" out of the human condition, and most especially those that involve an effort to "transcend" the human realm by "[deifying] what crushes [us] and [finding] reason to hope in what impoverishes [us]." Jaspers, for example, says Camus, finds "nothing in experience but the confession of his own impotence and no occasion to infer any satisfactory principle. Yet without justification . . . he suddenly asserts all at once the transcendent . . . and the superhuman significance of life. . . . Thus the absurd becomes god . . . and that inability to understand becomes the existence that illuminates everything." This is a kind of cheating that he finds not only in Jaspers but in many other modern thinkers—in Kierkegaard, in Shestov, in the religious existentialists generally: and he discerns a similar irrationalism in Husserl and Scheler and the phenomenologists. Here is a family of thinkers who, in the tradition of Tertullian, begin with the obscurantist proposition, *credo quia absurdum est*: that is to say, they begin with "a philosophy of the nonsignificance of the world": they see with great acuteness "that divorce between the mind that desires and the world that disappoints." Yet they prove the Absurd only to suppress it and to retreat from what they have brought to light. They are bent on escaping from the irremediable antinomies of the human condition: they are unwilling to endure the deserts of the Absurd: so, "starting from a philosophy of the world's lack of meaning, [they end] up by finding a meaning and a depth in it." The Absurd is used as a springboard to eternity, and this is a piece of sleight whose negation of human reason involves nothing less than "philosophical suicide."

There is, then, no humanly valid way, Camus asserts, of moving beyond the Absurd, of moving beyond the human. So what we must learn to do is to live with lucidity and without hope, nourished only by "the wine of the absurd and the bread of indifference." "Living," he says, "is keeping the absurd alive. Keeping it alive is, above all, contemplating it." This is what the absurd man consents to do: he is a man without nostalgia who consents to live *in* the Absurd, not acquiescently but defiantly, indifferent to the future, refusing all "supernatural consolations" and sustained only by his cold resolve not to relax the posture of rebellion.

Now this ethic of indifference entails a kind of stern hedonism, for, if "this life has no other aspect than that of the absurd . . . then I must say that what counts is not the best living but the most living"—which is to say that the notion of quantity will be of greater ethical significance than the notion of quality. And thus it is that, for Camus, Don Juan is one of the great "heroes of the absurd," for he goes from woman to woman not because he is guided by Ecclesiastes but because, having no hope of another life, he finds it logical to insist on satiety.

In his way of approaching the legend of Don Juan, Camus puts us in mind of the great portrait of the seducer in Kierkegaard's *Either/Or*, for he too insists on an unromantic perspective, refusing to regard Don Juan as a melancholy mystic in quest of an absolute love. He is a man, says Camus, who does not intend to be duped by the Absurd—which is perhaps simply to say that he is a man who does not intend to fidget over how his life might be given such a pattern and order as might guarantee some genuine self-fulfillment, for he is without the illusion of freedom. Knowing that beyond this limited universe "all is collapse and nothingness," he is a man who is determined to face the future with utter indifference and "to use up everything that is given." Since, for him, all experiences are equally important or equally unimportant, he takes it as his one rule of life to seek the greatest quantity of experiences and to live them through with the greatest possible intensity and passion. "If he leaves a woman it is not absolutely because he has ceased to desire her. A beautiful woman is always desirable. But he desires another, and no, this is not the same thing." In other words, possession, conquest, and consumption are his norms. And he is a "wise man"—his wisdom, however, not being some esoteric *gnosis* of the great tragic hero but being, rather, the wisdom of an ordinary seducer who, not having the merest vestige of any ultimate hope, is simply intent on enjoying this present life to the greatest possible degree. Nor does he have any regrets, for whatever the degree of lucidity he achieves, it never occurs to him to think of changing his vocation or altering his condition.

But Don Juan is not the only exemplary instance for Camus of *l'homme absurde*. The actor, too, is for him a great archetype of "absurd" living, for, as the practitioner of an art of simulation, of appearance, he incarnates the truth that the various fictitious lives he impersonates on the stage are no more real, have no greater significance, than his own. So, in a way, his very role as actor represents the absurdity of the general human condition.

In the iconology of the metaphysics of the absurd, the actor's position is perhaps somewhat different from Don Juan's. For Don Juan lives through the absurdity of life actually and existentially; whereas the actor is *l'homme absurde* only in a purely formal and analogical way. Yet he is for Camus a most powerfully evocative image, for

He abundantly illustrates every month or every day that so suggestive truth that there is no frontier between what a man

wants to be and what he is. Always concerned with better
representing, he demonstrates to what a degree appearing
creates being. For that is his art—to simulate absolutely, to
project himself as deeply as possible into lives that are not
his own. At the end of his effort his vocation becomes clear:
to apply himself wholeheartedly to being nothing or to being
several. The narrower the limits allotted him for creating his
character, the more necessary his talent. He will die in three
hours under the mask he has assumed today. Within three
hours he must experience and express a whole exceptional life.
That is called losing oneself to find oneself. In those three
hours he travels the whole course of the dead-end path that
the man in the audience takes a lifetime to cover.

So it is no wonder, says Camus, that the Church has so
often regarded the actor as a questionable figure. For it is his
body which is the actor's means of expression: he must trans-
late everything into physical and vocal gesture, and his culti-
vation of intensity at the level of the physical life presents a
standing challenge to Christianity's tendency to subordinate
the physical to the spiritual. And it is also in his commitment to
the immediacy of the present moment, the moment that exists
on the stage, and in his protean self-identification with many
dramatic roles that the Church has found a reality subversive
of its whole program for the management of life and for the
redemption of man.

From Don Juan and the actor, Camus turns to a third
exemplum of the absurd man which is incarnate in the adven-
turer or the conqueror who, in undertaking to carry out some
large program in the historical order, behaves "as if" the one
really useful action were possible—namely, "that of remaking
man and the earth." But, though his is a militant and activist
posture, Camus' conqueror, as he is portrayed in *Le Mythe*, is
not a mere gangster who plays the game of power simply to
satisfy a crude lust for empire and sovereignty. In the section
of the book which is devoted to his portrait, Camus makes him
speak in his own behalf and in the manner of a kind of theorist

(or even poet) of rebellion who, believing himself to have been "deprived of the eternal," has closed his heart, has chosen to ally himself with time, and has opted for the life of action rather than contemplation. "Between history and the eternal I have chosen history because I like certainties. Of it, at least, I am certain. . . ." And he seeks to make contact with the spirit of metaphysical insurrection through the decisive historical act, by "plunging into the seething soul of revolutions." But he knows that there are no victorious causes, that, in the face of death, all causes are lost causes: yet he maintains his lucidity, even in the midst of what negates it, determined never to relax the posture of protest and resistance. Like Garcia in Malraux's *L'Espoir*, he intends to "*organize* the apocalypse."

Then, finally, Camus finds the absurd to be crucially instanced in the artist or the "creator," because, though knowing the work of art to be only an impotent artifact, he yet persists in the practice of his craft, thereby exemplifying a type of revolt against the human fate: he is, indeed, among the most absurd of all men.

Perhaps the key sentence in Camus' meditation on the meaning of art is that in which he says: "If the world were clear, art would not exist": for this is the notion that is central to his whole understanding of the place of aesthetic creation in man's spiritual life. His premise is, of course, the world's absurdity, its defiance of every conceivable system of coherence, and the necessity that we face, therefore, of maintaining *our* lucidity, despite the incomprehensibleness of existence. It is just here that he locates the great significance of art. For, though it originates in the uselessness of "explanation" and is symptomatic of the mind's deepest ailment, it is far from being any kind of refuge from the bitter truth of our condition: it is, on the contrary, the great way in which *l'homme absurde* faces that truth and mimes the reality of our common fate. The world refuses to yield to the human spirit anything other than the stubborn fragmentariness of concrete phenomena, and the work of art therefore, in so far as it attempts simply to mime the concrete, attests, in its very being, to the impossibility of transcendence. Indeed, the truest work of art, Camus suggests, is that which consents to say the least, which is "devoid of lessons"; and he is the most exemplary of artists who simply "works up appearances and covers with images that which has no reason."

So it is, then, Don Juan, the actor, the conqueror, and the artist whom Camus offers as the great models of living in the absurd, and they all find their most concentrated image for him in the mythical Sisyphus who, for having attempted to conquer death itself, was punished in Hades by being compelled eternally, but unsuccessfully, to push a great rock to the top of a hill. Here, Camus feels, we have the full, grand human thing itself—impotence yet rebellion, overwhelming odds yet resolute endurance, defeat yet victory. He "teaches the higher fidelity that negates the gods and raises rocks. . . . One must imagine Sisyphus happy." It is, to be sure, a very tragic kind of happiness, but happiness it is, nevertheless, for Sisyphus maintains an intense awareness of the grim actuality that confronts him: he is unflinching in the face of his destiny: he knows that he will never reach the summit of his hill, but he never abdicates the struggle. And, in the rugged persistence of his refusal to allow the rock to remain at the bottom of the mount, he remains faithful to that essential *humanum* within himself, loyalty to which will bring a man the only sort of genuine happiness that is possible for humankind—namely, the happiness that comes from not betraying the dignity that belongs to one's nature as a man. He, therefore, *is*, and Camus regards the example of the Sisyphean Passion as an indication that the human spirit may not be utterly exhaustible by the Absurd: at least Sisyphus proves himself to be stronger than his rock, for "the rock is still rolling."

Now there is an element of glamorous titanism in all these figures—in Don Juan and the conqueror, in the artist and in the mythical Sisyphus. But Camus cautions us against mistaking the ethic of the Absurd as an aristocratic ethic appropriate only to an élite. He tells us quite plainly that it is lucidity alone that matters and that, in this, an obscure post office clerk can be the equal of a conqueror. Which means that he regards the absurd as something soberly to be faced throughout all the occasions and undertakings of the normal life of man. For— and this is the essential "democracy" of the human situation, as Camus understood it—whether he be a king or a chimney sweep, all that any man can count on for his soul's sustenance is the kind of courage that Hemingway liked to call "grace under pressure." And this is something of which the conqueror, Camus believed, had better be as careful as the post office clerk.

3

It was his first novel, *L'Étranger* (which appeared along with *Le Mythe de Sisyphe* in 1942, though it had been finished a few months before the completion of the essay), that established Camus' international reputation. Here, in the plot and the images of a work of prose fiction, we are made to experience the sensation of the Absurd with a degree of immediacy that is, I think, at no point equally realized in *Le Mythe*; and in Meursault, the little clerk in an Algerian shipping firm, we have one of Camus' purest renderings of the absurd man.

The narrative line of the novel is very simple. Meursault receives word of his mother's having died in a home for the aged, so he requests a brief leave from his business firm in order to go to her funeral in the country district in which the home is located. He is unmoved by the occasion and feels nothing other than the mild stupor that is induced by the summer heat. He returns to Algiers on a Friday evening and, the next morning, goes down to the beach for a swim. There he meets Marie, who used to be a typist in his office. After swimming together, they go to a Fernandel movie, then back to Meursault's room and bed and the beginning of a liaison. In the course of the summer, after an acquaintance of Meur-

sault's, Raymond, has beaten up his mistress, he consents to
testify in his behalf before the police. One weekend, while he
and Raymond are visiting Raymond's friends, the Massons, at
their summer cottage, they encounter this girl's Arab kinsmen
on the beach. In a scuffle that ensues Raymond is knifed by
one of them. Later, on the afternoon of that same day, Meursault returns to the beach alone, where he finds one of the
Arabs lying in the shade. He sees the Arab draw his knife: the
light of the blazing sun glints on the steel, and, says Meursault,
"I felt as if a long, thin blade transfixed my forehead. . . . I was
conscious only of the cymbals of the sun clashing on my skull.
. . . Then everything began to reel before my eyes. . . ." At this
moment he reaches into his pocket for the revolver which he
had taken from Raymond earlier in the day. "Every nerve in
my body was a steel spring, and my grip closed on the revolver. . . . I fired four more shots into the inert body. . . . And
each successive shot was another loud, fateful rap on the door
of my undoing."

The second part of the book is devoted to the interroga-
tion and the trial. Throughout the long proceedings, Meursault
displays the same indifference that he had shown toward his
mother's death. Indeed, it is his behavior on that earlier occasion by which those presiding over his trial seem chiefly to be
outraged, and one feels that he goes to the guillotine not so
much for having killed the Arab as for not having wept at his
mother's funeral.

Then, at last, he is visited in his cell by the prison chaplain
who comes to talk to him theologically about judgment and
redemption and to offer the comfort of the Christian faith. It is
at this moment that Meursault gains a new lucidity which
propels him out of his habitual indifference into a violent rejection of what he believes to be the thin ethereality of the chaplain's piety. As he faces the ultimate emergency of his own
ordained death, the wan spiritualism of the chaplain's religion,
in its conventional otherworldliness and sterile asceticism,

strikes him—to use a phrase of D. H. Lawrence—as really "doing dirt on life." So, as he says:

> I started yelling at the top of my voice. I hurled insults at him,
> I told him not to waste his rotten prayers on me. . . . He
> seemed so cocksure, you see. And yet none of his certainties
> was worth one strand of a woman's hair. Living as he did, like
> a corpse, he couldn't even be sure of being alive. . . .
> Actually, I was sure of myself, sure about everything, far
> surer than he; sure of my present life and of the death that
> was coming. That, no doubt, was all I had; but at least that
> certainty was something I could get my teeth into—just as
> it had got its teeth into me.

And it is in the light of this new clarity that he suddenly discerns what is really ultimate in his existence, that

> From the dark horizon of my future a sort of slow, persistent
> breeze had been blowing toward me, all my life long, from
> the years that were to come. And on its way that breeze had
> leveled out all the ideas that people tried to foist on me in
> the equally unreal years I then was living through. What
> difference could they make to me, the deaths of others, or a
> mother's love, or his God; or the way a man decides to live,
> the fate he thinks he chooses, since one and the same fate
> was bound to "choose" not only me but thousands of millions
> of privileged people who, like him, called themselves my
> brothers. . . . All alike would be condemned to die one day. . . .

In this final moment, once Meursault consciously perceives the utter futility of any kind of ultimate hope, it is as if a cloud had lifted: as he abandons himself to "the benign indifference of the universe," he suddenly realizes that his has indeed been a happy life and that he is even happy still. "It was as if," he says, "that great rush of anger had washed me clean. . . ." There is, to be sure, nothing other than this earthly existence, but the joys of this life, he now realizes, he has savoured even more deeply than he has known. He recalls the eternal Algerian summer, the sound of the rippling water at his feet down at the beach, the smooth feel of the water on his body as he struck out, the "sun-gold" of Marie's face—and he knows then that the glory of the world is its own justification. So, like Sisyphus, he is sustained by "the wine of the absurd and the bread of indifference," and he faces his last hour with the serenity of one who has moved forward, if not towards some brave new world, at least towards a calm acceptance of the present dispensation. And his final mood is very nearly the ecstasy of a pantheistic mysticism.

Now it is just this final transfiguration that fails to prove itself, either in terms of the logic of Camus' thought in this period of his career or in terms of the dramatic logic of the novel. What he succeeds in conveying to us—and with a more pungent vividness than any novelist since Kafka has achieved—is the very flavor and sensation that life takes on when (paraphrasing Yeats's famous line) things have fallen apart, when the center no longer holds, and "mere anarchy is loosed upon the world." In the universe that is inhabited by this obscure Algerian clerk all meaning has been displaced by the absurd equivalence into which all possible choices and actions have been collapsed by the death of God and "the cruel mathematics that command our condition." As Jean-Paul Sartre remarked in his fine review of the book in 1943, one is made uneasy by the very first paragraph. Meursault tells us that

> Mother died today. Or, maybe, yesterday; I can't be sure. The telegram from the Home says: YOUR MOTHER PASSED AWAY. FUNERAL TOMORROW. DEEP SYMPATHY. Which leaves the matter doubtful; it could have been yesterday.

We are made uneasy because we sense that we have suddenly entered a place in which the successiveness of time has somehow been canceled out or broken up: "Mother died today. . . . it could have been yesterday." It could have been the day before yesterday: the lifeless monotone of the speaker intimates that the issue is of no consequence to him. Or, again, when Marie asks him one evening if he'll marry her, he says:

> I said I didn't mind; if she was keen on it, we'd get married.
> Then she asked me again if I loved her. I replied, much as before, that her question meant nothing or next to nothing —but I supposed I didn't.
> "If that's how you feel," she said, "why marry me?"
> I explained that it had no importance really, but, if it would give her pleasure, we could get married right away.

Neither issue matters—neither the day on which his mother died nor whether or not he marries Marie—because, as he reasons at the end of the narrative, the "slow, persistent breeze" that blows in upon him from "the dark horizon of [his] future" levels out all distinctions and thus keeps any one action or experience from carrying more significance than others. He knows, in other words—long before the murder, the trial, and his condemnation—that he is going to die. So, when Raymond offers him friendship, when Marie offers him her love, when his employer offers him advancement, when a priest offers him the consolations of faith, he hunches his shoulders and says in effect, "It's all the same to me: makes no difference much: let it be as you will." And it is the unshakable taciturnity with which he faces the silence of the world that makes him a "stranger," an "outsider": he will have no traffic with the idols of the tribe, he will not give his suffrage to the illusions of those who cannot bear the cold, bitter stone of truth. The scandal that he therefore becomes is precisely what is at issue during his trial, in the abuse that is heaped upon him for his failure to weep at his mother's funeral. His refusal of the conventional emotions appears to the Algerian populace to be a kind of obscenity.

Now all this is conveyed with an uncanny shrewdness of dramatic gesture. The fragmentation and incoherence which are the basic ontological facts in Meursault's experience of life are present not simply in the assertions of his own broken rhetoric, but they are also present in the whole style and design of the novel. Recalling Francis Fergusson's definition of the tragic rhythm as a movement from *purpose* to *passion* to *perception*,[6] R. W. B. Lewis has very acutely observed that, in the case of *L'Étranger*, the movement is from a "carefully realized purposelessness through a prolonged absence of passion to the perception that makes them both right and appropriate. It is, in short, the absurd mimesis of the tragic."[7] Not only is the novel's dramatic structure suggestive of Camus' theme, but we encounter the abyss of nothingness in the very structure of his syntax. He wants to tell us that the dark breeze blowing in upon us from the future means that we really have no future at all, that all we have is the tenuity of the present instant. This is perhaps most powerfully intimated in the telegraphic laconicism of his syntax. As Sartre observed in his brilliant essay on the novel,

> The world is destroyed and reborn from sentence to sentence. When the word makes its appearance it is a creation *ex nihilo*. The sentences . . . are islands. We bounce from sentence to sentence, from void to void. . . . The sentences are not . . . arranged in relation to each other; they are simply juxtaposed. . . . [They have] neither ramifications nor extensions nor internal structure. . . . [They are all] equal to each other, just as all the absurd man's experiences are equal. Each one sets up for itself and sweeps the others into the void.[8]

We are, in other words, in a mute and abandoned universe: in Meursault we have an example of man living *in* the Absurd: this is, as the late Rachel Bespaloff said in her *Esprit* article,

[6] Francis Fergusson, *The Idea of a Theater* (Princeton: Princeton University Press, 1949), Chapter I.

[7] R. W. B. Lewis, *The Picaresque Saint* (Philadelphia: J. P. Lippincott Co., 1959), p. 71.

[8] Jean-Paul Sartre, "Camus' *The Outsider*," *Literary and Philosophical Essays*, trans. by Annette Michelson (London: Rider & Co., 1955), pp. 38–40.

"the world of the condemned man,"[9] the world that is portrayed with such poignant eloquence in the early sections of *Le Mythe de Sisyphe*. But, then, in the polemic against Kierkegaard and Shestov and Jaspers and in many other sections of that book, it is Camus' main purpose to invalidate all attempts to "leap" from absurdity into any kind of faith-ful affirmation. Yet this would appear to be precisely what is entailed in Meursault's final reconciliation. For he somehow moves from the sullen hopelessness and indifference in whose grip he is throughout most of the novel to the almost ecstatic affirmativeness of his final mood, and we find it difficult to understand what it is that explains and accounts for the passage. The passionate infatuation with life, the felicity, the sense of blessedness even, that Meursault somehow wrests out of his last hours—this all seems insufficiently prepared for in everything that has gone before: so it not only lacks dramatic cogency and credibility, but it seems also to be unsupported by what were the basic premises of Camus' thought in the early 'forties. But the forlorn, dispirited *isolé* who seeks with his own indifference to match the indifference of the world is a memorable figure, and his main story is one of the great philosophical myths in the literature of this century.

4

Two years after the publication in 1942 of *L'Étranger* and *Le Mythe de Sisyphe* there appeared the two major plays of Camus' early period, *Le Malentendu* and *Caligula*. These are works that, in a way, bring to a close the phase of his career in which, following the first books of the late 'thirties (*L'Envers et l'endroit*, 1937; *Noces*, 1939), he was attempting to explore the full depths of modern nihilism. And, of the two, it is in the somber, operatic brilliance of *Caligula* that we get the most

[9] Rachel Bespaloff, "Le Monde du comdamné à mort," *Esprit*, No. 163, January, 1950.

concentrated resumé of the early preoccupation with *l'absurde*.[10]

The young Caligula (who at the age of twenty-five became Emperor of Rome, and whose brief, tempestuous reign is chronicled in Suetonius' *Lives of the Caesars*) is overborne with grief following the death of his sister Drusilla, for whom he had conceived an incestuous love. His emotions, however, are not merely those of grief but of rage, anger, and indignation. For Drusilla's death, as he tells his friend Helicon, is but a symbol of the fact that "Men die and . . . are not happy." His loss, in other words, precipitates him into *l'absurde*, discloses how barren the world is of meaning and how absolutely death nullifies all human values. And, perceiving how shallow is the general understanding of this truth, he becomes a kind of missionary in behalf of the Absurd, deciding that the service he shall render Rome will be that of making known the metaphysical anarchy that dominates existence: he will wear "the foolish, unintelligible face of a professional god." So he arranges a drama that is intended to be a terrifying simulacrum of the unconscionable arbitrariness of fate itself. His method is the method of terror: he confiscates the property of both the rich and the poor; he murders the children and the parents of his friends; he humiliates and tortures distinguished patricians; he awards prizes to the citizens making the largest number of visits to the Roman brothels; he mercilessly decrees executions; he arbitrarily curtails food supplies for the populace; until finally, his malevolence reaches such insane proportions as to make it obvious that no one is safe.

The lesson that this frenzied pedagogue wants to teach is that the ultimate truth about the world is that it has no truth, and he proceeds to do this by creating a delirious kingdom of violence "where the impossible is king." He organizes a campaign against creation partly in order to give men access to the

---

[10] *Caligula*, though not published until 1944, had actually been written, at least in its first draft, as early as 1938, while Camus was still living in Algiers.

real facts of their condition in this world and partly as an act of revenge against a remote and criminal deity. So his demonic ardor is the passion of one who has undertaken an asceticism of absolute rebellion, and this furious adventure in sabotage does indeed at last begin to have its intended effect of unsettling the easy assumption of Caligula's patrician associates that the world has an order and a meaning that guarantee to them some fundamental security. The young poet Scipio is even so far converted, despite the murder of his father by imperial decree, that, when he is invited to join a plot against the Emperor, he refuses, declaring: "I cannot be against him. If I killed him my heart, at least, would still be on his side": for, as he says, "The same flame consumes our hearts." And Caligula's mistress, Caesonia, though she urges a course of moderation, does not really withhold her acquiescence in his program; whereas Caligula wants to enthrone "the impossible," she would like to see the "possible" given a chance: but they are essentially at one in their disillusion, and thus, in a way, she is without appeal when the time comes for her own destruction at his hands.

But, finally, this madman provokes a rising wave of revolt which culminates in his assassination. The plot is led by his friend Cherea, who becomes, in the dialectic of the drama, his major opponent. He chooses to join forces with the assassins "to combat a big idea . . . whose triumph would mean the end of everything." He acknowledges that Caligula's philosophy is "logical from start to finish," but the trouble with it, as he says, is that it converts itself into corpses—and, though it cannot be refuted, it must be opposed. He is a man in whom hope is as dead as it is in Caligula, but he silences all in his heart that is akin to the Emperor; for he is on the side of life, and he knows that Caligula is a prince of the powers of darkness who would make murder legitimate.

When Caligula is first seen on the stage, he has just returned to Rome, after having been away for three days following Drusilla's death. "His legs," says Camus, "are caked with

mud, his garments dirty; his hair is wet, his look distraught."
He tells Helicon that he has been reaching for the moon: "I
suddenly felt a desire for the impossible. . . . Really, this world
of ours, the scheme of things as they call it, is quite intolerable.
That's why I want the moon, or happiness, or eternal life—
something . . . which isn't of this world." He declares that the
real significance of Drusilla's death lies in the symbol which it
provides of "a truth that makes the moon essential"—the truth
that "Men die and . . . are not happy." But Cherea, though he
believes human existence to be as precarious and as threatened
as Caligula supposes, does not need the moon: he foregoes the
Emperor's Luciferian *dandysme* and chooses instead to dedi-
cate his own strength to fortifying the reign of man: he wants
to give the *possible* a chance.

In the great final scene of Act III, the two men, with a
certain wariness, approach each other for the last time, Caligula initiating the exchange with the somewhat wistful query,
"Do you think, Cherea, that it's possible for two men of much
the same temperament and equal pride to talk to each other
with complete frankness—if only once in their lives? Can they
strip themselves naked, so to speak, and shed their prejudices,
their private interests, the lies by which they live?" Cherea
replies: "Yes, Caius, I think it possible. But I don't think you'd
be capable of it." This is the signal for the fencing match
which ensues, in the course of which Cherea admits his inability to refute the logic of the Emperor's plan of life but insists,
nevertheless, that, were the Absurd to be pushed to its logical
conclusions, the world would then become "impossible to live
in, and happiness, too, would go by the board. And these, I
repeat," he says, "are the things that count, for me."

> *Caligula:* So, I take it, you believe in some higher principle?
> *Cherea:* Certainly I believe that some actions are—shall I
>   say?—more praiseworthy than others.
> *Caligula:* And *I* believe that all are on an equal footing.

Cherea: I know it, Caius, and that's why I don't hate you. I understand, and, to a point, agree with you. But you're pernicious, and you've got to go.

Given the insufferable anarchy into which Rome has been thrown, the time, in other words, has come for the Emperor's assassination. And, as this late stage of the action gets under way, he himself begins to show the signs of an inner disintegration: he shatters a mirror in which he beholds the intolerable image of his own hatefulness, and, at the very end, he acknowledges that he has taken a wrong turning, "a path that leads to nothing." Yet the last words are his: as the assassins fling themselves upon him with their daggers, he—"laughing and choking"—gasps out the cry: "I'm still alive!" Thus, like Melville's Ahab, he spits his last breath back at the Absurd, in frenetic and arrogant defiance.

Nor is it at all strange that one should at this point be put in mind of Melville and of *Moby Dick,* for Camus was careful to set down his conviction that the work of Herman Melville constitutes a "record of a spiritual experience of unequaled intensity"[11]; and he regarded *Moby Dick* as *the* exemplary instance in the history of prose fiction of *la création absurde*: it is, he said, "one of the most disturbing myths ever invented concerning the struggle of man against evil and concerning the irresistible logic which ends by first setting the just man against creation and the creator, then against his fellow-men and against himself."[12] And when, in the 'forties, *Caligula* was being first read and seen in performance by the French public, had it been generally known how deep an influence had been exerted on Camus by this great figure of the American nineteenth century, the broader implications of his Roman play might then have been more firmly grasped. It is natural, of

[11] Albert Camus, "Herman Melville," in *Les Ecrivains célèbres*, Vol. III (*Le XIXe Siècle-Le XXe Siècle*), ed. Raymond Queneau (Paris: Editions d'Art, Lucien Mazenod, 1953), p. 128.
[12] *Ibid.*

course, that, at the time when the play was first introduced to
France, it should have been interpreted in the light of the then
recent and tragic experience of the Hitlerian insanity and that
it should have been taken as a kind of political allegory, and so
indeed it was in part. But the artist who had conceived this
fearful pageant was a young man who knew the great account
of the fated *Pequod* and of its monomaniac old captain Ahab,
and he had therefore read, and doubtless been fascinated by,
that moving passage in *Moby Dick* in which Melville tells us
that "though in many of its aspects this visible world seems
formed in love, the invisible spheres were formed in fright."
Far more importantly than the social and political tragedy that
was precipitated by the Nazi experiment, it was the absurd
hero's invasion of these uncharted and horrific Melvillean re-
gions that Camus was attempting to dramatize in *Caligula*.

It is, indeed, this same metaphysical blackness that constitutes the pervading atmosphere of *Le Malentendu*, which,
though Camus' second play, was, at the time of its first performance in 1944, his first stage-piece to be presented in a
Parisian theatre. Here he gives us a full development of the
story which Meursault discovered on a scrap of old newspaper
under the mattress in his prison cell; and, in that version, it
goes like this, in Meursault's summary:

> . . . its scene was some village in Czechoslovakia. One of the
> villagers had left his home to try his luck abroad. After
> twenty-five years, having made a fortune, he returned to his
> country with his wife and child. Meanwhile his mother and
> sister had been running a small hotel in the village where
> he was born. He decided to give them a surprise and, leaving
> his wife and child in another inn, he went to stay at his
> mother's place, booking a room under an assumed name.
> His mother and sister completely failed to recognize him. At
> dinner that evening he showed them a large sum of money he
> had on him, and in the course of the night they slaughtered
> him with a hammer. After taking the money they flung the

body into the river. Next morning his wife came and, without thinking, betrayed the guest's identity. His mother hanged herself. His sister threw herself into a well.

Now it is, of course, the function of this brief passage in *L'Étranger* to be simply an odd bit of documentation of the general absurdity of life—the story in no way strains Meursault's credulousness: he takes it for granted that such things happen, and his only comment is that ". . . the man was asking for trouble; one shouldn't play fool tricks of that sort." And the more elaborate version of the tale that we get in *Le Malentendu* is intended to provide much the same sort of evidence that was originally communicated by an old newspaper clipping in a prison cell, the play's only departures from the narrative that is summarized in *L'Étranger* being that Jan, the murdered son, has no child, and he is not bludgeoned to death but is rather drugged and then tossed into a nearby river. Indeed, there is not a single character in the play who lives outside the realm of the Absurd—even though, as in the case with Jan and perhaps with the old manservant, there may not always be any highly developed consciousness of the true human condition.

The scene of the play is some claustral central European valley whose situation oppresses Martha, the sister, with a sense of being enclosed and shut-in: it is a dark, dreary, unfrequented place where it is always raining and where one dreams of open spaces by the sea that are bathed in a scorching sunlight which burns out the burden of the soul. With this dream in their darkened hearts, and most powerfully so in Martha's, she and her mother have systematically murdered the occasional patrons of their inn for the small sums that could be lifted from their persons, hoping eventually to acquire a hoard large enough to permit them to escape to the south—and to the sun and sea. So, when Jan appears, obviously well-to-do and apparently without connections, Martha's decision is immediate and automatic. "I have come here to bring them my money, and if I can, some happiness," says Jan to his wife Maria, whom he insists on leaving temporarily at a nearby hotel. But she contends that "there's something . . . something morbid" in the whole elaborate scheme of disguise and pretense and postponed recognition that he has planned: "No, there's only one way," she says, "and it's to do what any ordinary mortal would do—to say 'It's I,' and to let one's heart speak for itself." He ought, she tells him, to go to his mother and simply say: " 'I'm your son. This is my wife. I've been living with her in a country we both love, a land of endless sunshine beside the sea. But something was lacking there to complete my happiness, and now I feel I need you.'" Jan, however, cannot be shaken from his purpose, so he leaves Maria behind and, on arriving at his mother's inn, his purpose collides with that of Martha and the mother herself: before he has a chance to disclose his identity he is murdered, and is recognized by his mother and sister only after his death, when Maria comes and tells them whom they have killed. So the drama moves finally towards an unspeakably bitter irony of tangled purpose, the result of which is that Maria is robbed of her husband and Jan of his life and his mother and sister of their restoration to their long-lost son and brother. Thus it is no wonder that Martha, as she angrily contemplates their cruel defraudment, says at last to Jan's grief-stricken widow, just before she takes her own life: "Pray your God to harden you to stone. It's the happiness He has assigned Himself, and the one true happiness. Do as He does, be deaf to all appeals, and turn your heart to stone while there still is time."

It would appear that the central revelation which we are expected to perceive as emerging from the tragic denouement of *Le Malentendu* is that which is conveyed by Martha in her grim conversation with Maria at the end, when she says: ". . . it's now that we are in the normal order of things, [for] . . . in the normal order of things no one is ever recognized." This is a view of the human situation that the structure and atmosphere of the play enforce upon us, unquestionably, with a strangely

powerful and memorable intensity. Camus' *décor* is here something that is stripped and bare and utterly simple, with none of
the brilliant claptrap of drums and clashing cymbals and royal
banquets and plays within plays that marked his stage in *Caligula*: the scene is simply that of an isolated country inn
where the staff is prepared for murder. The action has a simple
linearity of structure that carries it forward with a relentlessness and inevitability not unlike that of Sophoclean tragedy:
the movement is from the son's return in disguise to his mother
and sister (with his intention to be their deliverer, and with
theirs first to murder and then to rob) through the murder and
the too-late discovery of Jan's identity to the final moment of
shock and mortification, with its divulgence of "the normal
order of things," the bleak wintriness of life in a world in
which God is absent and where, as Beckett says in *Molloy*, "all
wilts and yields, as if loaded down." It is indeed a stage, controlled as it is by the strange laws of dramatic irony and coinci-
dence, which leaves a permanent residue in the mind.

Yet, for all the hallucinative power with which the play
establishes its world in the imagination, its form, as many of
Camus' critics have remarked, is riddled with incoherence and
disjunction, particularly in that aspect of it which concerns the
delineation of the major characters. Why does Jan, for example, insist upon the guise of anonymity, instead of immediately
identifying himself to his mother and sister, as Maria quite
sensibly urges him to do? This is a question that the play never
really answers, and thus its fulcral point is couched in the most
exasperating—and damaging—ambiguity. Everything, to be
sure, would have been altered, had Jan simply said at the
beginning, as his wife counseled, "It is I." But this he refuses to
do, and for reasons not internal to the dramatic situation, but
rather, simply because Camus (as he very nearly admitted[13])
wanted to build an image of insincerity which is the exact

[13] *Vide* "Author's Preface" in Albert Camus, *Caligula and Three
Other Plays*, trans. by Stuart Gilbert (New York: Alfred A. Knopf,
1958).

opposite of that by means of which man can alone hope to
save himself in an absurd universe—that is, "practicing the
most basic sincerity and pronouncing the most appropriate
word."[14] But taking advantage of Jan in this way was for him,
in the most important particular, to make his character inex-
plicable in terms of what is intrinsic to the play itself.

Nor is Martha less opaque than her brother. Why has she
converted herself into so unfeeling and ruthless a criminal? Is
it because (as she suggests at the end) she has determined to
harden herself into stone, in order that, by her own deafness to
all appeals, she may offer a kind of resistance to a God whose
own happiness consists in being hard as stone? Or does she
murder simply as a way of winning an escape from her dreary
valley to some distant southern region that is bathed in sunlight and close to the sea? And why does she yearn so obsessively for the sun? What is it in her experience of life and in
her own nature that accounts for this preoccupation? Again,
these are questions which are not clearly and persuasively answered by the internal logic of Camus' play. And, in one final
particular, *Le Malentendu* is often marred by a curious kind of
excess of which Camus himself seemed to be obscurely aware,
for, in his Preface to the American edition, he assured us that
the play "is a work of easy access if only one accepts the
language"[15]—but this is, of course, precisely the acceptance
that it is frequently most difficult to manage, especially when
we are confronted by the mother and the sister who occasionally break out into a kind of stiff, elaborate, overly solemn
rhetoric that sounds strangely incongruous against the background of their rural simplicity.

The play, in other words, is not without its formal imper-
fections; yet, for all these, it possesses that strangely alchemical
power (of Kafka's *Der Prozess,* of Sartre's *Huis Clos,* of Beckett's *En attendant Godot,* of Ionesco's *Le Tueur*) of convincing
the men and women of Camus' generation that the distant and

[14] *Ibid.,* p. viii.
[15] *Vide* "Author's Preface" in *op. cit.,* p. viii.

unexampled world which it presents is somehow more real than that which will be reported on in tomorrow morning's newspaper.

5

Now it is in these early works—in *L'Étranger*, in *Le Mythe de Sisyphe*, in the plays *Caligula* and *Le Malentendu*—that we get what Rudolf Bultmann would call Camus' "sense of existence," his sense of what man is up against in this world. The crux of it, as I have been suggesting, is the idea of the world's absurdity. The definition of that in relation to which the human task is to be carried on does not, in other words, posit any specific hindrance or obstruction: it is, rather, simply the calloused "thickness and strangeness of the world" that constitutes our irremediable burden. *L'absurde* grows out of the fact that life is filled with meanings that are incomprehensible to man, that existence intransigently resists man's demand for rational coherence, and that man everywhere beholds the evidence of the fragility of his life. God is dead, and the sense of *angoisse*, of *l'absurde*, grows out of the absolute uncertainty as to whether or not there is any effective ontological warrant for the continuance of the human enterprise. The issue is the anxiety of emptiness, of meaninglessness; and the scene that is explored in Camus' early writings is the Abyss of *Nada* in whose servitude human life is caught at the end of the modern period—a world in which Nothing is at the center, the world of Hardy and Conrad, of Hemingway and Malraux and Sartre.

But, having defined what is centrally problematic in modern experience, Camus, from the mid-'forties on, was attempting to conceive a way of surviving and a strategem of resistance. Nathaniel Hawthorne once remarked of his friend Herman Melville that "he can neither believe, nor be comfortable in his unbelief." Something like this also comes near being true of this contemporary Frenchman, at least to the extent to which, in all of his work of the last fifteen years of his life, he

was attempting to find "the means to proceed beyond nihilism."
Like Cherea in *Caligula,* he believed that it is man's fate to live
without hope and without grace: yet no thinker of our time
has been more alert to the futility of the ethics that modern
nihilism has produced. Indeed, Camus' most cutting strictures
were reserved for those metaphysical rebels of the last hundred and fifty years who, like Ivan Karamazov, have concluded that, since God is dead, then "everything is permitted."
For to legitimize murder is to have allowed the Absurd to
intimidate us into unfaithfulness to humanity.

It was precisely Camus' most fundamental aim, however,
to find a way of affirming the human order. He wanted neither
the easy infinities of conventional religion nor the Manichaean
angelism of the modern nihilist, but, rather, he was looking for
"a form of order that orders indeed, but leaves reality, every
iota of yours and mine, intact—multitudinous, different and
free, but together at last."[16] It was this concern that unified his
work of the last fifteen years,[17] giving *La Peste* and *L'Homme
révolté* a privileged status among his writings of this period,
since it is in these books that we get the most concentrated
expression of his basic interest. Here, like Ignazio Silone, he
was asking the question as to what action will redeem the time
and re-establish the image of man: the focus, in other words,
had shifted from an analysis of the Absurd to an analysis of
how the world's disorder may be resisted and the life of the
human creature may be rectified and renewed.

The French Roman Catholic philosopher Gabriel Marcel
tells us that ours is today a world in which "the preposition
'with' . . . seems more and more to be losing its meaning."[18]

[16] William F. Lynch, S.J., "Theology and the Imagination,"
Thought, Vol. XXX, No. 116 (Spring, 1955), p. 34.

[17] Perhaps the one exception is the collection of stories that forms
the body of Camus' last published work in fiction, *L'Exil et le royaume,*
in which the preoccupation with the themes of exile and alienation to
some extent reaches back to the stress of the earlier books.

[18] Gabriel Marcel, *The Mystery of Being,* Vol. I, trans. by G. S.
Fraser (Chicago: Henry Regnery Co., 1950), p. 28.

But one feels that, on the contrary, the main lesson of *La Peste* is just that our solidarity with one another is the thing that we cannot possibly not know amid "this meadow of calamity,/ This uncongenial place, this human life. . . ."[19] "In an absurd world," says Camus, "the rebel still has one certainty. It is·the solidarity of men in the same adventure, the fact that both he and the grocer are baffled."[20] It is our involvement as men in a common fate that constitutes the principal fact for Camus in his book of 1947.

The setting of *La Peste* is the Algerian coast town of Oran, whose inhabitants begin to notice on a certain day an increasing number of rats in their dwelling places. In a short time rats are tumbling out of every hole and cranny in the town and dying by the thousands in the streets. Then the inhabitants themselves begin to die of a mysterious fever, and it soon becomes evident to the local physicians that all the horrible symptoms spell bubonic plague. So, after weeks of equivocation on the part of the authorities, it is apparent that there is no other course but to employ the most rigorous prophylactic measures and to place the town in quarantine. It is, then, separated from the rest of the world, and, with the closing of the gates, its people are shut in upon the long ordeal of isolation and suffering with which they have to live throughout almost an entire year.

In his epigraph from Defoe, Camus tells us that "It is as reasonable to represent one kind of imprisonment by another, as it is to represent anything that really exists by that which exists not." The allegorical nature of the fable is emphasized by the dull, provincial scene and by the dispassionate, matter-of-fact objectivity of tone from which Camus never varies in the chronicling of the events. When the book appeared in 1947, it was at first supposed, particularly by Camus' French readers,

---

[19] Matthew Arnold, "Empedocles on Etna," Act II, *Poetical Works of Matthew Arnold* (London: Macmillan and Co. Ltd., 1901), p. 472.

[20] Albert Camus, "La Remarque sur la Révolté," in the collection *Existence* (Paris: Gallimard, 1945), p. 18.

to be a rendering of the experience of the German Occupation. But so narrow a construction of its meaning is, I suspect, possible only if the novel is read without regard for the major consistencies of Camus' thought. For, once it is approached under this more spacious perspective, we cannot fail to discern that the plague itself is really but an emblem of everything that twists and betrays and otherwise outrages the human spirit in "this uncongenial place." The dilatoriness of the epidemic's progress is the massive inertia of the world, and its murderous malevolence is the disastrous irrationality of the Absurd itself.

In the gallery of characters whom Camus creates to carry his meaning, we are presented with a variety of responses to the crisis. For the little confidence-man, Cottard, the plague suddenly makes the fear and loneliness that he has known for so many years begin to be bearable: as Tarrou says: "He's in the same peril of death as everyone else, but that's just the point; he's in it *with the others.*" He is a hunted man: there is crime in his past; and, were it not for the emergency created by the epidemic, the future for Cottard would be something closed and annulled. But the crisis brings him a kind of ransom or deliverance, for it at once interrupts the normal procedures of justice, thus granting him at least a temporary reprieve, and, in the degree to which everybody is equally threatened by the pestilence, it restores to the outlaw a sense of involvement in the common tide of life: he can once again feel his neighbor to be his brother, and his own suffering is no longer a solitary suffering. So the plague is something with which Cottard wishes to cooperate, and, once its fury begins to lessen, he querulously impugns the validity of the death statistics which testify that the worst is over. Now Cottard, with his shabby little "black-market" operation and his emotional profiteering on human suffering, is, without doubt, an unattractive figure. Yet I suspect that to approach him as merely an object for excoriation is to be inattentive to the pathos of his fear and of his nervous insecurity. And, when one recalls Camus' own dis-

enchantment about the conventional machinery of social justice, as it was expressed, say, in *Réflexions sur la guillotine* or
as it is expressed by Tarrou in *La Peste,* one then also suspects
that perhaps he would even have preferred us to accord a
certain limited sympathy to this poor wretch who chose finally
to be shot by the police rather than surrender.

Then there is the obscure civil service clerk, Joseph
Grand, who has been writing for years a novel which never
advances beyond an introductory sentence that has been sub-
jected to endless revisions: Grand fights the plague by keeping
for the medical authorities a carefully detailed statistical account of its progress, and Camus says, half-whimsically, that
he is the real hero of the tale. Though he is stricken by the
disease, he manages to survive; and it is a survival of more
than the body alone, for, whereas Grand's life had for long
been trivialized and emptied of significance by his bondage to
the barren routine of his minor post in the bureaucratic machine of Oran, it is his participation in a great action, in a
collective effort, that reinvigorates his heart and his imagination—so that, at the end, he burns the great mass of manuscript on which he had recorded the countless versions of that
single sentence which he had ever managed to write of his
projected novel. It is no longer necessary in other words, for
him to perform this tic by way of forcing in himself something
that resembles genuine imaginative activity: the plague has
awakened new places in his heart, and the memory of his
beloved wife Jeanne is once again a rich and fecund presence
in his soul.

Or, again, there is the Jesuit priest, Father Paneloux, who
at first responds to the catastrophe by declaring in a sermon
that it is a divine chastisement visited upon the citizens of
Oran for the purging of their wickedness but who, after wit-
nessing the death-agonies of a little boy, gives up any attempt
at rational theodicy for blind faith. It is apparent that neither
the rationalist nor the fideist posture in the priest is anything
that can be easily accommodated to the basic premises con-

trolling Camus' novel. Father Paneloux is, of course, himself a radical, but his is the radicalism of a traditional supernaturalist faith: he lives outside the realm of the Absurd, and, though one may hesitate to say that he is *therefore* beyond the grasp of Camus' imagination, the fact is that the depth and inner complexity of the man are never deeply explored. He is one who unequivocally affirms the absolute sovereignty of a gracious and providential Presence. Indeed, so radical is his faith that he has for long been meditating on the question as to whether a priest has the right to consult a physician; and, in his death, he leads us to feel that he has at last decided that he does not have this right. But, of course, this unshakable trust in a Goodness that lies beyond the woe and desolation of this life could be understood by the author of *Le Mythe de Sisyphe* only as a form of "suicide" or abdication. In a world that seems to be governed not by Love but by Death, this obscure North African priest, in his unquestioning submission to the will of God, seems to be a frigid enigma; and it may be a measure of Camus' own failure to achieve, as a novelist, a certain sort of self-transcendence that Father Paneloux is so consistently approached externally and without charity.

Rambert, a Parisian journalist who is stranded in the city, embodies, in the poignancy of his separation from the woman in Paris whom he loves, one of the book's major themes, the powerlessness even of love before the terrors and disasters of history. He is a veteran of the Spanish Civil War, and his experience of various crimes throughout the world in the 'thirties has convinced him that one ideology deals no more adequately with the troubles of man than any other. Indeed, he has but one belief, and that is in love, not in the abstract idea of it but in his particular relation to the woman whom he adores and from whom, it seems, once the city is placed under quarantine, he is irremediably separated. No sooner, in fact, are the restrictions promulgated than he begins to plod away, "calling on all sorts of officials and others whose influence

would have weight in normal conditions," hoping against hope
that he can somehow get permission to leave Oran. "The gist
of his argument was always the same: that he was a stranger . . .
and, that being so, his case deserved special consideration,"
But the authorities turn a deaf ear to his pleas, and, finally,
after exhausting himself in fruitless interviews and going the
round of all the municipal offices, he falls into a period of sheer
lethargy and, in his despair, simply drifts aimlessly from café
to café. One day, when he tells Rieux, the chief physician in
the plague-infested city, that he has come to like "waking up at
four in the morning and thinking of his beloved Paris, the
doctor guessed easily enough . . . that this was his favorite time
for conjuring up pictures of the woman from whom he now
was parted . . . the hour when he could feel surest she was
wholly his." Yet, after desperately attempting to arrange an
escape from the quarantined city, when at last everything has
been made ready for his being smuggled out, Rambert suddenly decides to remain and to contribute his own strength to
the struggle against the plague. For he has discovered that no
man is an island and that he is himself diminished by the
sufferings that have befallen the people in this city, even
though he is a visitor and unconnected by personal ties with
the inhabitants.

It is, however, Jean Tarrou and Bernard Rieux who carry
the heaviest freight of the novel's meaning. Tarrou comes to
Oran just a few weeks before the onset of the plague: we do
not know from where. But, though apparently rootless and
unattached, he is a man whose human sympathies prevent his
living at any remove from the suffering of men. And, once it
becomes clear how disastrous is the emergency that Oran is up
against, he organizes teams of "sanitary squads" to fight the
ravages of the epidemic. As a result of this activity, he is soon
thrown close to Bernard Rieux, the leading physician in the
town, and, between the two, there grows up a deep sense of intimacy and friendship. One evening, after an exhausting day of

work, Tarrou suggests to Rieux that they take off an hour "for friendship," and then he tells Rieux something of what his life has been like. He was the son of a public prosecutor, and his father had wanted him also to go into the law. When he was barely seventeen years of age, his father had taken him to court to sit through a murder trial in which he, as prosecutor, was demanding the death penalty. He still remembers the cowering figure of the little red-haired defendant in the dock, and he tells Rieux that he was so filled with horror at the murder that his father in turn, as the representative of official justice, was pleading for, that he fled from his father's house, thereafter to devote his life to the subversion of a society which based itself on the death sentence. "I wanted to square accounts with that poor blind owl in the dock. So I became an agitator, as they say. I didn't want to be pestiferous, that's all." But then he found himself in revolutionary movements which themselves invoked the death sentence, and at first, he says, he accepted this as a necessary temporary expedient—till one day he witnessed a man's death under a firing-squad in Hungary and saw the hole that was left in the man's chest, a hole big enough to thrust one's fist into. It was in that moment, he says, that he realized that he had himself been a carrier of the plague which for years he had supposed himself to be fighting. From that point forward his pacifism became intransigent. He knows, of course, that "we can't stir a finger in this world without the risk of bringing death to somebody. . . . each of us has the plague within him; no one, no one on earth is free from it. . . . All I maintain is that on this earth there are pestilences and there are victims, and it's up to us, so far as possible, not to join forces with the pestilences." His path, he says, is "the path of sympathy," and "what interests me is learning how to become a saint . . . without God."

Though one feels that Camus' own vision of things is expressed more unequivocally by Tarrou than by any of the other characters in his fictions, one also feels that it may be

Rieux's kind of modest optimism that most nearly approximates the position to which Camus wanted always to be faithful. Like Cherea in *Caligula*, Rieux, though an atheist, has no taste for atheistical dialectic. The one occasion on which he evinces any irritation with his friend Tarrou is when Tarrou asks him if he believes in God. He replies that, of course, he does not, but he also indicates his principled impatience with this kind of question. The really vital point, he says in effect, is that Creation as we find it is something to be fought against and, when one joins this fight, then one is on the right road. All I know, he says to Tarrou, is that "there are sick people and they need curing." He has but one certitude, "that a fight must be put up, in this way or that, and there must be no bowing down. The essential thing was to save the greatest possible number of persons from dying and being doomed to unending separation." And, as he says to Rambert, "There's no question of heroism in all this. It's a matter of common decency"—by which, he says, he means simply doing one's job.

So, when Tarrou speaks to him of his interest in learning how to become a saint without God, Rieux bristles slightly and confesses: "Heroism and sanctity don't really appeal to me, I imagine. What interests me is being a man." To which, with a beautiful irony, Tarrou replies that he is "less ambitious." Or, again, when one day over the death-bed of the little son of the police magistrate, Monsieur Othon, Father Paneloux suggests to Rieux that, in a way, they are partners in working for man's salvation, the doctor replies: 'Salvation's much too big a word for me. I don't aim so high. I'm concerned with man's health; and for me his health comes first."

Thus it is that in Jean Tarrou and Bernard Rieux—and especially in the latter—Camus offers us an image of the kind of virtue, of the kind of holiness, that is possible for man in a time when God is absent. And what is clear is that it is a holiness that consists in a certain kind of resistance or revolt. The fundamental ontological realities, Camus seems to be saying, cannot be altered: the universe is not fully comprehensible and does not answer the human demand for clarity and coherence; nor is there any avoidance of that final annulment of the human enterprise in the death that awaits every living creature; nor is there even any way of guaranteeing man's protection from the brutal contingencies of nature and of history. But at least we may struggle *for* man and *against* whatever it is that would thwart or defeat or humiliate his humanity. The way, as Tarrou says, is the way of sympathy, of love, of compassion; and, when we see it as our human vocation to cherish and to defend the life of our fellow-creatures, we have then also undertaken the way of what Camus liked to call resistance, for we have set ourselves against a world-order that is indifferent to the hopes and aspirations of the human community.

It is, indeed, the purity of Christ's compassion that explains, I suspect, Camus' profound reverence for the human figure of Jesus. The French critic Roger Quilliot is probably right in saying that "cut off from his divine ascendance, Christ becomes for Camus what he was for Alfred de Vigny, the highest incarnation of . . . human grandeur."[21] He was one who attempted to heal what is broken in human life, to defend mankind against the powers of darkness, and, through the depth and scope of his charity, he became the great exemplar of *résistance*. We cannot, to be sure, alter the fundamental order of the world, but we can at least refuse to join forces with it and can thus at least, in a way, revolt against *l'absurde*. Each of us, as Tarrou says, carries "the plague" within him, but we can at least, through careful vigilance, try to make certain that we do not help to spread it—which is to say that, by dedicating ourselves to the relief of human suffering, we can to some extent contain and limit it. It is not a matter of heroism but just of common decency. This was the modest optimism that guided Camus' reflections on the human problem during the last years of his life.

[21] Roger Quilliot, *La Mer et les prisons: Essai sur Albert Camus* (Paris: Gallimard, 1956), pp. 103–104.

6

When we move from Camus' early works—*L'Étranger, Le Mal-entendu, Caligula,* and, particularly, *Le Mythe de Sisyphe*—to *La Peste,* it is apparent that his novel of 1947 signalizes a profound reorientation that was taking place in his thought throughout the 'forties and that is most fully presaged in his *Lettres à un ami allemand* which were published by Gallimard in 1945 (the first two having been written in 1943). For, in contrast to the author of *Le Mythe,* the Camus of *La Peste* is concerned to be a witness to something more ultimate even than the Absurd, this being simply the human spirit itself. This is a shift in his focus which, as he admits in the *Lettres,* was very largely a result of his experience as a participant in the Resistance against the German Occupation.

"If nothing had any meaning," said Camus to his young German friend in December of 1943 in the second of the *Lettres*—"if nothing had any meaning, you would be right. But there is something that still has a meaning," and that something he had come to believe to be none other than man himself. In the fourth *Lettre* of July, 1944, he admits to his former friend that "For a long time we both thought that this world had no ultimate meaning and that consequently we were cheated." He further admits the baffled unease that he at first felt, as his German contemporaries began to fill this void by a kind of anti-human politics whose only code was that of "the animal world—in other words, violence and cunning. . . . to tell the truth, I, believing I thought as you did, saw no valid argument to answer you"—except, he says, "a fierce love of justice which, after all, seemed to me as unreasonable as the most sudden passion." He was, in other words, in very much the same position as Cherea in *Caligula*—not being able, that is, to refute his opponent's philosophy which seemed "logical from start to finish," yet not being able to accept a doctrine which converted itself into corpses. But accept it he could not:

though he and his German friend had begun with the same premises, they had, finally, undertaken radically different commitments; and the one thing that Camus can say in substantiation of the course which he took is that he simply had "to remain faithful to the world." To be sure, this world, he continues to insist, "has no ultimate meaning. But," he declares, "I know that something in it has a meaning and that is man, because he is the only creature to insist on having one. This world has at least the truth of man, and our task is to provide its justifications against fate itself."

The Absurd, in other words, demands revolt: yet revolt, Camus is saying, must itself be subject to a principle of criticism, if it is not to become some form of sheer demonism whose consequences are utterly anti-human. This he believes to have been precisely the case with Nazism: though it was, perhaps in origin, an insurgence of rebellion against the Absurd, the violence of its racial particularism and the ruthless cruelty of its cynical politics converted its revolt against the Absurd into a revolt against man. Thus, he tells his former friend, "you . . . sided with the gods."

Now this is a Camus who had in some ways traveled a very considerable distance from the position that is recorded in *Le Mythe de Sisyphe*. For, having been scorched by the agony of France's subjection to the demonic satanism of Nazi Germany, he had come to know that Don Juan is not a sufficient guide through the wilderness to which man is condemned in this late, bad time. The world is still under the dominance of the Absurd. But the Nazi experiment had taught him the folly of allowing one's despair to turn into intoxication. In the fourth *Lettre*, it is clear that he had begun to suspect that, if one is to face Evil writ large and disastrous upon the human polity, one must derive some more fruitful conclusion from the Absurd than that "what counts is not the best living but the most living." For this merely quantitative morality is hardly a doctrine that would have permitted any significant ethical discriminations at all between, say, the Resistance movement and the massive evil which it was opposing. It was out of just this kind of dilemma that Camus, urged on by the exigencies of life in occupied France, began to seek in the early 'forties some principle by means of which the absolute ethical relativism of an "absurd" metaphysic might be modified toward a more genuinely humane end.

It is in the brilliant book that he produced in 1951 on the history of resistance (or "rebellion"), *L'Homme révolté*, that we get the most explicit rendering of this phase of his thought. Here, as in *La Peste*, Camus appears as the celebrant of the human communion, and a communion that is itself established by and in "rebellion." He suggests that the "slave who has taken orders all his life [and who] suddenly decides that he cannot obey some new command" furnishes perhaps the purest instance of rebellion. For when he says "No, you are going too far," he is saying "that there is something in him which 'is worth while . . .' and which must be taken into consideration," that for him to do what he is now ordered to do would be for him to consent to a violation of that in him which makes him a man. He acts, in other words,

> in the name of certain values . . . which he feels are common to himself and to all men. . . . It is for the sake of everyone in the world that the slave asserts himself when he comes to the conclusion that a command has infringed on something in him which does not belong to him alone, but which is common ground where all men—even the man who insults and oppresses him—have a natural community.

Thus it is, as Camus says, that, when a man rebels, he "identifies himself with other men and so surpasses himself. . . ." Rebellion, then, in the widest sense, "goes far beyond resentment," for not only does it reveal "the part of man which must always be defended," but it also reveals some essential respect in which the human individual is involved in the family of mankind. "I rebel, therefore we are."

The trouble, however, with the great strategists of rebellion in the modern period has been, Camus felt, that whether, out of a metaphysical radicalism, they have rebelled against the human condition itself or whether, out of a social radicalism, they have rebelled against humanly perpetrated injustice, they have tended, in too many instances, to ignore the idea that is most basically involved in the logic of rebellion, the idea of *mésure*, of balance, of moderation. If one turns to the tradition of metaphysical rebellion—the tradition of Sade and Lautréamont, of Rimbaud and the Surrealists, of Feuerbach and Nietzsche—one encounters a type of rebel whose belief that God is dead convinces him that man is absolutely free and entitled therefore to do anything that promises to hasten the establishment of the dominion of man. And if one turns to the tradition of historical rebellion—the tradition of Rousseau and Saint-Just, of Bakunin and Marx and Lenin—one encounters a type of rebel who also believes that God is dead and who concludes that history is, therefore, to be "written in terms of the hazards of force." What is tragic in each case is that, given the desacralization of life in the modern period, a rebellion that was initiated *for* man turns in the end *against* man, its demonized purposes being consecrated in blood. What is lost is the *mésure* which makes intemperate fanaticism in behalf of any kind of absolute impossible, whether it be the dream of absolute freedom or the dream of absolute justice. This was the essence of Camus' critique of the major programs of rebellion that have been developed since the eighteenth century.

Yet, though no orthodox apologist of our time has been more expert than Camus in discerning the fetters that modern secularism has forged for the human spirit, it is significant that he did not conclude that "rebellion" itself has been invalidated. On the contrary: he believed that ours is an age irretrievably *désacralisé* and that rebellion, therefore, remains "one of the essential dimensions of man." Even in his last years Camus never repudiated the basic lesson of *Le Mythe de Sisyphe*: to be sure, he did not any longer want to think of himself as an atheist, for, as he said in *Le Monde* in 1955, irreligion had come to strike him as entailing an unseemly kind of presumptuous vulgarity: but God *has* disappeared, and the world *is* absurd. Yet, as I have already noticed, he did want to avoid Ivan Karamazov's conclusion that, therefore, "everything is permitted." He wanted, in other words, to go "beyond nihilism," and it is in this attempt—by the way of the reinstatement of the doctrine of *mésure*—that he expected us to discern his departure from the dominant traditions of modern rebellion.

Now by *mésure*, by the idea of "limit" or "border-line," Camus meant something quite simple: he meant that rebellion can never be in behalf of total freedom (whether for Sade's aristocrat of libertinism or the Romantic dandy or the Nietzschean Superman or the Marxist proletarian or for anyone else) and that it serves the human communion only when it "puts total freedom up for trial" and acknowledges that

> freedom has its limits everywhere that a human being is to be found—the limit being precisely that human being's power to rebel. . . . The rebel undoubtedly demands a certain degree of freedom for himself; but in no case, if he is consistent, does he demand the right to destroy the existence and the freedom of others. He humiliates no one. The freedom he claims, he claims for all; the freedom he refuses, he forbids everyone to enjoy. He is not only the slave against the master, but also man against the world of master and slave.

The logic, then, of true rebellion, as Camus understood it, forbids any principle or doctrine that promises to legitimize murder even as a temporary expedient, and this is so, he maintained, because "rebellion, in principle, is a protest against death." Yet Camus was no conventional pacifist, for he recognized that, the world being as it is, were the rebel absolutely to claim not to kill or lie, he would be

> renouncing his rebellion and accepting, once and for all, evil and murder. But no more can he agree to kill and lie, since the inverse reasoning which would justify murder and violence would also destroy the reasons for his insurrection. Thus

the rebel can never find peace. He knows what is good and, despite himself, does evil. The value that supports him is never given to him once and for all; he must fight to uphold it, unceasingly.

But at least, like Tarrou, "he can put his conviction and passion to work at diminishing the chances of murder around him." And, in thus dedicating itself to a relative justice, rebellion may prove that it is neither mere resentment nor some form of disguised imperialism but "love and fecundity" and compassion: it is at this "meridian of thought" that the rebel "rejects divinity in order to share in the struggles and destiny of all men."

7

From the two central books of his career (*La Peste* and *L'Homme révolté*), then, Camus emerges, in the line of Antoine de Saint-Exupéry and André Malraux, as a great French poet of *fraternité* for an age that has known the malaise of the Absurd. Throughout his career he remained, to be sure, a poet of *rébellion*, but, in the last fifteen years of his life, there was a noticeable deepening of his concern that the act of revolt should not so generalize itself as to betray the human sodality, making (to paraphrase the language of Jesus' parable of the empty house) the rebel's last state worse than the first. In his work for the theatre, this is the presiding interest in *L'État de siège* (1948) and in *Les Justes* (1950), the two plays which immediately preceded *L'Homme révolté* and which carry forward into the concrete terms of dramatic action many of the central themes of his book of 1951—just as the earlier plays, *Caligula* and *Le Malentendu,* bore a similar relation to *Le Mythe de Sisyphe*.

L'État de siège was first produced in the autumn of 1948 by Jean-Louis Barrault at the Théâtre Marigny, and, though by no means a popular success, it was, in its dramaturgy, the most ambitious theatrical venture that Camus had ever under-

taken, with a musical score by Honegger and a stage-décor by
the painter Balthus, the arts of mime and burlesque, the devices of monologue and conventional dialogue, ingenious lighting and aural effects and the simultaneous presentation of
many scenes being all combined into a spectacle more showy
and brilliant even than that of *Caligula*. The setting is the
Spanish city of Cadiz, over which, as the play opens, a buzzing
comet flies, portentously and to the people's consternation.
Since "good governments are governments under which nothing happens," the Governor informs the populace that "nothing
has occurred to justify alarm or discomposure" and that they
are even to deny that a comet has ever risen on the horizon.
But when, in the town market place, we begin to hear the thud
of the falling bodies of those who have been mysteriously and
fatally stricken, it is apparent that disaster is at hand; and it is
soon impossible to deny that the city has been overtaken by a
deadly plague. Indeed, Camus himself, overtaken, it seems, by
an uncontrollable allegorical passion, chooses to put the Plague
into his cast of characters, this blustering and sinister presence
appearing in the city shortly after the epidemic gets under
way, being accompanied by a young woman who is his secretary.

The Plague immediately sets to work, with the help of his
secretary, to organize lists of the inhabitants, then directing her
to check first one and then another off—and no sooner does
her scrawl go down into her notebook than the thud of a
falling body is heard: ". . . from today," says the Plague, "you
are going to learn to die in an orderly manner."

> Until now you died in the Spanish manner, haphazard—
> when you felt like it, so to say. . . . Yes, you muffed your
> deaths. A dead man here, a dead man there, one in his bed,
> another in the bull ring—what could be more slovenly? But,
> happily for you, I shall impose order on all that. There will
> be no more dying as the fancy takes you. Lists will be kept
> up—what admirable things lists are!—and we shall fix the
> order of your going. Fate has learned wisdom and will keep

its records. You will figure in statistics, so at last you'll serve some purpose.

It is not surprising that the Plague should appoint as his chief lieutenant the local iconoclast and wiseacre, Nada, the self-appointed mocker of Cadiz philistinism and of all the established pieties. For Nada's part, in the total design of the play, is to represent that despair grown intoxicated with itself which Camus was attacking in *Lettres à un ami allemand*. "Suppression—that's always been my gospel," he says. "But until now I had no good arguments to back it up. Now I have the regulations on my side." So, dreaming of a total "suppression," wanting to annihilate everything since Nothing "is the only thing that exists," he makes the Plague a most willing and efficient henchman.

The young medical student Diego is the character who finally emerges as the man with sufficient strength to rally the forces of revolt. He, like all the other citizens of the town, is at first simply terrified by the kind of delirious violence which the Plague enacts into law, with its suppression of freedom, its requirement of men's betrayal of one another, its fraudulent rhetoric, and its venomous and endless assassinations. But at last the emotion of fright is overborne by the more powerful emotion of disgust at the obscene capriciousness with which human life is being destroyed: so, when the Plague's secretary discovers him in the act of attempting to escape from the city, instead of cowering before her in groveling abjection, having been tried beyond the point of further tolerance, he flings into her face his outrage, his anger, his indignation. She, having grown weary of killing and having come, as she admits, to have a "soft spot" for Diego, confides that the Plague's whole system "has a weak point. . . . As far back as I can remember the machine has always shown a tendency to break down when a man conquers his fear. . . . I won't say it stops completely. But it creaks and sometimes it actually begins to fold up." In other words, once a man ceases to be afraid, the Plague then ceases to have any power over him—and, when that time comes, it is thereafter pointless for the Plague to order his secretary to scratch the man's name off her list: the thud of a falling body will not be heard.

With this assurance, then, Diego takes heart—and, in this moment, the prophecy that the wind's blowing from the sea would signalize the city's liberation begins to be fulfilled, for, as Diego, enheartened by the secretary's disclosure, begins to urge his fellow townsmen to join him in an act of revolt, a breeze is felt. The play then quickly moves toward the great scene of confrontation between Diego and the Plague, who holds Diego's fiancée Victoria as a hostage. The Plague proposes a bargain: Victoria's life for the liberty of Cadiz: "I'll give you that girl's life and let you *both* escape, provided you let me make my own terms with this city." But Diego refuses, and, in exasperation, the tyrant cries out: "You fool! Don't you realize that ten years of this girl's love are worth far more than a century of freedom for those men? . . . No one can be happy without causing harm to others. That is the world's justice." But Diego persists in his rejection of a logic that would permit him to purchase a private fulfillment at the expense of the city's enslavement, and, to the Plague's definition of "the world's justice," he simply replies: "A justice that revolts me and to which I refuse to subscribe." He chooses, in other words—like the Camus of the *Lettres à un ami allemand*—"to remain faithful to the world," to "the truth of man": he will not side with the gods, for the supreme and single *mésure* to which he gives his suffrage is the human community itself, and to consent to his revolt being converted into a betrayal of his brethren would be for him to overpass the one limit to which he owes an absolute obedience. Thus it is that in the young medical student of *L'État de siège* Camus embodied that spirit whose tough humaneness he counted on to withstand not only the rampant oppressiveness of political tyranny (the Plague) but also the rampant self-destructiveness of a self-intoxicated nihilism (Nada). Diego is, in other words, the *exemplum* that

Camus offers in this play of the rebel doing what is pleaded for
in the great final section of *L'Homme révolté*—namely, going
"beyond nihilism," in fidelity to the human communion.

It is a similar preoccupation with the morality of *rébellion*
which is at the heart of *Les Justes,* the play which was produced for the first time by Paul Œttley at the Théâtre-Héber-
tot in Paris in December of 1949 and which is modeled very
closely on Boris Savinkov's account of Socialist terrorism in
Moscow in 1905.[22] The particular movement with which
Savinkov was affiliated was the Organization for Combat of
the Socialist Revolutionary Party, and the focal point of his
book is his narrative of the group's plot against the Grand
Duke Sergei Alexandrovitch. Two members of the organization, Voinarovski and the student Kaliayev, were selected to
toss a bomb into the carriage of the Grand Duke as he drove to
the theatre on the second day of February. But, as the carriage
passed the spot where Kaliayev was stationed, he, whose as-
signment it was actually to throw the bomb, could not bring
himself to do it, for the Grand Duke was accompanied by the
Grand Duchess and their little niece and nephew, and this
was an eventuality that had not been anticipated in the group's
calculations. His colleagues afterward agreed with Kaliayev,
that he was right not to have taken the lives of innocent children. So they set up a new plan to kill the Grand Duke two
days hence when, as they knew, he would again be driving to
the theatre, and, on this second occasion, the assassination,
encountering no obstacles, was successful. Later, in prison,
Kaliayev refused to purchase his freedom by informing on his
fellow conspirators; nor would he be moved by the Grand
Duchess's appeal that he submit himself to the Church's disciplines of contrition and penance. For, having taken a human
life in what he believed to be a just protest against the tyran-
nous oppressiveness of the Russian Establishment, he was in-
sistent that he should pay with his own.

[22] *Vide* Boris Savinkov, *Souvenirs d'un terroriste,* trans. by Bernard
Taft (Paris: Payot, 1931).

Now, as he tells us in *L'Homme révolté*, Camus had the highest admiration for "the men of 1905," for nowhere else in the history of modern terrorism could he find assassins in whom the moral imagination conducted so sensitive an inquiry into the question as to whether murder, in any circumstances, could be justified as a technique of revolt. Indeed, these were, he says, the *meurtriers délicats*, the fastidious assassins, for they never forgot that, prompted by whatever motives, the destruction of human personality does itself increase the burden of man's woe and is therefore something that must cause the wielders of bombs and revolvers the profoundest unease and chagrin. In *L'Homme révolté* Camus recalls, for example, that Savinkov decided on one occasion, as he was escaping from a Czarist prison, "to shoot any officers who might attempt to prevent his flight, but to kill himself rather than turn his revolver on an ordinary soldier." Of Dora Brilliant, another terrorist, he recalls that Savinkov said that "terror weighed on her like a cross" and that he said of Rachel Louriée that, though she believed in terrorist action, "blood upset her no less than it did Dora." Camus cites numerous other instances in support of his contention that, in the history of modern revolutionary action, these people of 1905 represent a truly remarkable high-mindedness, a moral nobility that was a consequence of the fact that, though revolution was for them "a necessary means," it was not "a sufficient end": though they found murder necessary, they also found it to be inexcusable. "History offers few examples," says Camus, "of fanatics who have suffered from scruples, even in action. But the men of 1905 were always prey to doubts. The greatest homage we can pay them is to say that we would not be able, in 1950, to ask them one question that they themselves had not already asked and that, in their life or by their death, they had not partially answered." When Voinarovski declared in his turn: "If Dubassov is accompanied by his wife, I shall not throw the bomb," he was expressing what Camus found to be characteristic of the entire movement—namely, the profound self-abnegation and the fastidious consideration for the lives of others which mark (in its Greek nomination) that *sophrosyné*, that moderation, in the power of which *rébellion* can alone hope to be delivered from its own desperateness.

So it is not surprising, then, that Camus should have found in Savinkov's memoirs the material for what is perhaps his most moving work for the theatre. The character Boris Annenkov is modeled directly on Savinkov himself, as is Kaliayev on the original, Dora Dulebov on Dora Brilliant, and Alexis Voinov on Voinarovski. The central line of the play's action hews very closely to the actual sequence of the original events. In the opening act the terrorists (Dora, Annenkov, Stepan Fedorov, and Kaliayev) are together in a sparsely furnished Moscow apartment, where they review the last details of the Grand Duke's assassination which is to be carried out by Kaliayev; and, in the second act, he returns with the news that the plan was aborted by the presence of the Grand Duke's nephew and niece in the carriage. Stepan, grown irascible after years in prison and bearing on his body the print of the lashings he has suffered, is infuriated by Kaliayev's idealistic temporizing. "Not until the day comes when we stop sentimentalizing about children," he says, "will the revolution triumph, and we be masters of the world." Dora reminds him that "When that day comes, the revolution will be loathed by the whole human race." But his brutal realism is unmoved. Annenkov, however, speaks for all the others when he asserts that the slaughter of the children would have served no purpose: so it is decided to make another attempt in two days' time, and the second act closes with Stepan sneering at what he believes to be the stupid scruples of his associates in terror. In the third act the conspirators gather once again in the same apartment; then Annenkov and Kaliayev, who are to perform the deed, depart, and, at the close of the act, Dora is peering through the window and describing the event as it occurs in the street below. The fourth act takes place in Kaliayev's prison cell where both the police chief Skuratov and the grieving Grand Duchess attempt in various ways to elicit from him a renunciation of the deed, Skuratov by promising an amnesty for information on the fellow conspirators and the Grand Duchess by invoking the dogmas of the Christian faith. But, as we learn in the final act which is very largely given over to Stepan's account of the execution as he witnessed it, Kaliayev, to the very end, remains faithful to his comrades and to their vision of the future.

Now, in the unfolding of this action, there are several scenes which are of focal importance. The first of these is, of course, the terrible *agon* in Act II in which the chief contestants are Stepan, on the one side, and Kaliayev and Dora, on the other. Stepan's passion for an abstract justice and an abstract future has destroyed in him all scruples about means, and he regards the sense of honor and responsibility that led Kaliayev to refrain from murdering innocent children as merely luxurious self-indulgence: he will not complicate the pragmatic issue of expediency and success with fastidious moral considerations. When Dora cries out: "Even in destruction there's a right way and a wrong way—and there are limits," Stepan, with equal passion, vehemently declares: "There are no limits!" But this is a fanatical ruthlessness that leaves Voinov and Annenkov and the others aghast with horror. And Kaliayev speaks for them all, when he says:

> Killing children is a crime against a man's honor. And if one day the revolution thinks fit to break with honor, well, I'm through with the revolution. If you decide that I must do it, well and good; I will go to the theatre when they're due to come out—but I'll fling myself under the horses' feet.

What he refuses, in other words, to do is to brutalize his fellow human being for the sake of an uncertain and unknown future: ". . . those *I* love are the men who are alive today. . . . it is for them I am fighting, for them I am ready to lay down my life." Though he must sometimes take the part of assassin, he will not be a murderer—a distinction he insists upon. There is, in short, a *mésure*, a limit, which must not be overpassed.

It is precisely this idea of limit, of a border-line beyond which a man of honor does not trespass—it is precisely this which Skuratov is incapable of understanding, as is shown in the great scene of his confrontation with Kaliayev. His is a mind that knows only the simplest logic, and he ridicules what he takes to be the illogic of a terrorist whose ideal permits him to murder a Grand Duke but which makes him balk at murdering children. "If an ideal balks at murdering children, is one justified," he asks, "in murdering a Grand Duke on its behalf?" But, of course, the only answer which Kaliayev could give to this question is one which would entail the notion of *mésure* that the police chief, in his commitment to a simple common-sense ethic, has ruled out of hand.

Indeed, what we feel most strongly in the moving encounter between Kaliayev and the Grand Duchess at the end of Act IV is, again, his fidelity to the idea of *mésure*. The Grand Duchess, in her sorrow, now views the world as a "desert," as a place "empty" and "cruel," and, inevitably, as she faces her husband's murderer, she identifies him with the blighting forces. Yet—though she, from her perspective, could not be expected to regard Kaliayev differently—it is, ironically, just this view of the world as a "desert" that, in his own way, he resists: Stepan is prepared to make a desert in order that Russia may some day be "a land of freedom that will gradually spread out over the whole earth": but Yanek, though he is ready to shed blood, despises murder. As he says in his great scene with Dora in Act III, "I can see the vileness in myself. . . . I've got to kill—there are no two ways about it. But . . . I shall go beyond hatred."

Both *L'État de siège* and *Les Justes*, then, particularly in the persons of Diego and Kaliayev, give us images of the rebel "at the meridian." Both plays are to some extent disfigured by a certain rhetorical bombast which, as Albert Sonnenfeld has remarked with some irritation in a brilliant essay on Camus' dramaturgy,[23] is consistently characteristic of his work for the theatre. But both are plays which speak powerfully of the honor and the generosity and the "strange form of love" which are ingredients of true rebellion; and, in speaking also of the necessity of rebellion being consecrated in moderation and in the acknowledgment of *la mésure,* they summarize, along with *La Peste* and *L'Homme révolté,* one of the central themes of Camus' thought.

8

Christian students of Camus' work, in tending generally to overreact to *La Chute* and to read it as a kind of gloss on the Pauline theology of the Fall, have been by way of convincing some that his novel of 1956 represents a major departure from the basic consistencies of his previous work. It may be, of course, that, through the embarrassingly acute analysis of pharisaism undertaken in this book, Camus was to some extent, as R. W. B. Lewis suggests, groping "toward a new basis for solidarity with his fellows: to what might be called the fellowship of those ashamed, the democracy of the guilty."[24] But I suspect that we shall be closer to the truth about *La Chute,* if we approach it in the manner that Camus himself recommended, as a satirical study of a perverted and unhealthy kind of *solidarité:* it is not that Camus was without a doctrine of sin, for this I shall shortly be wanting very strongly to emphasize: the issue is rather perhaps his distaste for a definition of what is unitary in the human community in terms of a principle of evil. Rieux tells us at the end of *La Peste* "what we learn in a time of pestilence: that there are more things to admire in men than to despise." But Clamence tells

[23] Albert Sonnenfeld, "Albert Camus as Dramatist: The Sources of His Failure," *The Tulane Drama Review,* Vol. V, No. 4 (June, 1961), pp. 106–123.

[24] R. W. B. Lewis, *op. cit.,* p. 107.

us precisely the opposite, that there is in the human soul nothing but malice and brutish nastiness. It is through his twisted
misanthropy, I suspect, that Camus wanted to complete the
dialectic of his message, by presenting an inversion of the
heroism (which is not so much heroism as simply common
decency) that he had theoretically expounded in *L'Homme révolté* and that he had dramatized in various ways in *La Peste,
L'État de siège,* and *Les Justes.*

In the intense and bitter monologue that Clamence deliv-
ers to a nameless acquaintance whom he meets in an Amsterdam bar, he reviews his brilliant legal career in Paris and the
handsome liberality with which he defended the benighted
and the penniless, bestowing his charity on the needy and
lending his assistance to the unfortunate. "I freely held sway,"
he says, "bathed in a light as of Eden. Indeed, wasn't that
Eden, *cher monsieur*: no intermediary between life and me?"
But, as he says, there came a time when all this was over-
turned, for, one evening as he was walking along the banks of
the Seine, he heard a drowning woman's terrified cry for help
coming out of the darkness, and he ignored it. From that point
onwards, he says, the discovery of his own cowardice slowly
led him to the realization of how false and farcical had been
the beneficent role that he had hitherto been playing. His
charities had simply been a way of winning a sense of superiority over people—but, once this was shattered, he began to
feel himself a *pauvre type,* and it becomes apparent that his
only way of enduring the wound to his pride was to become
what he calls a "judge-penitent." That is to say, amid the foggy
gloom of Amsterdam, he now satisfies his need for condescension by gloatingly convicting others of the guilt that festers in
his own soul. The more he accuses himself, the more, he believes, he has the right to judge other men, and thus the doctrine of sin becomes an instrument of aggrandizement and
exploitation. He is, in other words—Jean-Baptiste—like his
ancient progenitor, a voice crying—*clamans*—in the wilderness, but, unlike the man who entered Judaea, his is a proph-

ecy that promises not salvation but debasement and humiliation. So Camus, in *La Chute,* was not flirting with any kind of
neo-Jansenism, as some of his Christian readers have supposed,
but was rather intending to exhibit the kind of morbid perver-
sion of *solidarité* that may be promoted by a soured Mani-
chaeism.

Whether Jean-Baptiste is called a Manichaean or a nihilist
does not greatly matter, for, in the end, it comes to pretty
much the same thing: like that bilious and exacerbated little
cypher whom we meet in Dostoievski's *Letters from the Underworld,* his dominant emotion is one of hatred and contempt
for his fellow men, and, with him, the accusation of self is but
a pretext for launching such an attack on the human community as will have the effect of subverting all values, all established pieties, indeed all confidence in man's capacity for truth
and decency. Of all the admissions which he makes about
himself the one which is perhaps most revealing is that in
which he says: "I, I, I is the refrain of my whole life. . . ." And
not only everything he says but the very form of the novel
itself is calculated to convince us that this is so. There is,
presumably, an interlocutor by whom Jean-Baptiste is confronted; but we do not hear this second presence directly—
and, once we have grasped the real fibre of the *juge-pénitent,*
we begin to feel that the interlocutor is never heard simply
because Jean-Baptiste is too much of a bully to allow him to be
heard and is too intent on using his doctrine of universal guilt
to bludgeon this person into some definitive act of self-abnegation. As he says:

> With me there is no giving of absolution or blessing. Every-
> thing is simply totted up, and then: "It comes to so much.
> You are an evildoer, a satyr, a congenital liar, a homosexual, an
> artist, etc." Just like that. Just as flatly. In philosophy as in
> politics, I am for any theory that refuses to grant man in-
> nocence and for any practice that treats him as guilty. You see
> in me, *très cher,* an enlightened advocate of slavery.

But it is a slavery to which he does not submit himself, for, despite all his confessing, he is careful, as he says, never to accuse himself crudely. "No, I navigate skillfully . . . in short, I adapt my words to my listener and lead him to go me one better." Which is Jean-Baptiste's way of exempting himself from judgment, of coming out better than the next fellow, and thereby of permitting everything to himself. And this, as he admits, is what is most essential for him—"being able to permit oneself everything, even if, from time to time, one has to profess vociferously one's own infamy." So it is that a Manichaean premise brings him round to the nihilistic freedom of Ivan Karamazov—"Everything is permitted": and this is not a logic which makes any room at all for *la mésure*. In short, Jean-Baptiste Clamence is to be viewed as representing in the universe of Camus' fiction the absolute antithesis of the true rebel.

La Chute, which, in its size, barely surpasses the length of the *novella,* was first planned to be a part of the collection of stories that Camus published in 1957 under the title *L'Exil et le royaume.* Had it been somewhat briefer, it might well have entered into that volume to form an interesting contrast with such pieces as "La Pierre qui pousse" and "Les Muets." For, whereas Camus in *La Chute* is dissecting and evaluating a kind of rampant egoism that is destructive of the human communion, in these stories he is once again celebrating, as in *La Peste,* the sacrament of the brother as the single means of grace and hope of glory. "La Pierre qui pousse," for example, tells of a French engineer, D'Arrast, who has come to Iguape to build a bridge. Here he meets a native, a mulatto ship's cook, who, in gratitude for his survival of a shipwreck, has vowed to carry on his head a great slab of stone in a ceremonial procession to the church, and there to place it at the feet of Christ. But, on the day when he attempts this, he labors and labors, and staggers, and finally collapses under the great weight, in tears, "defeated, with his head thrown back" —whereupon D'Arrast picks up the stone and carries it himself, not to the cathedral but back to the little hut in which the man lives. "And there, straightening up until he was suddenly enormous, drinking in with desperate gulps the familiar smell of poverty and ashes, he felt rising within him a surge of obscure and panting joy that he was powerless to name." Refusing, in other words, to perform an act of Christian oblation, he finds his fulfillment in taking upon himself the burden of a fellow human being and in thus serving what the late Charles Williams called the Companionship of our Coinherence.

Or, again, the beautifully composed little story called "Les Muets" centers upon M. Lassalle, the proprietor of a small cooper's shop, who, in a time when cooperage is shrinking with the building of great tankers and tank trucks, refuses to grant his workmen the wage-increase that they so desperately need because of rises in living costs. So they strike. But, having no financial reserves to see them through the strike, they are forced to return to the shop after only a few days' stoppage of work. On the morning of their return, to their great surprise, they find that the doors of the shop are closed: never had this been so before. But M. Lassalle has wanted to emphasize that he has the upper hand: so it is only after their arrival that he allows his foreman slowly to push open the heavy doors on their iron rails. As they enter the shop, they are silent and humiliated, "furious at their . . . silence, but the more it was prolonged the less capable they were of breaking it." Then, during the course of the day, M. Lassalle's little girl suddenly becomes critically ill, and, in the late afternoon, as the men are preparing to return to their homes, M. Lassalle comes into their washroom, dishevelled and racked with anxiety about his child: they feel his sorrow, and their first impulse is to give their sympathy to the distraught father. But they are still unable to break the silence into which they had been plunged by the humiliation that they had suffered at his hands at the beginning of the day. So, having sinned against the fraternity that is constituted by the little shop (not because he had been unable to increase his workmen's wages but because he had calculatedly submitted them to a cruel snubbing), the man goes out, uncomforted and unsustained by the encouragement by which he would have been upborne had his previous behavior permitted his fellow human beings to give him the solace which their natures craved to offer.

This, then, is the one type of story in *L'Exil et le royaume,* which we get not only in "La Pierre qui pousse" and "Les Muets" but also, somewhat more obscurely and obliquely, in the piece called "L'Hôte"—the type, that is, which speaks of the human communion itself as that in the sustaining power of which man can alone hope to prevail and to endure beyond the time when, as William Faulkner says, "the last ding-dong of doom has clanged and faded from the last worthless rock hanging tideless in the last red and dying evening." The three other stories in the volume—"La Femme adultère," "Le Renégat," and "Jonas"—are stories whose images of loneliness and abandonment and travail are reminiscent of the emphatic absurdism of Camus' early period. Being a late product of his literary effort, they may well remind us that, for all of the piety toward *la présence humaine* and *solidarité* that informs the work of his last years, he remained a poet of dereliction and a philosopher of *rébellion.*

9

Now, apart from André Malraux and possibly Jean-Paul Sartre, Camus seemed more ready for dialogue with the Christian community than any other French writer of our day who stands outside Christian perspectives. This was so because, perhaps beyond all his major contemporaries, Camus, both as artist and philosopher, canvassed the human problem with a singular attentiveness to what is implied for it by the modern crisis of faith. He had, to be sure, in the course of his meditations discovered that, even in the midst of winter, there was in himself an invincible summer. Those of his Christian critics who want to go in for the closest kind of bargaining have, therefore, been quick to conclude that his was a position outside the realm of grace. But I wonder to what extent it was not rather, in very large part, simply outside what Dietrich Bonhoeffer liked to call "cheap grace"—that is, grace as a spatialized and objectified God, as the old metaphysic of transcendence, as bourgeois respectability without discipleship.[25]

It is true, of course, that Camus, for all of his affinity with modern Existentialism (with which his quarrels were always family quarrels), lived very much in the universe of classical Stoicism and of the neo-Stoicism which has been so powerfully expressed in our own period by such writers, superficially so different, as Conrad and Hemingway and Faulkner and Malraux. His was not, to be sure, the metaphysic that generally prevailed in ancient Stoicism, for he could not be so certain of the rationality of the world-process as an Epictetus or a Marcus Aurelius, and he was unconvinced that human life is steadied and protected by anything transcendent to itself. But the indifference, the austerity, the *apatheia,* with which Camus' rebel faces the silence of the universe is a Stoic *apatheia,* a Stoic courage: it is, as it was for Seneca, a way of safeguarding what is right and reasonable in the human soul against everything in existence by which it might be mutilated or undone. The rebel, as Camus said, "opposes the principle of justice which he finds in himself to the principle of injustice which he sees being applied in the world."

Yet, despite the heavily Stoical cast of Camus' mind, there is one very important respect in which his moral and religious vision is profoundly different from that of classical Stoicism. It is a difference of which we may be put in mind by an observation which Paul Tillich makes of the Stoics:

> The Stoic as a Stoic does not experience the despair of personal guilt. Epictetus quotes as an example Socrates' words in Xenophon's *Memorabilia:* "I have maintained that which is

---

[25] Dietrich Bonhoeffer, *The Cost of Discipleship,* trans. by R. H. Fuller (New York: Macmillan Co., 1949), Chapter I.

under my control" and "I have never done anything that was wrong in my private or in my public life." And Epictetus himself asserts that he has learned not to care for anything that is outside the realm of his moral purpose. But more revealing than such statements is the general attitude of superiority and complacency which characterizes the Stoic *diatribai*, their moral orations and public accusations. The Stoic cannot say, as Hamlet does, that "conscience" makes cowards of us *all*. He does not see the universal fall from essential rationality to existential foolishness as a matter of responsibility and as a problem of guilt. The courage to be for him is the courage to affirm oneself in spite of fate and death, but it is not the courage to affirm oneself in spite of sin and guilt.[26]

For Camus, however, we are all, as Tarrou says, *dans la peste*, and nowhere in recent literature can we find a more trenchant analysis of the depth of the moral problem than in the closing pages of *L'Homme révolté*. Here he evinces a profound awareness of how deeply every life is involved in a violation of the law of love and of how tragically contaminated is every expedient man uses to secure a tolerable justice. The rebel wants "to serve justice so as not to add to the injustice of the human condition": so "he cannot turn away from the world and from history without denying the very principle of his rebellion." Yet to involve oneself in the drama of history is to be overtaken by the uneasiness of conscience resulting from our discovery of the moral ambiguity that inheres in every choice, in every option: there is no "motive that does not have its limits in evil." To renounce the project of making the human person respected is to "renounce rebellion and fall back on an attitude of nihilistic consent." Yet to "insist that human identity should be recognized as existing" is to undertake a commitment that will prevent my unqualifiedly rejecting violence. "If the rebel makes no choice, he chooses the silence and slavery of others. If, in a moment of despair, he declares that he opts both against God and against history, he is the witness of pure

[26] Paul Tillich, *op. cit.*, p. 17.

freedom; in other words, of nothing." But, then, to ally oneself with the struggle *for* man is to pledge oneself to an effort that may in some sense entail a vindication of murder—despite the fact that "rebellion, in principle, is a protest against death." Thus, as Camus says in the passage from which I have already quoted, "the rebel can never find peace. He knows what is good and, despite himself, does evil." "Rebellion . . . sets us on the path of calculated culpability," and it is in *la mésure* that we have the one hope of its being redeemed.

So, though in some measure the vision of this Frenchman has its affiliation with the Stoic tradition, he very clearly in no wise represents the moral complacency of classical Stoicism. On the contrary: he tells us that the rebel must face the moral ambiguity of human existence "indefatigably." The question therefore arises as to how, within the perspectives of Camus' thought, this is possible. What was it, in other words, that enabled him to affirm the human enterprise as passionately as he did, "in spite of sin and guilt"?

The answer to this question is, I believe, to be found in its clearest form in his early book *Noces* (published in Algiers by Charlot in 1938), in the volume of essays called *L'Eté* (published in Paris by Gallimard in 1954), and in the final chapter of *L'Homme révolté*. We are reminded, when we turn to the book of 1938, that Camus, having grown up in Algeria, was by birth and nurture a North African, and the four essays that comprise this slender volume are devoted to the Mediterranean countryside which formed the scene of his youth. They are a veritable "manual of happiness," and what is celebrated is a "loving alliance" between man and the earth—the riot and play and fecundity, the glory and the grandeur of the world. Camus speaks of places, of Tipasa and Djémila and Algiers and Florence; he speaks of the heat of the sun, of the magnificence of the sea, of the tanned bodies on the beach, of the cool evenings and the quiet Mediterranean dusks. He makes us smell the heavy fragrances of North African plants; he makes us see the riotous colors of the Tuscan landscape; and we are drenched in the rich, sensual carnality of wind and rain, of gardens and the desert, of sky and sea. He records how, as a youth, he "learned to consent to the earth and to burn in the dark flame of its celebrations." And, in one characteristic sentence, he says: "I must be naked and plunge into the sea . . . and consummate on my own flesh the embrace for which, lips to lips, earth and sea have for so long been sighing."

The message, in other words, of *Noces* is that "if there is a sin against life, it is perhaps not so much in despairing as in hoping for another life, and in concealing the implacable grandeur of this one." Thus the author of this book was bent on surrendering himself utterly to "the happy lassitude of my nuptials with the world." In what is perhaps the key essay in the volume, the opening essay which is called "Noces à Tipasa," he records how, on one gloriously beautiful spring day, amid the melodious sighings of the Algerian countryside, he opened his "eyes and heart to the intolerable grandeur of that sky gorged with heat." And it is a similarly "lucid attention" before the great enchantments of the earth which is called for in the other meditations—"Le Vent à Djémila," "L'Eté à Alger," and "Le Désert"—which comprise this beautiful and moving little book.

It is this same opulence of language, of emotion, of love, that animates the essays written between 1939 and 1953 which were brought together in *L'Eté*. In *Noces* Camus was attempting to express the "simple accord" that he felt between himself and the rich, luxuriant field of life, and it is this same purpose which controls the rhetoric of the eight meditations that form *L'Eté*. "In the center of our work," he says in this book, "shines an inexhaustible sun," and it is this—the dazzling brilliance and beauty and splendor of the world—it is this, he confesses, that protects him against despair. In the essay called "Retour à Tipasa," there occurs a crucial passage in which he says:

At noon on the half-sandy slopes covered with heliotropes like a foam left by the furious waves of the last few days as they withdrew, I watched the sea barely swelling at that hour with an exhausted motion, and I satisfied the two thirsts one cannot long neglect without drying up—I mean loving and admiring. For there is merely bad luck in not being loved; there is misfortune in not loving. All of us, today, are dying of this misfortune. For violence and hatred dry up the heart itself; the long fight for justice exhausts the love that nevertheless gave birth to it. . . . But in order to keep justice from shrivelling up like a beautiful orange fruit containing nothing but a bitter, dry pulp, I discovered once more at Tipasa that one must keep intact in oneself a freshness, a cool well-spring of joy, love the day that escapes injustice, and return to combat having won that light. . . . In the middle of winter I at last discovered that there was in me an invincible summer.

Now this "invincible summer" is not any mere Stoic *apatheia*, it is no mere capacity for endurance, for martial fortitude, for preserving the stiff lip despite the assaults of experience; it is, instead, something glowing and positive and does, indeed, I believe, partake of what Paul Tillich, with his genius for definition, has called "absolute faith," the faith which creates the courage of self-affirmation not only "in spite of fate and death" but also "in spite of sin and guilt." "An analysis of the nature of absolute faith," says Dr. Tillich,

reveals the following elements in it. The first is the experience of the power of being which is present even in face of the most radical manifestation of nonbeing. . . . The vitality that can stand the abyss of meaninglessness is aware of a hidden meaning within the destruction of meaning. The second element in absolute faith is the dependence of the experience of nonbeing on the experience of being and the dependence of the experience of meaninglessness on the experience of meaning. Even in the state of despair one has enough being to make despair possible. There is a third element in absolute faith, the acceptance of being accepted. Of course, in the state of despair there is nobody and nothing that accepts. But there is the power of acceptance itself which is experi-

enced. Meaninglessness, as long as it is experienced, includes
an experience of the "power of acceptance." To accept this
power of acceptance consciously is the religious answer of
absolute faith, of a faith which has been deprived by doubt
of any concrete content, which nevertheless is faith and the
source of the most paradoxical manifestation of the courage
to be.[27]

I wonder if we have not here an analysis that very nearly
describes Camus' prehension of human life. Was not the invincible summer that he discovered in the midst of winter his
testimony to an "experience of the power of being . . . in face
of the most radical manifestation of nonbeing"? And were not
the hymns in *Noces* and *L'Eté* to the beautiful plenitude and
splendor of the world his testimony to an experience of being
at one with Being-itself, an experience that went deeper even
than the experience of the Absurd? He speaks in *Noces* of "the
smile of complicity" that he "exchanged" with the brilliant
smile of the Mediterranean sea and sky and wind and stars,
and I wonder if this may not have been his obscure testimony
to a deep intuition of something like that which Dr. Tillich
calls "the power of acceptance." Perhaps this was what *enabled* him to bear the knowledge that, though the rebel is not
ignorant of what is good, nevertheless, he does evil. Rebellion,
he says in the final chapter of *L'Homme révolté*, "cannot exist
without a strange form of love"—the love, that is, of "the real
grandeur" of the world; and it is out of this love that there is
born "that strange joy which helps one live and die." So perhaps this was a modern man who did not altogether live outside the realm of grace.

Camus was, of course, in mid-career at the time of his
death; and it is said that there was then a vast novel in
progress that was to be called *Le premier homme*, and also a
long essay to be called *Le Mythe de Némésis*; and there are
still other rumors of additional works that were at various

[27] Paul Tillich, *op. cit.*, p. 177.

stages of accomplishment on his desk. So the circle of definition that is to be drawn about his testimony is not that at
which he himself aimed, and it must, unhappily, forever remain incomplete. But at least an attentive reading of the work
that he was spared to finish ought to indicate how shortsighted
it is to understand the version of the modern story that he
produced as entailing nothing more than might be suggested
by such old counters as "neo-paganism" or "existentialist
nihilism."

In an eloquent statement in *The Atlantic Monthly* in the
spring of 1958, Charles Rolo spoke of Camus as "a good
man,"[28] and, though I suspect that he may himself have been
embarrassed when his critics responded to him as though he
were "a moral force," it is, nevertheless, something of the sort
that we feel. For here was a man who in no way chose to live
at any comfortable remove from the tension and unrest of his
age. As participant in the French Resistance during the war
years, as newspaper editor and political ideologist, as theatrical
director in the Parisian theatre, as artist and thinker, he lived
in the very center of the maelstrom of contemporary history,
and he did this without recourse to any of the false safeties and
securities by which European intellectuals in this century have
sometimes been compromised: he did this only with the courage of a kind of "absolute faith" which passionately affirmed
the worthfulness of the human enterprise in spite of its apparent "absurdity." Through him we have a noble example of "the
courage to be" in a representative man of our age—rooted,
perhaps, "in the God who appears when God has disappeared
in the anxiety of doubt,"[29] but rooted also in a profound and
moving reverence for what he could descry of the Sacred in
man himself. So the Swedish Academy was, I believe, on the
right track when, in the Nobel Prize citation of 1957, it honored this remarkable Frenchman for illuminating "the prob-

[28] Charles Rolo, "Albert Camus: A Good Man," *The Atlantic
Monthly*, Vol. 201, No. 5 (May, 1958).
[29] Paul Tillich, *op. cit.*, p. 190.

lems of the human conscience in our time," for this was precisely the feat that he had achieved. "Had I been on the Swedish jury," he said, "I would have voted for Malraux." In his acceptance speech in Stockholm he chose to speak of the idea by which he had been comforted and sustained throughout his life, even in the most difficult and trying circumstances, the idea of his art and of the writer's vocation. "To me," he said, "art is not a solitary delight. It is a means of stirring the greatest number of men by providing them with a privileged image of our common joys and woes." And so he declared his conviction that the artist

> by definition . . . cannot serve today those who make history; he must serve those who are subject to it. Otherwise he is alone and deprived of his art. All the armies of tyranny with their millions of men cannot people his solitude—even, and especially, if he is willing to fall into step with them. But the silence of an unknown prisoner subjected to humiliations at the other end of the world is enough to tear the writer from exile, at least whenever he manages, amid the privileges of freedom, not to forget that silence but to give it voice by means of art.

Here indeed, we feel, was an artist who had found his voice. So it was with the profoundest sorrow that men and women all over the world learned, January 4, 1960, that early that day Camus had been killed. The car in which he was riding with his publisher Michel Gallimard had struck a tree near Sens, about seventy-five miles southeast of Paris: not only France but the whole civilized world felt diminished. For everyone had known that, in the little village of Lourmarin at the foot of the Alps, where he now lies buried and where he spent his last years, one of the great spokesmen for the human spirit in this century was in the midst of a career than which there was none more promising.

V

Beckett's Journey into
the Zone of Zero

J'écrivais des silences, des nuits,
je notais l'inexprimable. Je fixais
des vertiges.
—Rimbaud, *Une Saison en Enfer.*

But it is not at this late stage . . .
that I intend to give way to literature.
—Beckett, *Molloy.*

All writing is rubbish.
—Antonin Artaud.

In a brief passage that has since become one of the famous
lessons on modern literature, the French critic and early editor
of the *Nouvelle Revue Française,* Jacques Rivière, many years
ago remarked:

> If, in the seventeenth century, it had occurred to anyone to
> ask Molière or Racine why he wrote, neither would probably
> have found any other answer than this: "To entertain cultured
> people." Only with Romanticism did the literary act begin
> to be thought of as a sort of attempt to reach the absolute,
> and the literary product as a revelation. At that moment
> literature garnered the heritage of religion and organized itself
> upon the model of what it replaced: the writer became a
> priest; all his gestures tended toward one thing only—the

157

introduction of the "divine presence" into that eucharistic host which the work of art became. All the literature of the nineteenth century is a vast incantation toward the miracle.[1]

Now it was undoubtedly the French tradition of the nineteenth century that was at the center of Rivière's attention when he made this statement, and it may at first strike us as strange that this should have been so. For it is the German intelligence that is commonly supposed to have a kind of racial monopoly on the headier forms of metaphysical adventure; whereas it is the qualities of clarity and lucidity and logicality that it is our habit to regard as characteristically French. But these are clichés that quickly crumble when we think of the impulses that were released in the French nineteenth century by the writers whom Rivière very probably had in mind, by such men as Baudelaire and Rimbaud and Lautréamont, the great *poètes maudits* of the period.

French Romanticism had, it is true, in the generation of Chateaubriand, Lamartine, and Musset an elegiac phase that was comparable to the English movement represented by Wordsworth, Keats, and Shelley. But by the time a later generation had awakened to the barren emptiness that appeared to be at the center of the world, as it was represented to them by the great secularizing movements of Comte and Darwin— by this time the quiet melancholy of Lamartine and the lachrymose sentimentality of Musset had to give way before some desperate and blasphemous stratagem of "metaphysical revolution" or "sabotage."[2]

It is in the career that produced *Les Fleurs du Mal* that we have the great type and example of this disaffection, for, though Baudelaire does not represent its extremest forms, it was he who gave to the new sensibility its vocabulary and its

---

[1] Jacques Rivière, "Questioning the Concept of Literature," in *From the NRF*, ed. Justin O'Brien (New York: Meridian Books, Inc., 1959), p. 41.

[2] The phrases are Albert Camus': *vide The Rebel* (New York: Vintage Books, 1956), Chapters I and II.

defining style. The atmosphere in which he lived was, of course, one that was very largely formed by the influences of Comte and Bernard and Renan and Taine and Herbert Spencer: which is to say that Baudelaire's was "an age of bustle, [of] programmes, platforms, scientific progress, human-itarianism, and revolutions which improved nothing, an age of progressive degradation. . . ."[3] It was, in other words, a time in which all the complex multi-dimensionality of existence was being scaled down to the univocal simplicities with which posi-tive science could deal. In such a time as this a man like Baudelaire, in whom there remained so large a residue of theo-logical preoccupation, was bound to assert that human reality is something immensely more rich and complicated than was implied to be the case by the *Cours de philosophie positive.* Baudelaire's way of making this insistence was to declare that the world is a "forest of symbols." This is the central phrase in "Les Correspondances," which is one of the central poems of his career, and the phrase was, I take it, for him a way of asserting that our deepest and intensest experiences are always suffused by a sense of encounter with dimensions of reality transcending the immediate data presented by the world itself. The most interesting phenomena in our experience, that is, are distinguished by a kind of inexhaustibility—which is not sim-ply a matter of their having a structural complexity that we generally have not sufficient time in our lives fully to examine; no, their inexhaustibility strikes us rather as a consequence of their pointing to depths within themselves that are essentially and radically mysterious. I encounter *this* person or *this* ex-pression of the natural universe in the fullness of his or its essential being, and in the moment of this encounter I am conscious of this particular finite reality "half-revealing a transfinite dimension within itself, a tap root which seems to connect it . . . with . . . the ultimate Source, Ground, and Abyss of all finite reality . . . from which . . . [the created order]

[3] T. S. Eliot, "Baudelaire," *Selected Essays: 1917–1932* (New York: Harcourt, Brace and Co., 1932), p. 342.

derives its being and its vitality."[4] This is, I think, something of what Baudelaire intended to be the real meaning of "Les Correspondances." The world is a "forest of symbols," and so the task of poetry is that of deciphering the obscure revelations of "infinite things" that are offered by the vast field of existential reality.

It is, indeed, just when we understand in this way the message of "Les Correspondances" that we can see the relation between this central concept in Baudelaire's poetics (of the world, that is, as a "forest of symbols") and the idea of the *gouffre* which gains its definitive expression in the great poem "Le Voyage," whose closing lines advise us to

> Plonger au fond du gouffre, Enfer ou Ciel, qu'importe?
> Au fond de l'Inconnu pour trouver du nouveau!

We must plunge into the *gouffre,* into the Abyss, for, if the world is resonant of "infinite things," then we cannot be satisfied with the forest of symbols, since it is but a point of departure and a way of moving into the unplumbed depths of Being-itself. But, though the poet's function is to locate "les splendeurs situées derrière le tombeau," he must never cease to be on guard against the treacherous uncertainties of life: he is *le dandy* who forges a mask of feigned indifference and hauteur wherewith to defend himself against the taciturn indifference of the world. And it is in the theory of correspondences, the idea of the *gouffre,* and the theory of dandyism that we have the basic premises of Baudelaire's understanding of the poetic enterprise.

Now Baudelairean dandyism moves into an even more strident and high-pitched key in the Comte de Lautréamont (Isidore Ducasse), whose *Les Chants de Maldoror* is perhaps one of the half-dozen most important poetic texts of the nineteenth century. What is decisive about this dandy who is the hero of Lautréamont's poem is that *il voudrait égaler Dieu.* In

[4] Theodore M. Greene, "The Ontological Dimension of Experience," *Thought*, Vol. XXIX, No. 114 (Autumn, 1954), p. 374.

one of the great scenes of the poem, for example, Maldoror is seated at the seashore, when a sudden storm batters a ship against a reef, scattering the sailors amid the wreckage in the water. As the men are attacked by sharks, Maldoror assists the sharks with his gun in finishing them off, so that the men might enjoy the benediction of returning to their piscatory ancestors of the deep. Then, when the ship has sunk and the water is crimson with the sailors' blood, a monstrously fierce female shark turns on the other sharks to destroy them—whereupon Maldoror comes to her assistance with his gun and his knife. When they have all been slain, he then, alone now in the water with the female shark, embraces her with the ardor of a lover. Thus it is that he seeks to recreate himself, to give himself a new form of being, and, in doing so, to assert his equality with the great Enemy: his stratagem, in plunging into the sea, is to forsake the earth and to wage an open war against creation; and his "frightful copulation" with the shark is but the sign of his desire to descend into the *gouffre* and, by an act of rape and sabotage, to take possession of the prehistoric mysteries of existence.

Like the dogs whom he sees howling, as though they were raging against life itself, Maldoror tells us that he too feels "le besoin de l'infini," and, in his quest of it, he does not propose to be hindered by anything at all, not even by reason itself: indeed, if reason is inhibiting, then it must be systematically unhinged. For the great thing is "le rêve surnaturel," and, for this, the poet must be prepared to convert himself into a monster—this is Lautréamont's terrible and insolent lesson: reason must be prepared to become unreason, man must be prepared to become a beast, poetry must be prepared to become non-poetry for the sake of "le rêve surnaturel."

But for all of the dark and horrible audacity of Lautréamont, this French drama of baptism in the *gouffre* finds its great theoretician in the nineteenth century in the boy-poet of Charleville, A.thur Rimbaud, who assisted Baudelaire, says Jacques Maritain, in making "modern art pass the frontiers of the spirit."[5] And the key to both his masterpieces, *Les Illumi-nations* and *Une Saison en Enfer*, is to be found in his *Lettre du 15 mai 1871* to his friend Paul Demeny, written at the age of seventeen.[6] Here is the crucial passage:

> The first study for a man who wants to be a poet is the knowledge of himself, entire. He looks for his soul, inspects it, learns it. As soon as he knows it, he cultivates it: it seems simple: in every brain a natural development is accomplished: so many egoists proclaim themselves authors; others attribute their intellectual progress to themselves! But the soul has to be made monstrous, that's the point:—like *comprachicos*, if you like! Imagine a man planting and cultivating warts on his face.
>
> One must, I say, be a *seer*, make oneself a *seer*.
>
> The poet makes himself a *seer* through a long, a prodi-gious and rational disordering of *all* the senses. Every form of love, of suffering, of madness; he searches himself, he con-sumes all the poisons in him, keeping only their quintessences. Ineffable torture in which he will need all his faith and superhuman strength, the great criminal, the great sickman, the utterly damned, and the supreme Savant! For he arrives at the unknown! Since he has cultivated his soul—richer to begin with than any other! He arrives at the unknown: and even if, half crazed, in the end, he loses the understanding of his visions, he has seen them! Let him croak in his leap into those unutterable and innumerable things: there will come other horrible workers: they will begin at the horizons where he has succumbed.

Now here we have a most candid expression of a kind of radicalism in French tradition of the nineteenth century of which Rimbaud is perhaps the extreme instance. And, in this

[5] Jacques Maritain, *Art and Scholasticism*, trans. J. F. Scanlan (New York: Charles Scribner's Sons, 1943), p. 99.

[6] Quotations are from the translation by Louise Varèse which forms a part of the prefatory material in her version of *Les Illuminations* (*Prose Poems from the Illuminations* [New York: New Directions, 1946]).

present context, what is chiefly significant is that he, like Lautréamont, in defining the poet's task as that of mapping out the *gouffre*, converts him into a priest whose work becomes an "incantation toward the miracle." The poet, he says, must make himself a seer, even if this means that reason is capsized utterly: and if reason is deranged, then surely language itself will also begin to disintegrate. But these are consequences which Rimbaud faced with complete fearlessness and lack of regret, for he was bent on turning poetry into a technique of *science*,[7] a technique whereby the whole fabric of things might be somehow conquered and made accessible to poetic cognition. As Marcel Raymond puts it, "he lived for the sake of those exceptional adventures in which the universe, finally given back to itself, is experienced from the inside like an imponderable blazing mass whence flaming forms gush forth, to fall endlessly."[8] Which is to say that this demon-ridden sorcerer was gambling on a kind of divine omniscience that would finally make poetry unnecessary. So it is no wonder, despite the occasional contact that they make with the world of familiar experience, that his poems are so elusive, so baffling, so strange. "Resting on precarious foundations and always uncertain of their own identity, things escape from themselves and burst the framework in which we enclose them; despite their relief, their density in each of the situations in which the poet places them, they glide from one form to another like the ephemeral images in a kaleidoscope."[9] This was, of course, Rimbaud's way into "the voluptuousness of nirvana,"[10] into the Zone of Zero, into a state of mystical clairvoyance in which poetic discourse would be superfluous—and the point is that the gymnastics of this way involved such an overstraining of language till it had finally to become sim-

---

[7] *Vide* Jacques Maritain, *Creative Intuition in Art and Poetry* (New York: Pantheon Books, 1953), pp. 184–195.

[8] Marcel Raymond, *From Baudelaire to Surrealism* (New York: Wittenborn, Schultz, Inc., 1950), p. 33.

[9] *Ibid.*, p. 35.

[10] *Ibid.*, p. 33.

ply an object of exasperation. So we are not surprised that this choreographer of the word should have gone on to exhaust not only "every form of love, of suffering, of madness," but should have gone on to exhaust even his medium itself and should have lapsed into silence at the age of nineteen, spending the remaining eighteen years of his unhappy life in an aimless vagabondage over the European and African continents.

Baudelaire, then, Lautréamont, Rimbaud—they are the three main sources of a tradition in modern literature which, in various ways since their time, has been extended by Mallarmé and Valéry and the Surrealists. Despite the enormous diversity of aim and method that is contained within this tradition, its unitary principle is a result of the fact that it is a tradition which always manages to accede to the demurrer which Jean Cocteau entered many years ago when he said: "Literature is impossible. We must get out of it. No use trying to get out through more literature. . . ."[11]

These three Frenchmen of the nineteenth century were among the first of the great pioneering visionaries of their period (Dostoievski, Van Gogh, Nietzsche, Melville) to face the precariousness of human existence and the remoteness of meaning in the time of the absent God. Being unable to accept the self-evident certitudes of the complacent positivism of their age, they turned to poetry itself as the "sacred action" best calculated to break the silence of the *gouffre,* to guarantee "the blessed emergence of the exceptional moment in which all the energies of life are polarized around a single focus, and nothing in the world exists except its luminous radiance."[12] They conceived the poet's mission to be one of subverting, of sabotaging, the banal immediacies of nature and human society, of transcending all the conventional possibilities of experience, in order that access might be won to that "really real" which lies beyond what Coleridge called "the world of familiarity and selfish solicitude." Like Hölderlin, they defined the

---

[11] Quoted in Jacques Maritain, *op. cit.,* p. 182.
[12] Marcel Raymond, *op. cit.,* p. 350.

office of the poet in terms at once priestly and prophetic, agreeing with their German progenitor that poetry's business is with the "naming" of the gods and that its primary function is not *mimesis* but revelation, the bringing forth of creation, as it were, all over again, as if God had never acted, or as if his original action now required repetition.

The tradition, in other words, that extends from the great *poètes maudits* of the mid-nineteenth century through Mallarmé and Valéry to Pierre Reverdy and the Surrealists André Breton and Louis Aragon is a tradition in our literature whose aim it has been to liberate the mind from the fragmentation and illusoriness of finite reality, in order that it might somehow gain an entry into the dark and primitive depths of Being-itself: the goal is that cosmic point where all the scattered leaves of life are into one volume bound, where substance and accidents, and their modes, are all fused together into one blazing flame. "Poetry," said Valéry, "is an attempt to represent or to restore, by articulate language, *those things or that thing*, which tears, cries, caresses, kisses, sighs, etc. try obscurely to express."[13] And, in his *Second Manifeste*, André Breton declared:

> Everything suggests the belief that there is a certain point of the mind where life and death, the real and the imaginary, the past and the future, the communicable and the incommunicable, the high and the low are no longer perceived as contradictions. It would be vain to look for any motive in surrealist activity other than the hope of determining that point.[14]

Or, as this ultimate goal was classically put by Rimbaud in *Une Saison en Enfer*: "I wrote of silences, of nights, I noted down the inexpressible. I pinned down fits of giddiness."

Now, having converted poetry into a species of magic, this is a line of writers who have had to practice a most radical

[13] Quoted in Marcel Raymond, *op. cit.*, p. 156.
[14] André Breton, *Second Manifeste du Surréalisme* (Paris: Editions Kra, 1930), p. 10.

kind of chemistry on their inherited language. Whether we turn to Rimbaud or to Mallarmé or to Valéry or to Breton, we are in the presence of artists who believe that what the new Oxford philosophers call "ordinary language" is a language too wooden and fossilized to serve as anything other than a kind of rough tool of the market-place. For the hazardous adventure of poetry a very much finer medium is needed: words must be divested of their conventional significations, in order that their original innocence may be restored. Standing, as he does, at a point of intersection between the plane of the familiar banalities of normal experience and the plane of "le rêve surnaturel," the poet must derange not only his senses perhaps, as Rimbaud advised, but also his language, if he is to do justice to his vision. For words cannot be vehicles of supernature, if they are used by the poet as they are used by the butcher, the baker, and the candlestick-maker: they must be liberated from the tyranny of reason and allowed to chase one another into the kinds of subtle modulations and ensembles whereby we may win the ultimate transverberation by the Divine Dark. And this is, indeed, the perilous experiment that was fostered by this tradition. "Real life," said Rimbaud, "is *elsewhere*," and, in the line of modern writers running from Baudelaire and Lautréamont through Mallarmé and Valéry to André Breton and Paul Eluard, the work of art was conceived to be a kind of demiurgic passport to this uncharted and distant region.

But, of course, language, even at its volatile best, is a most frail and imperfect instrument of the miraculous. However relentlessly the artist seeks to make it the servant of some sacral grammar and logic of his own creation, it does persist, with its clumsy inflexibility, in performing its customarily mundane and ostensive functions. So it was inevitable that the kind of radicalism we have been canvassing should issue in a profound despair of language and of literature, for what had been sought was an ineffable ultimacy of Being that had necessarily to be betrayed by the concretions of verbal discourse. The difficult paradox in which these writers had become enmeshed was a result of the fact that, through *poetic* forms, they were seeking to transcend *all* forms: through language, they were seeking to liberate themselves from all the distortions of reality that inhere in language as such: and this, however, exhilarating the attempt might be, was something which, in the nature of the case, could never be quite managed. So, after completing *Une Saison en Enfer* in the summer of 1873, Rimbaud abdicated from poetry altogether. After finally facing his own ultimate inability to bully language into conquering the primordial Mystery, Mallarmé had to confess his disenchantment with "the literary game." Paul Valéry came to speak of the work of art as a "forgery." The distinguished critic Marcel Arland, in an early essay which appeared in the *Nouvelle Revue Française* in 1924, noticed the fact that "literature . . . no longer charms us very much."[15] One could fill up several pages with the indictments and denials and rejections of literature with which the modern French tradition is bestrewn: the very word *littérature* has, in fact, become a pejorative for the *avant-garde,* and it is one of the great ironies in the literary life of our time, that a tradition which expected more of literature than any other had ever done has, over the last fifty years, been developing a most profound and deep-seated aversion to it, the feeling, as Cocteau says, that it "is impossible," that "we must get out of it. No use trying to get out through more literature."

It is, indeed, this despair of "the literary game" that constitutes what is undoubtedly the basic premise of many of those writers of the present time in France who, in the years since the close of the Second War, have emerged into prominence as the chief creators of what Claude Mauriac calls the new *alittérature.*[16] I do not think that we can hope to "place"

[15] Marcel Arland, "Concerning a New 'Mal du Siècle,'" in *From the NRF,* ed. Justin O'Brien (New York: Meridian Books, Inc., 1959), p. 35.

[16] *Vide* Claude Mauriac, *The New Literature,* trans. Samuel I. Stone (New York: George Braziller, Inc., 1959), pp. 11–13.

novelists like Alain Robbe-Grillet and Nathalie Sarraute or dramatists like Arthur Adamov and Eugène Ionesco except in terms of the kind of distrust of the literary enterprise that is bequeathed to them by the classic generations of modern France: this is what they take for granted, and this is the essential clue to all the new projects that they are attempting to devise. In the theatre of Ionesco, it is drama itself that is under attack; in the fiction of Michel Butor and Nathalie Sarraute, the novel itself is something that, in effect, we are asked to regard as questionable and problematic; and their contemporaries are, most of them, "anti-dramatists" and "anti-novelists." So it is not surprising that for many of the strategists of "the new literature" that strange book *Le Théâtre et son double* should have attained a kind of kerygmatic status, for the mad genius from whose pen it came, Antonin Artaud, was a theorist who, with his characteristic perversity, insisted on placing at the center of his poetics the notions of the emptiness and futility of literature.

But though this disenchantment with literature that characterizes the new heroes of the *avant-garde* in France is, as a habit of mind, a bequest which they receive from their classic modern tradition, it is something that, in them, has not the same roots that it had in a Rimbaud or a Mallarmé. For, in the great innovating pioneers, it was a result of a thwarted nostalgia: they were writers who, having heard a disastrous retreat in the heavens above, experienced the world as "a desert of loss,"[17] and they hoped to find in the rich resources of poetic art a means of satisfying their ontological hunger, a way of bridging the Abyss or of *invoking* into it a good and gratifying Presence: and the inadequacy of *poiesis* to the burden which they imposed upon it was the cause of their despairing of literature. But the generation of Ionesco and Robbe-Grillet is a generation that takes the death of God for granted as casually as it does the fact that Tuesday follows Monday, and

[17] Ralph Harper, *The Sleeping Beauty* (New York: Harper & Bros., 1956), p. 23.

its lack of confidence in the literary project, far from being a result of a frustrated Prometheanism, is simply a consequence of its assumption of the fundamental meaninglessness of human existence. The dourness of the new temper does not, in other words, follow so much upon the frustration of a Promethean effort as it does upon a sense of the futility of all Prometheanism which has metaphysical ambitions.

It is, indeed, this strict astringency of their vision that impels these writers to practice a most ruthless kind of *askésis* upon their art. For, given the essentially incoherent character of existence, they feel that, insofar as the novelist, for example, imposes such order upon experience as traditional structures of plot and character involve, he does to that extent falsify reality and is guilty of dishonesty: he produces mere "literature." Of all this—the old eloquence, the old psychological analysis, the old "stories"—the novel must be purified. And, similarly, in the drama, neither the tradition, say, of Ibsen nor of Chekhov can any longer avail, for the theatre must be stripped of every representational pretension, if it is to be, in Giraudoux's phrase, "an evening school for adults": indeed, Eugène Ionesco speaks of his play *La Cantatrice chauve* (*The Bald Soprano*) as an "anti-play," and the whole new *avant-garde* theatre in France might be said to be an anti-theatre, a theatre deliberately disdaining subject-matter and "anthropomorphism" and intent upon exposing the veritable nothingness that is at the center of human life. Roland Barthes is one of the recognized spokesmen for the new program, and he is eager for his colleagues to bring us "to the doors of a world without literature about which, however, it will be up to the writers to testify"—and to testify by way of what he calls *le degré zéro de l'écriture* ("the zero degree of writing"): only thus can the writer be an honest man—by expunging from his books every last iota of message, of significant action, and of "style." For writing, says M. Barthes, "is in no way a means of communication": he agrees with the novelist Jean Cayrol that ours is a "desolate world of *absence*," and he also agrees with the Sartre who sometimes seems to feel that the writer's sole business today is to be a kind of laconic witness to the death of man.

Perhaps the chief theorist of this new attitude is the young writer Alain Robbe-Grillet, whose drastic conclusions exemplify a complete fearlessness of their own rigorous and insolent logic. His major concern has been with the novel, this being the field of his own creative practice; and the basic presupposition on which his own literary career is based is that "the art of the novel . . . has achieved such a degree of stagnation . . . that it is scarcely imaginable that it can survive for long without radical changes."[18] What it must be liberated from is the tradition of "psychological analysis," for this is a tradition whose assumptions about the unity of personality have long since lost any genuine relevance to the modern experience: the tradition, in other words, of Madame de la Fayette, of Stendhal, of Flaubert, of Proust, has reached a point of utter exhaustion, and what is required now is "a revolution more total [even] than those from which such movements as romanticism and naturalism were born."

M. Robbe-Grillet's prescription for the present *malaise* involves what is, for him, the most radical request that can be made—namely, the request that *le nouveau roman* be done in such a way as to discard the old "sacrosanct psychological analysis" and to invite the reader "to look at the world which surrounds him with entirely unprejudiced eyes." For surely, he contends, the most remarkable thing about the world is simply that it *is*. "Around us, defying the mob of our animistic or protective adjectives, things *are there*. Their surfaces are clear and smooth, *intact*, neither dubiously glittering, nor transparent. All our literature has not yet succeeded in penetrating their smallest corner, in softening their slightest curve."

Now it is in the cinema that M. Robbe-Grillet finds the best clues to the direction that the novel of the future must

[18] Alain Robbe-Grillet, "A Fresh Start for Fiction," *The Evergreen Review*, Vol. I, No. 3, p. 98. The quotations from M. Robbe-Grillet that immediately follow are drawn from this essay.

take. It too is an heir of the psychological tradition, and very often it "has as its sole purpose the transposition of a story into images." But "the very conventions of the photographic medium" have a way of drawing us out of our comfortable interiorities—so that, however much, in the literary text that forms the basis of the scenario, the empty chair may have been a sign of absence or the hand placed on a shoulder a sign of friendliness or the bars on a window a sign of the impossibility of leaving,

> in the cinema, one *sees* the chair *too*, the movement of the hand, the shape of the bars. What they signify remains obvious, but, instead of monopolizing our attention, it becomes something added, even something in excess, because what touches us, what persists in our memory, what appears as essential and irreducible to vague intellectual concepts, are the gestures themselves, the objects, the movements, and the contours, to which the image has suddenly (and unintentionally) restored their *reality*.

It is, in other words, in its tendency to move away from a "universe of 'signification' (psychological, social, functional)" that the cinema suggests a method of renewal for the novel, and a method whereby the novel may attain to greater truth to the actualities of man's being-in-the-world. For the movie camera, in vivifying the sheer *thereness* of familiar gestures and objects and in making them appear, through their very vividness, somehow alien and strange, has the effect of making us look at the actual world that surrounds us, as it were for the first time, so that we become aware of its strangeness and of its imperviousness to every system of meaning. This, M. Robbe-Grillet believes, must be the purpose of the novel of the future: it must become *le roman objectif,* exhibiting the world in its brute givenness and in its unyielding resistance to all our characteristic habits of apprehension and order.

So, in his own novelistic practice, and notably in *Le Voyeur* and *La Jalousie,* M. Robbe-Grillet does not, as he insists, "set out to create characters or tell stories." He wants instead to focus our attention upon the external world, and what we are struck by in his fictions is the virtual disappearance of the human protagonist: the world of his novels is a world, it seems, in which there is no room for man, all the available room being taken up by the hard, resistant materialities with which the ghostly remnants of men collide. Indeed, in *La Jalousie,* though the angle of narration is that of the "first" person, there is not a single reference in the entire novel to "I" or "me," so that one critic speaks of the book's narrative point of view as that of the "absent I."[19] Or *Le Voyeur,* for example, opens with the docking at a pier of a ship which carries the central personage of the novel, Mathias, and here is a passage dwelling on details of the sort to which the novelist devotes himself, with an absolutely incredible single-mindedness, for page after page after page:

> The pier, now quite close, towered several yards above the deck. The tide must have been out. The landing slip from which the ship would be boarded revealed the smoother surface of its lower section, darkened by the water and half-covered with greenish moss. On closer inspection, the stone rim drew almost imperceptibly closer.
>
> The stone rim—an oblique, sharp edge formed by two intersecting perpendicular planes: the vertical embankment perpendicular to the quay and the ramp leading to the top of the pier—was continued along its upper side at the top of the pier by a horizontal line extending straight toward the quay.
>
> The pier, which seemed longer than it actually was as an effect of perspective, extended from both sides of this base line in a cluster of parallels describing, with a precision accentuated even more sharply by the morning light, a series of elongated planes alternately horizontal and vertical: the crest of the massive parapet that protected the tidal basin from the open sea, the inner wall of the parapet, the jetty

[19] Bruce Morrissette, "New Structure in the Novel: *Jealousy,* by Alain Robbe-Grillet," *The Evergreen Review,* Vol. III, No. 10, p. 104.

along the top of the pier, and the vertical embankment that plunged straight into the water of the harbor. The two vertical surfaces were in shadow, the other two brilliantly lit by the sun—the whole breadth of the parapet and all of the jetty save for one dark narrow strip: the shadow cast by the parapet. Theoretically, the reversed image of the entire group could be seen reflected in the harbor water, and, on the surface, still within the same play of parallels, the shadow cast by the vertical embankment extending straight toward the quay.

At the end of the jetty the structure grew more elaborate; the pier divided into two parts; on the parapet side, a narrow passageway leading to a beacon light, and on the left the landing slip sloping down into the water. It was this latter inclined rectangle, seen obliquely, that attracted notice; slashed diagonally by the shadow of the embankment it skirted, it showed up as one dark triangle and one bright. All other surfaces were blurred. The water in the harbor was not calm enough for the reflection of the pier to be distinguished. Similarly the shadow of the pier appeared only as a vague strip. . . .

Here, indeed, is a refusal of "psychological analysis"—and with a vengeance. But M. Robbe-Grillet is nothing if not consistent; and, since he has no interest in the feelings, in the thoughts, in the inwardness, of his characters, he proceeds, with a most astonishing relentlessness, to describe simply the strange opaqueness and density of the world's surfaces, and this is done with a thoroughness that is surely without parallel in the history of the novel. He "intends," says the French critic Bernard Dort, "to stick to zero,"[20] and his "objectal" catalogues are designed to undo what he calls "the old myth of depth,'" by converting human reality into a kind of frozen "still life" in which there is not the merest trace of *la présence humaine*, but only angles and planes and streets and houses and skies—and objects and gestures. It is, we might say, an art

[20] Bernard Dort, "Are These Novels 'Innocent'?," *Yale French Studies*, No. 24, p. 24.

which mimes the act of suicide: the novelist opts for things and against man.

Now, among the writers on the French scene today who are commonly regarded as the chief practitioners of *le nouveau roman* (Nathalie Sarraute, Jean Cayrol, Claude Simon, and Michel Butor being perhaps the chief figures), Alain Robbe-Grillet has been highly publicized. The more scrupulous critics are often at pains, and rightly so, to remind us that this is a group which contains within itself a very great degree of diversity and that all its members cannot, therefore, be subsumed under the program of any single figure. This is, of course, a salutary caution, and one which we ought by no means to disregard, but it ought not to intimidate us into disregarding the significant affinities that these writers have with one another. It is true that, in language and composition and structure, Nathalie Sarraute's procedures differ sharply from Michel Butor's, as do Claude Simon's from Marguerite Duras'. But, careful as we must be about discriminations of this sort, it would, at the same time, be foolish for us to ignore the fact that all these writers live out of and evoke essentially the same general ethos, and it is of this that M. Robbe-Grillet is a representative, though perhaps by no means the most impressive, instance.

As I think of this whole effort that is being undertaken today in France, I am at times put in mind of the somewhat parallel effort in modern painting that began with Cézanne and that culminated in the great adventure of Cubism. Admittedly, the "objectivism" of M. Robbe-Grillet makes the parallel much more exact in his case than in that of certain of the other writers with whom he is associated. But, in them all, we feel that the literary project is being directed by the need to dismantle the world and put it back together again—perhaps in order that it might be discovered where we are, and possibly who we are. They are all bent upon reconstructing either the raw materiality of the external world (as in the case of Alain Robbe-Grillet) or the elementary forms of consciousness itself (as in the case of Nathalie Sarraute); and, in this way, they are all, in one degree or another, systematicians. But, at the same time, though they all have a certain passion for reconstruction, they are eager to dispense with what Claude Simon disapprovingly calls "la merveilleuse illusion." They do not want, by means of the conventional "verisimilitudes" of prose narrative, to impose order and structure upon a world in which, as they experience it, there actually is no order or structure. This is why so often they deliberately refuse to look at anything other than the surfaces of the world: and this is also why, deliberately refusing "the myth of 'depth'" (with its fictions of "character" and "story"), their novels are often like a sentence which, despite its complex and ingeniously woven texture, remains suspended in mid-air. Indeed, in a universe which is absurd and in which therefore we cannot escape from despairing of literature, finally, they all do what Bernard Dort describes Alain Robbe-Grillet as doing: they "stick to zero." And the emphasis, as M. Dort reminds us, is to be placed on the *sticking*. For the generation of Joyce and Kafka and Musil did not, as he says,

> banish meanings. Anything but. They piled one meaning on the other so that in the end these might exterminate each other. They did not repudiate the idea of a totality. Anything but. But their totality had a minus sign. It was indeed an addition of the greatest possible number of meanings, but the total always tended to zero.[21]

But, as he says of M. Robbe-Grillet, and as we might also say of many of the other new heroes of the French *avant-garde*—they *stick* to zero, and this it is which defines their literary and spiritual position in the cultural life of our time.

Now it is one of the oddities of modern literature that the most impressive representative of this radical French contemporary tradition is the man from Ireland, Samuel Beckett, who has lived in France off and on for more than thirty years and

[21] *Ibid.*

whose most important works have been written in the French language (many of which, however, he has himself translated into English, which is his native tongue). In him the dark, seedy, claustral universe of the new nihilism has its most ingenious and resourceful cartographer.

There is perhaps no single point at which it is necessary to begin either the reading or the analysis of Mr. Beckett's books. For, though the author of the trilogy *Molloy, Malone Dies,* and *The Unnamable* (written in the years since the Second World War) has won a kind of rhetorical brilliance and expertise that the author of *Murphy* (1938) had not yet achieved, the entire body of his work is characterized by a singularly unchanging mood and orientation. His novels and his plays, from beginning to end, evoke a world in which the despair and the defeat of man are so absolute as to be almost beyond the possibility of dramatization: it is a world in which the individual lives in those "perilous zones . . . dangerous, precarious, painful . . . [where] the boredom of living is replaced by the suffering of being."[22] It is a world of utter destitution, of utter indigence; his protagonists are old men—half blind, stinking, lame and physically broken, bedridden or dependent on crutches or even at times reduced to crawling about over the surface of the earth. Not only are they cripples who fart incessantly and who cannot control their bladders: they are also paupers whose nakedness is barely covered by castoff rags and whose residence is under a withered tree or in garbage cans or insane asylums or on some cold and forsaken patch of ground under a vacant, unconsoling sky. They are impotent and ignorant, uncertain who they are or where they are and unable to hold the present moment in any kind of coherent relation to the past. They are lonely and without connections, and, even when they do stumble across another derelict in their wilderness, having lost the knack of communication, their stutterings and stammerings cannot be an instrument of communion. So the domi-

[22] Samuel Beckett, *Proust* (New York: Grove Press, Inc., 1957), p. 8.

nating image that is formed by Murphy and Watt, by Molloy and Malone, by Vladimir and Estragon, is an image of denudation, of divestment, of abortion and loss. A by no means uncharacteristic scene is that formed by the "mime for one player" called "Act Without Words," which is appended to the American edition of *Endgame*:[23] its single actor is situated on a stage which is described as a desert of dazzling light. Time and again, he hears whistles first from the right and then from the left wing. But, each time he goes out into either wing, he is flung back onto the stage—though, each time, he gets up, dusts himself, and, after reflecting, goes off to respond to the whistle from whichever direction it comes. Finally, however, he thinks better of this and ignores a whistle that comes from the left wing. Then, to the accompaniment of whistles from above, various objects begin to be lowered—which are snatched upwards, however, each time he reaches for them. So, at the last, he simply "remains lying on his side, his face towards auditorium, staring before him," and, though a carafe continues to be lowered and dangled before his face, he disregards it now: "he does not move" and simply "looks at his hands," his position being rather like that of Moran (Molloy's pursuer) in *Molloy*, who, as his leg begins to stiffen with paralysis, thinks to himself:

> Such are the advantages of a local and painless paralysis. . . . To be literally incapable of motion at last, that must be something! My mind swoons when I think of it. And mute into the bargain! And perhaps as deaf as a post! And who knows, as blind as a bat! And as likely as not your memory a blank! And just enough brain intact to allow you to exult! And to dread death like a regeneration.

This is, indeed, the position of the poor *isolés* whom we meet in Beckett's plays and fiction: they are bereft of every imaginable security, and, in their cheerless, hopeless world of Zero,

[23] Samuel Beckett, *Endgame* (New York: Grove Press, Inc., 1958), pp. 87–91.

they have only enough vitality remaining to summon a dry and feeble gesture of irony, the suggestion that, maimed though they are, they can still perhaps exult in Nothingness.

Murphy, the book of 1938, which was Beckett's first venture into the novel (his previously published work having consisted of the essay on Proust; the poem of 1930, *Whoroscope*; the volume of stories *More Pricks Than Kicks*; and the collection of verse *Echo's Bones*), gives a statement of the world's absurdity which is uncharacteristic of the later novels only in the relatively greater lucidity of its plot and characters; but, in the disenchantment of its vision, it is of a piece with the entire body of his work. Murphy is a Dubliner living in London on hand-outs, a "seedy solipsist" who believes his mind to be "a large hollow sphere, hermetically closed to the universe without." He wants to shut out the world because its irrationality and disorder leave him no hope at all of coming to terms with it successfully: the only kingdom, he feels, in which he has any kind of chance is the kingdom of his own mind, and this it is, therefore, into which he seeks to withdraw. He wants to be "but a mote in the dark of absolute freedom," and his way of inducing this nirvana-like euphoria in himself is to strap himself naked into a rocking chair, and then to rock and rock and rock and rock until he "comes alive in his mind."

His progress, however, away from the insecurities of the world of "extension" and into the dark, inner room of the self is complicated by his love for the prostitute Celia, a voluptuous creature who, in her locomotions, is "accompanied delightedly by her hips, etc." She, loving Murphy but also wanting respectability and an assured place in society, insists upon his getting a job—which, when at last it is secured, turns out to be a post as orderly in an insane asylum. "What more vigorous fillip could be given to the wallows of one bogged in the big world than the example of life to all appearance inalienably realized in the little?" Indeed, Murphy does "call sanctuary what the psychiatrists called exile," finding a strange sort of happiness amongst the mad and the deranged, since they have already entered the zone which he attempts to reach by means of his rocking chair. But this happiness is short-lived, for, one day, while tied to his rocker in one of his self-induced trances, he burns to death.

In his will he had left the following directions regarding the disposal of his remains:

> I desire that they be burnt and placed in a paper bag and brought to the Abbey Theatre, Lr. Abbey Street, Dublin, and without pause into what the great and good Lord Chester-field calls the necessary house, where their happiest hours have been spent, on the right as one goes down into the pit, and I desire that the chain be there pulled upon them, if possible during the performance of a piece, the whole to be executed without ceremony or show of grief.

But, unfortunately, Cooper, to whom the ashes are entrusted, before he can flush them down the toilet in the Abbey Theatre, becomes involved in a barroom brawl, and, in a moment of anger, takes the packet of ash from his pocket, "where earlier in the evening he had put it for greater security," and throws it at the man who had offended him:

> It bounced, burst, off the wall on to the floor, where at once it became the object of much dribbling, passing, trapping, shooting, punching, heading and even some recognition from the gentleman's code. By closing time the body, mind and soul of Murphy were freely distributed over the floor of the saloon; and before another dayspring greyened the earth had been swept away with the sand, the beer, the butts, the glass, the matches, the spits, the vomit.

Now this is the kind of ghastly concatenation of events that the logic of Beckett's fiction persuades us to regard as natural and expectable in a universe that is utterly absurd and probably even maleficent. It is the world of the "underground man," the best of all possible worlds perhaps, but a world blanketed by irrationality and gratuitousness and grotesquerie. And had Murphy been asked to define his idea of eternity, one imagines that he might well have agreed with Dostoievski's Svidrigailov, that the other world in all probability is "peopled with spiders," a sort of "dark recess . . . [or] bathroom crammed with spiders in all the corners."

So it is no wonder, then, that the protagonist of *Watt* (written in the Vaucluse during the German occupation of France, and published in 1953) is a man who is continually shuffling and reshuffling the most elementary percepts of his experience, in an effort to descry some merest vestige of a pattern beneath the disarray and fracture of existence. Watt is a seedy little cypher with a "big red nose and no fixed address" whom we suddenly see one evening disembarking from a tram and making his way on to the railway-station, where he takes a train and begins a journey. Then, with no explanation of where it is that he gets off the train, we find him continuing his journey by hiking across a countryside. Like all of Beckett's heroes, he is physically maimed and crippled—so that his

> way of advancing due east, for example, was to turn his bust as far as possible towards the north and at the same time to fling out his right leg as far as possible towards the south, and then to turn his bust as far as possible towards the south and at the same time to fling out his left leg as far as possible towards the north, and then again to turn his bust as far as possible towards the north. . . . The knees . . . did not bend. . . . The arms were content to dangle, in perfect equipendency.

In the course of this trip by foot—which he interrupts to rest in a ditch—he is assaulted by a Lady McCann, who throws a stone at him, "with all her might, which, when she was roused, was not negligible. . . . And it is to be supposed that God, always favourable to the McCanns of ? , guided her hand." But Watt, "faithful to his rule . . . [takes] no more notice of this aggression than if it had been an accident. . . . For it was an attitude become, with frequent repetition, so part of his being, that there was no more room in his mind for resentment."

Then, at last, he arrives at nightfall at the house of a Mr. Knott, and it appears that in this establishment there is a job waiting for him. He at first finds both the back and the front doors locked, but, on returning to the rear entrance, discovers, to his astonishment, that, though lately locked, it is now open: how this happened he never learns. After managing to get in, he takes a seat in a parlor, apparently intending to sit there through the silent gloom of the night, "picking his nose, waiting for the dawn to break." But his vigil is soon interrupted by the appearance of a loquacious fellow named Arsene, who is being replaced in Mr. Knott's house, it seems, by Watt. The remainder of Part I of the novel is devoted to a long monologue in which, presumably, it is Arsene's intention to orient his successor to his new situation. But his tips are fringed with irony, for, as he says, he once knew a Mr. Ash, whom he met one evening on Westminster Bridge and who announced the time to him as "seventeen minutes past five exactly," whereupon Big Ben then immediately struck the hour of six o'clock—and that, says Arsene, is "the type of all information whatsoever, be it voluntary or solicited."

With the beginning of Part II, Watt is already an established retainer in Mr. Knott's household, and from this point on he is involved in an unending struggle to understand the logic or the illogic that forms the basis of all the various arrangements of life in this strange house. He is, for example, baffled by what seems to be the very incommensurateness of language itself with the realities of existence in the world of Mr. Knott: he finds himself "in the midst of things which, if they consented to be named, did so as it were with reluctance":

> Looking at a pot, for example, or thinking of a pot, at one of Mr. Knott's pots, of one of Mr. Knott's pots, it was in vain that Watt said, Pot, pot. Well, perhaps not quite in vain, but very nearly. For it was not a pot, the more he looked, the more he reflected, the more he felt sure of that, that it was not a pot at all. It resembled a pot, it was almost a pot, but

it was not a pot of which one could say, Pot, pot, and be comforted. It was in vain that it answered, with unexceptionable
adequacy, all the purposes, and performed all the offices, of a
pot, it was not a pot. And it was just this hairbreadth departure from the nature of a true pot that so excruciated Watt.

Indeed, now that he is a denizen of Mr. Knott's establishment,
he even makes "the distressing discovery that of himself too he
could no longer affirm anything that did not seem as false as if
he had affirmed it of a stone."

This helpless bafflement of Watt before the irrationality of
life in Mr. Knott's house is most especially instanced by his
response to the visit of the Galls, the father and son who come
to tune the piano. The senior Gall is blind: so it is his son who
tunes the piano, while his father simply stands in the center
of the music-room. Then, when the work is done, the son
speaks of the mice having returned and of the piano being
doomed—and, these cryptic remarks being concluded, they
leave. The incident strikes Watt as being like so many other
happenings in Mr. Knott's house—in that "it was not ended,
when it was past, but continued to unfold, in . . . [his] head,
from beginning to end, over and over again." It was not simply
a matter of two piano-tuners having come to the house and
tuned the piano, exchanged a few words, and then left: no,
this was simply the outer image of how *something else* had
happened—but he can never determine what this something
else is. Yet the mere fact of his being unable to determine the
meaning of this and similar occurrences does not distress him
so much as does his hunch that in incidents such as this

> a thing that was nothing had happened, with the utmost
> formal distinctness, and that it continued to happen, in his
> mind. . . . Yes, Watt could not accept . . . that *nothing* had
> *happened*, with all the clarity and solidity of *something*, and
> that it revisited him in such a way that he was forced to
> submit to it all over again. . . .[24]

[24] The italicizations are mine.

But most baffling of all in this odd, eerie house is the master, Mr. Knott himself. He is an absolute enigma whom Watt rarely even glimpses, and when he is occasionally seen for a brief moment, we are reminded of the castle-bureaucrat Klamm in Kafka's *The Castle,* for, like the strange personage with whom K. has to deal, it seems impossible ever to be certain under what aspect Mr. Knott will present himself: sometimes he is fat and sometimes he is thin, on some occasions tall and at other times short. His face forever remains indefinite; and we do not hear him speak. His gestures are awkward and erratic, and, for Watt, he is simply a tantalizing and not altogether unsinister question-mark. Indeed, Beckett's unheroic little hero exhausts every last ratiocinative resource in an effort to figure things out. There is, for example, the bell which he hears in the night summoning Erskine, the other servant, to Mr. Knott's room. But is it Mr. Knott who presses the bell, and, if so, is it with his finger or his thumb or his nose or his toe or his elbow? It is with investigations into such questions as these that we are occupied through several pages —only for Watt finally to discover, after breaking into Erskine's room, that, though there is a bell in the room, it is broken.

Or, again, there is the tantalizing mystery of how it is that the establishment manages to arrange for a famished dog to eat the remains of Mr. Knott's supper. Mr. Knott's meals always and unvaryingly consist of a single dish, a kind of soup which is prepared by numerous ingredients being mixed together and boiled in a pot—

> fish, eggs, game, poultry, meat, cheese, fruit, all of various kinds, and of course bread and butter, and . . . the more usual beverages, such as absinthe, mineral water, tea, coffee, milk, stout, beer, whiskey, brandy, wine and water, and . . . many things . . . for the good of the health, such as insulin, digitalin, calomel, iodine, laudanum, mercury, coal, iron, camomille and worm-powder, and of course salt and mustard,

pepper and sugar, and of course a little salicylic acid, to delay fermentation.

We are told that "Mr. Knott was never heard to complain of his food, though he did not always eat it." And, on those occasions when he left some portion of this brew in his bowl, Watt's instructions were to give the remains to a hungry dog. But, since there was no dog in the house, it was necessary, therefore, "that a dog from outside should call at the house at least once every day, on the off chance of its being given part, or all, of Mr. Knott's lunch, or dinner, or both to eat." In his effort to find a hypothesis that would explain the means whereby it could be guaranteed that a dog would always appear at the appropriate times, Watt is finally led to conceive of a family named Lynch, whose fantastically degenerate members are maintained by Mr. Knott through generation after generation, solely in order that they might provide the necessary dogs. It takes almost thirty pages for Watt to win some small measure of comprehension as to how it is that "the dog and the food . . . [are] brought together," and this is a statistic that is significant of the incredible lengths of tedium to which Beckett is willing to risk submitting his reader, in order fully to document the diligence with which his hero attempts to come to terms with the bizarre and extraordinary world of Mr. Knott.

So it is no wonder that, faced as he is on all sides by what is ambiguous and undecipherable, Watt has to teach himself to live merely "among face values": nor is it any wonder also that, under the pressure of the knotty ravelment of his situation, even his speech at last becomes shapeless and disordered—

Most of day, part of night, now with Knott. Up till now, oh so little seen, or so little heard. From morning till night. This I heard, this I saw then what. Thing, dim, quiet. Now also failing, Ears, eyes. In hush, in mist, moved I so. . . . Abandoned my little to find him. My little to learn him forgot.

My little rejected to have. To love him my little reviled. This
body homeless. This mind ignoring. These emptied hands.
This emptied heart. To him I brought. To the temple. To the
teacher. To the source. Of nought.

Though he is aware of these "cracks" in his speech, he is "too
tired to repair [them]," and the scene of his final collapse
appears to be, as in the case of so many of Beckett's other
heroes, an asylum for the insane.

At the end of the material which Beckett has appended to
Watt—addenda whose incorporation into the novel was prevented, he says, by "fatigue and disgust"—he wryly remarks,
"no symbols where none intended." Which may indeed be his
characteristically sardonic way of underlining the symbolic intention. But though the tenuities of *Murphy* and *Watt* may
make this kind of cryptic footnote necessary, it could perform
no essential function in the novels that form the trilogy—
Molloy, Malone Dies, and *The Unnamable* (written between
1951 and 1953). For the central characters in these books—
and most especially Molloy—employ in their speech a kind of
rhetoric which obviously wants to bear the full freight of "the
human condition." This is not to say that Beckett's precise
meanings are any more accessible here than in the earlier writings, for they are not: indeed, these books move towards an
impatience with "literature" that is so severe as finally to make
the art of fiction, as in *The Unnamable*, an art of unintelligibly
orchestrating the ultimate Silence. But, for all of the extrava-
gant funambulism, these books are drenched in the imagery
and language of contemporary existentialist nihilism. And
though, as we inch our way along from page to page, their incredible tediousness converts the aesthetic transaction into a
grim struggle on the part of the author to hang on to the
reader's attention, they yet haunt us in memory, and their
characters speak to us with a pathos, and at times an eloquence,
rarely equalled in the *Angst*-ridden literature of modern aliena-

tion. When Molloy listens, "the voice is of a world collapsing endlessly, a frozen world, under a faint untroubled sky. . . . And," he says,

> I hear it murmur that all wilts and yields, as if loaded down. . . . For what possible end to these wastes where true light never was, nor any upright thing, nor any true foundation, but only these leaning things, forever lapsing and crumbling away, beneath a sky without memory of morning or hope of night.

And when morning does come, he knows what he must do, for, as he says, "Morning is the time to hide."

The entire trilogy might well have been called, by way of a general title, *Portrait of the Artist in a World Collapsing*, for this, we gradually discover, is what it is Beckett's intention to give us through the characters of Molloy and Moran and Malone and the Unnamable. Molloy, in his decrepitude and destitution, bears upon himself the hallmarks of the Beckett hero: he is old and crippled and bedridden and nearly blind. We first meet him in his mother's room, where he is writing in bed. "There's this man who comes every week. Perhaps I got here thanks to him. He says not. He gives me money and takes away the pages. So many pages, so much money. . . . Yet I don't work for money. For what then? I don't know. The truth is I don't know much." But, in one of his essays on Beckett,[25] Hugh Kenner has suggested that, given the fundamental logic of his fictional universe, the explanation of Molloy's literary activity may be regarded as gaining a kind of adumbration at least in a passage in *Watt*, where, in connection with the mystery of the dogs, we are told that

> Not . . . for a moment [did] Watt . . . [suppose] that he had penetrated the forces at play, in this particular instance, or even perceived the forms that they upheaved, or obtained

the least useful information concerning himself, or Mr. Knott, for he did not. But he had turned, little by little, a disturbance into words, he had made a pillow of old words, for a head.

And this is, indeed, what the heroes of the trilogy are bent on doing—on turning, little by little, a deep and irremediable disturbance into words.

The narrative that Molloy is writing is intended by him to be an account of how, by bicycle and on foot, he came to this room: it had been, it appears, a grim and desperate journey in the course of which one leg became stiff, the toes of the foot of the other leg then falling off—so that, finally he had to turn from the bicycle to his crutches, and then to crawling, being mysteriously rescued from complete immobility in a ditch at the last. This harrowing odyssey is paralleled in the second part of *Molloy* by a similar journey undertaken in search of Molloy by one Moran, who also starts out with a bicycle; but, after a time, his knees grow stiff, and then his legs become paralyzed—so that, in the end, he too must crawl or simply roll along inch by inch. And, when we meet him, Moran also has a pencil in his hand and is writing the story of his journey.

Now we begin to get these two figures straight when we discover that the one is but the *alter ego* of the other. Like the hero of Kafka's *The Trial*, before his arrest, Moran too, before he is bidden by the mysterious Youdi to set out in search of Molloy, lives a meticulously ordered and self-contained life, in a neat little cottage with his son and housekeeper. He insists upon having his meals served on the clock's exact stroke of the appointed hour. After dinner, he enjoys a quiet nap in his bed. He most carefully tends the little garden behind his house. He is scrupulous in performing the religious observances ordained by his church. He is a man "patiently turned towards the outer world as towards the lesser evil, creature of his house, of his garden, of his few poor possessions." But amid the tidiness and triviality of his little world, he has, from time to time, uneasy

intimations of a life within himself that is deeper and darker
and less rational than that of the simple diurnal self with
whom he customarily has dealings: indeed, sometimes he hears
echoing within himself "a first syllable, Mol, very clear, followed almost at once by a second, very thick, as though gob-
bled by the first, and which might have been oy as it might
have been ose, or one or even oc." And, as Edith Kern has
pointed out in her perceptive essay, it is significant that "as
Moran advances upon his road into the Molloy country, he
slowly changes into that other self and comes to resemble
Molloy."[26]

But what is perhaps most significant of all about Moran is
that he is a writer: the record of his adventures which we read
is a record of his own composition—which permits us then to
regard him as Beckett's *exemplum* of the artist, of the man
who turns a deep disturbance into words. What is most significant about Molloy (that dimension of Moran's own selfhood
for which he is searching) is that his is a life given over to
searching for his mother's room—or, as Professor Kern so
acutely suggests,[27] for those Mothers of Being who, according
to Nietzsche,[28] preside over "the innermost heart of things."

So, then, in a time when the world is frozen and "all wilts
and yields," the artist's turning (Molloy-Moran) must be towards Mother's room, towards the dark and original source of
Being: the journey there is difficult and dangerous, and, in his
wanderings over and through the Mountains and Valleys of
Primal Pain, he may be stripped of every security and racked
by infinitely excruciating hurts and humiliations. But he smarts
under none of this, for, as Heidegger says,

> It is the time of the gods that have fled *and* of the god that
> is coming. It is the time of *need*, because it lies under a double

[26] Edith Kern, "Moran-Molloy: The Hero as Author," *Perspective*,
Vol. XI, No. 3 (Autumn, 1959), p. 186.

[27] *Ibid.*, pp. 190–191.

[28] Friedrich Nietzsche, "The Birth of Tragedy," *The Philosophy of
Nietzsche* (New York: Modern Library, 1937), p. 1033.

lack and a double Not: the Nomore of the gods that have fled and the Not-yet of the god that is coming.[29]

In this time of breakdown and reorientation, journeying and risk are the portion appointed him by his vocation. "Zero" is the terse reply that is spoken by Clov to Hamm in *Endgame,.* when Hamm asks if there is anything on the horizon. When this is all that can be seen, the artist must seek to return into proximity to the Mothers of Being, there to await, with patience and cunning, some brave new world—and the book that he writes will be, like the jottings of Molloy and Moran, a record of how he did finally manage to arrive within the precincts of that original Room.

The Malone of *Malone Dies* is but another phase or aspect of Molloy-Moran. In the first book of the trilogy we are shown the artist journeying back through the Wasteland into those primal precincts wherein alone he stands a chance of grasping the dilapidation and turning it into words; and, in the second book, we see him actually engaged in the creative process. Malone is somewhat nearer even to extinction than Molloy, and, as he lies paralyzed in his bed waiting for death, he writes in a notebook with the stub of a pencil sharpened at both ends, resolved to be "neither hot nor cold any more"—"I shall be tepid, I shall die tepid." He intends to tell three stories—one about a man and a woman, another "about an animal, a bird probably," and the third about a thing, "a stone probably." Then, having got through these, he will prepare an inventory of the few wretched possessions—an old hat, a crooked stick, one boot, etc.—that he has in his hospital room; and, having done this, he will be finished.

One suspects, though, that there could never be world enough and time for the completion of this project, and Malone does not live to finish even the first of the three stories which concerns a certain gentleman named Saposcat (gen-

[29] Martin Heidegger, "Hölderlin and the Essence of Poetry," *Existence and Being* (Chicago: Henry Regnery Co., 1949), p. 313.

erally referred to as Sapo [which is perhaps, as Hugh Kenner suggests, a diminutive form of homo sapiens])[30] and his wife who are anxious about the outcome of an examination which their son faces. In the course of the narrative, Sapo's name becomes Macmann (Son of man), and his picaresque adventures reenact the earlier misfortunes of Molloy and Moran. Like Watt, he ends his days in an institution for the insane: he is picked up one day, rolling in the rain, and taken to the asylum at Stillorgan, County Dublin, where, in his old age, he senescently fumbles at sexual fun-games, with Moll and is watched over by his keeper, Lemuel. But the main focus of the book is to be found far less in Sapo-Macmann than in Malone himself, his interest in Macmann's story being so intermittent as to permit him to leave out whole portions of it for the sake of making periodic notations on the steadily advancing deterioration of his own body—whose final expiration leaves the tale suspended in mid-sentence. But till the emission of that last breath, agonized though he is both physically and spiritually, this insane and absolutely lucid genius never ceases to investigate and to chart the limitless void against whose sheer emptiness his life has been irremediably wrecked. Or at least he does not do so until a penultimate moment in which, imagining himself dealt a terrible blow by an unidentified presence, in a kind of raging fury against the universal dearth, he plunges the whole narrative into a blood bath, with Lemuel, the madhouse-keeper, hacking up some of the internees and shoving the rest out to sea.

In *The Unnamable* we are hermetically sealed up within the absolute and self-contained world of the artist's imagination; and, whereas the hegemony of this world was to some extent broken in upon and invaded by the larger human universe in *Molloy* and *Malone Dies*, in the final novel of the trilogy it is utterly shut up and impermeable: so it is no wonder that of this book Beckett himself has said that it has

[30] Hugh Kenner, "The Absurdity of Fiction," *The Griffin*, Vol. VIII, No. 10 (November, 1959), p. 15.

brought him into "a situation that I can't extricate myself from." And so indeed we are persuaded that it has, for all that we encounter is the discarnate imagination of the artist churning away, over the Void. "I am obliged to speak," says the Unnamable: "I shall never be silent. Never." And through almost two hundred pointless pages in which the last pretense at the invention of sustained narrative has been dropped, this disembodied intelligence, dreaming its dream of absolute freedom and of absolute nothingness, speaks. "What was I going to say? Never mind, I'll say something else, it's all the same." Sometimes he wonders how it is that he goes on writing and what there is to write about. But, though he never achieves any clarity about these basic questions, he keeps on going, for about at least one thing he is in no doubt at all, and that is that he "must go on . . . must say words, as long as there are any," for they, the words, may bring "me to the threshold of my story." So the voice is kept launched, and the authorial pen is kept moving, telling "the story of the silence" that is within the Unnamable and without—

> the silence, full of murmurs, distant cries, the usual silence, spent listening, spent waiting for the voice, the cries abate, like all cries, that is to say they stop, the murmurs cease, they give up, the voice begins again, it begins trying again, quick now before there is none left, no voice left, nothing left but the core of murmurs, distant cries, quick now and try again, with the words that remain, try what, I don't know, I've forgotten, it doesn't matter, I never knew, to have them carry me into my story, the words that remain, my old story, which I've forgotten, far from here, through the noise, through the door, into the silence. . . .

Indeed, says M. Mauriac,

> We fall here . . . into absolute silence. . . . By means of a literature that, by negating all literature, annihilates itself in the catastrophe it has created, Samuel Beckett, an exemplary *alittérateur*, opens a door in us which, even after Joyce and Kafka, might perhaps have remained closed. . . . One cannot

deny, at any rate, the extraordinary impression, I dare not say of enrichment, since it concerns awareness of an absolute poverty, that Samuel Beckett creates. Poverty that is our only wealth. Inexhaustible, fascinating poverty.[31]

Here, then, we have the major design of Beckett's fiction. Briefly schematized, it might be said to entail a definition in *Murphy* and in *Watt* of his sense of the objective human situation, in all its hopelessness and abandonment and absurdity. Then, in the trilogy, "spiraling inward to the center of . . . [his own] solitary world,"[32] the artist, in contemplating the processes of his own creativity, reaches the conclusion that, given the chaotic absurdity of human existence, he is himself, as artist, his sole reliable datum: as the Unnamable puts it,

All these Murphys, Molloys and Malones do not fool me. They have made me waste my time, suffer for nothing, speak of them when, in order to stop speaking, I should have spoken of me and of me alone. But I just said I have spoken of me, am speaking of me. I don't care a curse what I just said. It is now I shall speak of me, for the first time. I thought I was right in enlisting these sufferers of my pains. I was wrong. They never suffered my pains, their pains are nothing, compared to mine, a mere tittle of mine, the tittle I thought I could put from me, in order to witness it. Let them be gone now, them and all the others, those I have used and those I have not used, give me back the pains I lent them and vanish, from my life, my memory, my terrors and shames. There, now there is no one here but me, no one wheels about me, no one comes towards me, no one has ever met anyone before my eyes, these creatures have never been, only I and this black void have ever been. And the sounds? No, all is silent.

The day, in other words, that is disclosed in these fictions is (as Hamm puts it in *Endgame*) "an extra-ordinarily bitter day . . . zero by the thermometer."

[31] Claude Mauriac, *op. cit.*, pp. 81–82.
[32] Hugh Kenner, "The Beckett Landscape," *Spectrum*, Vol. II, No. 1 (Winter, 1958), p. 22.

Of all Beckett's fiction, though, it is his novel of 1961, *Comment c'est* (American edition, *How It Is*, 1964), that offers the extremest instance of his impatience with literature and of his determination to produce a fiction that will be against the very idea of fiction itself. Here we encounter a novel that is not only stripped of every vestige of plot and action and character, but one in which even the last remaining props of syntax have collapsed and in which therefore the narrator simply "says it as he hears it"—

> my life last state last version ill said ill heard ill recaptured when the panting stops ill murmured to the mud brief movements of the lower face losses everywhere.

It is Pim, whoever he is, who gives the book something like a fixed center, and that this is Beckett's intention is announced in the opening lines, in which the narrator says: "how it was I quote before Pim with Pim after Pim how it is three parts I say it as I hear it." Pim's role here is very much like that of the Absent One in *Godot*: it is, presumably, in his image that the narrator dimly descries (as do Gogo and Didi in Godot) a presence and a power to be united with which is to be no longer wholly under the dominance of meaninglessness and despair: so his diary begins with the record of his journey towards Pim—through a "vast stretch of time," in the dark, and by way of his crawling naked over terrains of mud and slime: "ten yards fifteen yards half on my left side right foot right hand push pull flat on my belly mute cries half on my right side left foot left hand push pull flat on my belly mute cries not a syllable to be changed in this description."

But, after the narrator does finally reach Pim, their "vie en commun" in no wise proves to be the radiant blessing that one might have expected it to be. Indeed, after crawling eastward through great stretches of mud, this naked pilgrim with a sack tied round his neck finds Pim's condition to be identical with his own: he, too, lies prone in the mud with his sack. It may well be the rage of disappointment that leads the narrator to take up with respect to him a relation very much like that of Pozzo to Lucky in *Godot*: in any event, he becomes Pim's scourge and torturer, varying his blows to the head with sharp jabs of a can opener into Pim's anus. But the fist and the can opener are instruments of instruction as well as of anger, for it is through a carefully administered ritual of beatings and stabbings that the mute narrator teaches Pim when to sing and when to speak, himself responding by tracing out his replies on Pim's back, letter by letter.

Part I of the book is devoted to the journey in search of Pim, and Part II to the encounter; then, in Part III, we gather that a radical reversal of things is under way, for Pim is now crawling across the muddy wastes of the world in search of one whom he in turn shall torment—while the narrator is waiting for still another personage called Bom, to whom he will be apprenticed in much the same way that Pim was apprenticed to him. It is suggested that these reversals are periodic, so that the narrator may look forward to still another time when he will again be the torturer, as Pim may again be destined to be the tortured. The moral judgment, in other words, behind which the book lines itself up is as clear as it is bleak: Beckett's intention would seem to be to say that, though life in the human City is comprised of manifold relations, they all move within the single polarity involving torturer and victim, both roles being enacted in turn by all men in the various relations with one another into which they are brought by the adventures of life. As it is put by the narrator: ". . . each of us is at the same time Bom and Pim executioner victim schoolmaster dunce plaintiff defendant dumb and theatre of a word found again in the dark the mud there nothing to correct."

This is the sense of existence that is exteriorized in Beckett's stage-pieces—in such works as *Waiting for Godot* (1952) and *Endgame* (1957) and the sketch for radio *All That Fall* (1957). They are all suffused with the purest nihilism and are appalling metaphors of what human life is like in the Zone of Zero, in the time of the absent God. They are bereft of the merest vestige of plot and action, and when, in *Waiting for Godot*, Estragon remarks, "Nothing happens, nobody comes, nobody goes, it's awful!" he summarizes the whole of Beckett's theatre. In *Waiting for Godot*, for example, two Chaplinesque hobos simply wait under a tree on an untraveled heath for someone called Godot, who never arrives. Though the prefix of this name has encouraged some of Beckett's critics to interpret the play theistically, we ought perhaps to remember the passage in *Molloy*—in which the protagonist tells us that he called his mother Mag because, he says, "the letter 'g' abolished the syllable *ma*"—and, similarly, the suffix *ot* (with its heavy aural implication of naughting scepticism) may be intended to negate *God*, as the actual content of the play would certainly lead us to suppose. Or, again, in *Endgame*, we are in an unfurnished room suffused with a gray light, with two small windows too high up to be seen through; and in this room there are four grotesques. Nagg and Nell are two legless ancients who occasionally poke up their heads from the ashcans in which they are confined to ask for their pap and sugar plums. Hamm, their blind son, is an invalid whose station is a wheel chair, and there he remains throughout the play, stanching his wounds with a bloody handkerchief and, from time to time, irascibly demanding his dose of "pain-killer" from Clov, his adopted son and attendant, who, despite his game legs, is the sole member of the quartet who is able to hobble about the room. When Clov climbs up his ladder to peer out one of the windows through his telescope, he reports to Hamm that "All is Zero." And when Hamm petulantly asks, as he often does, "What's happening, what's happening?" Clov's unvarying answer is, "Something is taking its course." But Hamm has no illusions about the providential beneficence of this unfoldment, whatever it is of, for, as to God, he says, "The bastard doesn't exist." So they simply sit there in the "infinite emptiness," watching their "light dying," abusing each other, telling their bitter jokes (about the tailor, for example, who, when asked by an irate customer why he couldn't make a pair of trousers in three months when God made the world in six days, replied, "But my dear Sir, my dear Sir, look—at the world—and look—at my TROUSERS!"), and reminding themselves of the hopelessness of their condition. "Outside of here," says Hamm, "it's death," and we are reminded of Vladimir's word to Estragon in *Godot*, "There's no way out. . . ."—as we are also reminded of that claustral Second Empire living room in Sartre's *No Exit* which is Hell.

I have already referred to that passage in *Watt* in which the protagonist worries over the meaning of the visit paid to Mr. Knott's house by the Galls, the piano-tuners, and I am put in mind of it again, as our circle begins now to be completed. For, among the many reverberations in us that Mr. Beckett's writings release, there is a certain particular resonance that this passage has which makes us feel that here perhaps is a clue to the primary intention that executively controls the entire *oeuvre*. Watt, it will be recalled, as he contemplates the fact that the piano-tuners simply came and then left, is troubled by "the utmost formal distinctness" with which "*nothing* had *happened*": he is not yet an adept, says Beckett, in the art of eliciting "*something* from *nothing*." But this, he goes on to imply, is precisely the challenge that faces the human intelligence, of learning how to elicit *something* from *le Néant*. And is not this, we may now begin to wonder, precisely the end to which his whole effort as an artist is devoted—the elicitation, that is, with "the utmost formal distinctness," of some little something from the great environing Nothingness that perpetually threatens to smother us out?

Beckett reminds us, of course, that

> the only way one can speak of nothing is to speak of it as though it were something, just as the only way one can speak of God is to speak of him as though he were a man, which to be sure he was, in a sense, for a time, and as the only way one can speak of man, even our anthropologists have realized that, is to speak of him as though he were a termite.

This is, indeed, just what he seems to have tried to do in book after book, to speak of man, yes, but to speak of him in such a way that we shall know, through all the images and metaphors of illness and senescence and decay, that Man is nothing, and that Man is nothing because there is Nothing either in or beyond existence that sanctions or gives any kind of warrant or dignity to the human enterprise. Indeed, the nihilism of this writer is not only present in the images and situations which he selects as the vehicles of his meaning, but is operative even in the nervous rhythms of his sentences. In one of the most acute observations that any of his readers have made, Miss Christine Brooke-Rose has noticed how frequently the word *not* is to be heard throughout his work, "like a constant echo":[33] "Not that Watt was ever to have any direct dealings with Mr. Knott, for he was not" or "Not that many things remain to be said, on the subject of the Galls father and son, for they do not" or "Not that the garden was so little, for it was not," etc. This is the language, as Miss Brooke-Rose puts it, of one who is "the poet of *le Néant*"[34] and, his spiritual residence being in that cheerless and unpromising Zone of Zero, it is the language of one who distrusts and despairs of literature, since to work within any form is always to run the risk of coming to believe in *something* rather than *nothing*, at least in *something* sufficient enough to give a kind of existential accreditation to literary form itself. But not even intending to relax his nihilism to this minimal extent, Beckett's is, therefore, a poetry determinedly formless and stammering, full of "slightly surrealistic tricks, [of] the things which are and are not, [of] the detailed and serious treatment of pointless incidents, [of] the introduction of characters in a familiar tone, whom we are supposed to know, and who never reappear."[35] It is, in other words, a

[33] Christine Brooke-Rose, "Samuel Beckett and the Anti-Novel," *The London Magazine*, Vol. V, No. 12 (December, 1958), p. 41.

[34] *Ibid.*, p. 43.

[35] *Ibid.*, p. 44.

literature uninformed by any faith in literature itself, and Mr. Beckett's profound scepticism about the Word and about *Mythos* is, at bottom, rooted in a profound despair of *Logos*, of the possibility of any system of meaning being able to introduce any kind of ultimately valid and satisfactory order into a universe in which "the bastard doesn't exist."

One is also struck by the remarkable absence of any kind of piety in Beckett's books. Amid all the broken furniture of the world and amid all the maimed and stunted grotesques who masquerade as men, there is nothing that commends itself as deserving of reverence, of honor, or even of respect: the human scene, like that in the novels of Céline (with whom Stephen Spender is right in thinking Beckett deserves more to be compared than with Kafka or Joyce),[36] is always nasty and brutish and hateful and absurd. The light is always dying, and the temperature is always Zero.

So one wonders how appropriate it is, in this particular ambiance, to contemplate the possibility of "grace at zero point." A good deal has been said (outside the contexts of literary criticism) by Christian writers in recent years, particularly on the European scene, about "grace at zero point." This is a kind of witness which it is by no means improper to recall in this present context, since, given the actualities of our culture, it is impossible for agnosticism to go as deep as Beckett's without its becoming involved in polemic against Christian premises. But, now, when Christian theologians like Karl Barth or the late Dietrich Bonhoeffer speak of "grace at zero point," they have in mind the possibilities for radically new beginnings that come into existence when, by some extreme and thoroughgoing crisis, the life of men is so stripped of every proximate and spurious security as to compel them to submit to the cleansing processes of judgment and to rebuild their life on some fresh and new structure of meaning that is given of God. And, unquestionably, the austere tragic vision in much of

[36] Stephen Spender, "Lifelong Suffocation," *New York Times Book Review*, 12 October 1958, p. 5.

the great literature of our period has had the effect, as Amos Wilder has remarked, of saying to men:

> You must change your life! Such art represents a demand, even a rebuke. It sees through us. . . . There is an interesting analogy between the surgical acerbity of much modern art and the inexorable sobriety of neo-orthodox theology. In any case, the modern writer challenges men to revise their mood and attitude. He says that cherished decorums are misconceived, and that cherished securities are not enough.[37]

Thus it is that, despite the various ways in which the authors of *The Castle, The Sound and the Fury, The Old Man and the Sea,* and *The Plague* bring us to a kind of "zero point," it is, nevertheless, a point at which new beginnings are in view and a point to which, therefore, those who live in traditional communities of religious faith had better make a journey, if their certitudes are not to lapse into irrelevant banality.

In the writings of his last years, Dietrich Bonhoeffer liked to tell us that "now that it has come of age, the world is more godless, and perhaps it is for that very reason nearer to God than ever before."[38] But, as one of his recent interpreters has reminded us, he was not himself intending to sponsor or to promote the world's godlessness but was, rather, attempting only to elicit from us the recognition that the godlessness of contemporary agnosticism is very often a profoundly "*hopeful* godlessness"[39] and therefore points beyond itself to fresh redintegration. It is indeed just here that we may see the tremendous difference between a Camus, say, and a Beckett. For, though both are situated within the perspectives of modern secular existentialism, the godlessness of a Camus is a pro-

[37] Amos N. Wilder, *Theology and Modern Literature* (Cambridge: Harvard University Press, 1958), p. 59.

[38] Dietrich Bonhoeffer, *Letters and Papers from Prison,* ed. Eberhard Bethge; trans. Reginald H. Fuller (London: SCM Press Ltd., 1953), p. 167.

[39] John D. Godsey, *The Theology of Dietrich Bonhoeffer* (Philadelphia: The Westminster Press, 1960), p. 272.

foundly hopeful godlessness, whereas that of Beckett is soured and bitter and utterly hopeless. Erich Heller says of Kafka that "he knows two things at once, and both with equal assurance: that there *is* no God, and that there *must* be God."[40] But Samuel Beckett is in that line of contemporary writers— Nathanael West, Louis-Ferdinand Céline, Eugène Ionesco— who not only begin at Zero but who *stick* to Zero. And at this point—no grace, but only the sound of "a world collapsing endlessly, a frozen world, under a faint untroubled sky. . . . And . . . all wilts and yields."

[40] Erich Heller, *The Disinherited Mind: Essays in Modern German Literature and Thought* (Philadelphia: Dufour and Saifer, 1952), p. 162.

VI

Graham Greene: Christian
Tragedian

Graham Greene's first novel—*The Man Within*—appeared in
1929, and, as we stand now at a remove from it of nearly forty
years, it is clear that the enormous body of work which he has
accomplished in the intervening period gives him a stature
which requires that we judge him in the terms that we use for
judging the major novelists of this century. Yet he has rarely
been fortunate in the quality of the discriminations which his
critics have brought to bear upon his fiction; and, over a
long period now, he has often in fact been submitted to a
strangely rancorous kind of condescension at the bar of contemporary criticism—a malice so captious and depreciative indeed as to give rise to the suspicion that it may be prompted,
in a predominantly secular literary community, by a sense of
scandal, that so manifestly gifted an artist should be so radically committed to Catholic Christianity.

There is no gainsaying what is obviously the primary fact
about his career, that Mr. Greene does have a profound allegiance to Catholic belief. And wanting, as a Christian artist,
like Dante in the fourteenth century, to disclose the point of
juncture between nature and grace, he has often used violence
and melodrama as instruments for awakening his age out of its
lethargies, for destroying its specious securities and revealing

its underlying turmoil and nightmare. He has wanted to "prohibit sharply the rehearsed response,"[1] to resurrect the heart through terror and to exhibit the world itself, in all of its degradation, as the country wherein we must realize "New styles of architecture, a change of heart."[2] But since he has known at what a discount a Christian reading of the human situation has been held in the modern world, he has resorted to those devices of indirection which the Christian writer has frequently employed in our period, himself often concealing the true motives of his work beneath the conventions of the "thriller."[3] There is little doubt but that the furtive lust and the shabby little slum rooms, the vitriol and the razor blades, the chases and the explosions have effectively hidden his larger purposes from many of his readers. Too frequently the verdict has been that his main contribution to the furniture of the contemporary imagination is simply a "shabby Inferno" of "soured virginity, soured spirituality, soured kindliness . . . the world of the Slump, as well as of the Fall."[4]

Mr. Greene belongs, of course, to that English generation of W. H. Auden and Stephen Spender, Rex Warner, and Christopher Isherwood, which grew to maturity in the years between the two great wars and which was profoundly affected, at an impressionable age, by the general European *malaise* that was brought overwhelmingly into focus by the call to arms in Spain in the summer of 1936. It was a world unforgettably described by Mr. Auden in his *New Year Letter* of 1940, where he speaks of how,

---

[1] W. H. Auden, "Petition," *The Collected Poetry* (New York: Random House, 1945), p. 110.

[2] *Ibid.*, p. 111.

[3] Among the major novels, the exceptions are *It's a Battlefield* (1934), *The Heart of the Matter* (1948), *The End of the Affair* (1951), *The Quiet American* (1955), *A Burnt-Out Case* (1961), and *The Comedians* (1966).

[4] Donat O'Donnell, "Graham Greene," *Chimera*, Vol. V, No. 4 (Summer, 1947), p. 30.

> taut with apprehensive dreads,
> The sleepless guests of Europe lay
> Wishing the centuries away,
> And the low mutter of their vows
> Went echoing through her haunted house,
> As on the verge of happening
> There crouched the presence of The Thing.

But Mr. Greene's response to the developing crisis differed from that of his contemporaries who were bent on invoking all the militant formulas of leftist politics and who were seeking a way out of their own disquiet through Freudian psychology. It was not that he turned away from the contemporary world, but, rather, that the ruined cities and the putsches and mobilizations of western Europe in the 'thirties—which he looked at as steadily as did the early Auden and Spender and Orwell, or Continental writers like Malraux and Silone—pointed, for him, not simply to a breakdown in the machinery of modern society but to something in the nature of man which could not be grasped by the mathematically precise assignations of guilt and innocence characteristic of leftist liberal thought. As Mr. Auden, again, was to say in the *New Year Letter,* himself now having passed through his youthful Marxism and expressing here, one feels, a sensibility very close to Mr. Greene's: "The situation of our time/Surrounds us like a baffling crime." And all of our equipment for the detection and containment of the malevolent forces only

> Extends the area of the crime
> Until the guilt is everywhere,
> And more and more we are aware,
> However miserable may be
> Our parish of immediacy,
> How small it is, how far beyond,
> Ubiquitous within the bond
> Of one impoverishing sky,
> Vast spiritual disorders lie.

It is as Arthur Rowe, the hero of *The Ministry of Fear*, says: "The world has been remade by William Le Queux." Released from imprisonment for the mercy-killing of his wife, Arthur is first met against the background of war-torn London, stumbling into a charity bazaar in a Bloomsbury square where he wins a cake which contains the microfilms of a naval secret that is being sought by Nazi spies. Before he is fully sensible of his plight, he has become involved in an intricate web of espionage and murder and is himself an outlaw, having been framed by the ruthless amoralist, Willi Hilfe, for a nonexistent murder. In the midst of this macabre entertainment[5] he cries out to his dead mother in a dream: "I've killed my wife and the police want me."

> His mother smiled at him in a scared way but let him talk: he was the master of the dream now. He said, "I'm wanted for a murder I didn't do. People want to kill me because I know too much. . . . It sounds like a thriller, doesn't it?—but the thrillers are like life . . . it's what we've made of the world since you died. I'm your little Arthur who wouldn't hurt a beetle, and I'm a murderer too. The world has been remade by William Le Queux.

So Mr. Greene has chosen in many of his novels to render the contemporary world through the medium of the "thriller" —not at all, though, as some of his critics have hinted, because he wishes to cater to the plain reader's desire for circuses, but, rather, because he has felt that it makes possible a more effective imaginative seizure of the infernal realities of our time. It is this searching moral purpose behind the frequently Gothic exterior of his books that gives him the kind of importance as a

---

[5] Mr. Greene has designated certain of his novels as "entertainments" (*Stamboul Train, The Third Man, Loser Takes All, A Gun for Sale, The Confidential Agent, The Ministry of Fear, Our Man in Havana*), by which, presumably, he intends to suggest some relaxation of serious purpose. But, as Walter Allen has reminded us in an essay cited in the following note, "just as the little girl wrote of Shakespeare that his comedies were as good as tragedies by anybody else, so Mr. Greene's 'entertainments' are at least as good as most people's novels."

novelist to which only a very few of his contemporaries can lay any claim.

In his earlier novels—*Stamboul Train* (1932), *It's a Battlefield* (1934), *England Made Me* (1935), and *A Gun for Sale* (1936)—Mr. Greene created (as did T. S. Eliot in his early poems) a kind of abstract of our modern Inferno, and it is the adjective "seedy," recurring again and again, which is the focally descriptive term. We are brought up against a whole series of displaced persons, lonely and uprooted, whose seedy world, in all of its moral neutrality, is—as it is said of the Swedish industrialist Krogh in *England Made Me*—a wilderness of their own contriving. In *Stamboul Train* there is, for example, the hypochrondriacal Mrs. Peters who whines ceaselessly about her digestion: "Get me a sandwich. . . . I'm so empty I can hear my stomach. . . . No, I won't have any more of this foreign beer. My stomach won't stand it. Ask them haven't they got a Guinness. I'd just fancy a Guinness." Or there is the joyless lesbian relationship between Mabel Warren, the foreign correspondent, and the beautiful and vacuous Janet Pardoe, who is "lovely." We also have the vain and smug little writer of popular fiction, Savory, whose bit of success has very greatly enlarged his sense of the role he must play in the world. In *It's a Battlefield* there is Kay Rimmer, the sister-in-law of the doomed Communist murderer, Jim Drover, who comes alive only in the moment of copulation, who "never felt more at home than in a bed or a man's arms." She is in love with the young Frenchman, Jules Briton, but she cannot resist the exquisite flat and the luxurious rose-colored, semicircular bed of Surrogate, whom she meets at a Communist meeting. And there is the pathetic figure of Conder, who, in the loneliness of his squalid little bed-sitting room, seeks to redeem his sense of failure in fantasies of being a successful journalist and business magnate, and particularly, of being a family man.

It is perhaps in *England Made Me*—which Mr. Greene himself rightly regards as being among his most successful books—that he gives us his finest evocation of our "fallen" world. Kate Farrant, the mistress and secretary of the Swedish financier, Krogh, brings her weak, shifty, but charming scapegrace brother Anthony to Stockholm (and there are hints of incest in their relation), where she hopes to place him in Krogh's organization. The great man takes him on as his personal bodyguard and is soon captivated by Anthony's debonair amiability. But Anthony meets the English tourists, Mr. and Mrs. Davidge, and falls in love with their daughter, Lucia, whose teenage frankness about sex and whose prattling simplicity make her a little pathetic and yet, perhaps because of the very freshness in her unformed youth, somehow desirable. Her background of Coventry, Woolworth's, and Wotton-under-Edge represent "home" to Anthony, and for this he proposes to break with Krogh and Kate, promising Lucia, on the morning he sees her off at the railway station, to meet her on a certain day not far hence at the Moroccan Cafe in the High Street at "home." But he never arrives there, for before he can leave Stockholm he is murdered by Hall, Krogh's devoted henchman, who fears that Farrant, having made so many discoveries about the precariousness of their financial enterprises, may betray them all. After Anthony's death, Kate decides to leave Stockholm. But she does not intend to return to England: "I'm simply moving on," she says to Minty, the newspaperman. "Like Anthony."

Now this is the basic situation of the novel into which Mr. Greene draws a host of memorable figures whose wretched loneliness very largely defines the tone of the book. There is Krogh, the self-made business magnate, whose vast wealth cannot purchase for him any felicity of soul, whose exterior presents to the world the formidable solidity of success, but who is really, as Kate realizes in a moment of sympathy, ". . . one of us, fighting for his own security like one of us, he's not the future, he's not self-sufficient, just one of us, out of his proper place." He lives, without love, in a "wilderness of his own contriving," his deepest pleasure consisting in gazing at the initials of his own name flashing at him in the electric lights that adorn every doorway in his great office building. Or there is the little newspaperman Minty, an expatriate, who lives on Krogh, since everything that happens to Krogh is "news"—a man utterly without connections, without roots, who hopes, that morning when Anthony takes Lucia to his room simply because there is nowhere else for them to go, that they have come to see him as a friend, and who is bitterly disappointed when he realizes that it is only his bed that they want. "Poor devil," they say, as he leaves. "It's a dreary world." And finally there is the "depraved innocence" of Anthony, who has emerged from a long series of seedy, disreputable confidence games with his slick, shiny exterior unscathed but without either wisdom of the mind or peace of heart. Ironically, he dies by drowning—ironically, because his baptism comes too late. Kate Farrant says of them all (including, one imagines, Hall, who makes her think of "some great pain hopelessly demanding sympathy"): "We're all thieves. . . . Stealing a livelihood here and there and everywhere, giving nothing back. . . . No brotherhood in our boat. Only who can cut the biggest dash and who can swim."

So it is not surprising that betrayal, as Walter Allen has observed, is a frequently recurring theme in Mr. Greene's earlier books.[6] There is Conrad Drover, for example, in *It's a Battlefield*, who sleeps with his doomed brother's wife, as there is also in the same book the habitual infidelity of the effete Communist intellectual, Surrogate, to the memory of his wife who had known the inner falseness of his life for what it was. Or there is the hare-lipped killer of *A Gun for Sale* who is betrayed by Anne, the first person he ever dares to trust. It is a world of violated trusts and broken loyalties—such a world as Gauguin was thinking of when he remarked (and Greene has quoted this sentence): "Life, being what it is, one dreams of revenge." Which is perhaps the explanation of another characteristic theme in these books: namely, criminality, the violent

[6] Walter Allen, "Graham Greene," in *Writers of Today*, ed. by Denys Val Baker (London: Sidgwick and Jackson, 1946), pp. 22–23.

lawlessness of those like Josef Grünlich in *Stamboul Train* or Conrad Drover in *It's a Battlefield* or Raven in *A Gun for Sale* who strive toward further self-definition through an act of revenge.[7] They have, of course, significant affinities with many of the major heroes of modern literature—with Lafcadio of Gide's *Les Caves du Vatican,* with Joe Christmas of Faulkner's *Light in August,* with Jeremiah Beaumont of Penn Warren's *World Enough and Time,* and with Meursault of Camus' *L'Étranger,* to name only a few.

The shabby little shyster lawyer of *Brighton Rock,* Mr. Prewitt, reminds us at one point that, when Faust asked Mephistopheles where Hell was, Mephistopheles replied: "Why, this is Hell, nor are we out of it." And so too does it seem that many of Mr. Greene's early novels are, at bottom, saying: "Why, this is Hell, nor are we out of it." For he is always juxtaposing the special personal failures recorded in these books against the background of the collective tragedy of the modern world—the furious schismatism of the Communist Party in *It's a Battlefield,* the unconscionable incitation of international war by armament manufacturers in *A Gun for Sale,* the internecine struggles generated by Franco-feudalism in *The Confidential Agent,* the Mexican church suppression in *The Power and the Glory,* and the Nazi fifth column in *The Ministry of Fear.* "Each of these novels," says Mr. Allen, "is the microcosm of the violence of a continent," and each is "reminiscent in a very real way of the world of the old Icelandic sagas and eddas. Though he believe it, no man is strong."[8]

It is that hauntingly memorable book of 1938, *Brighton Rock,* which marks a kind of transition in Mr. Greene's work from the early novels to the major books of his maturity—*The Power and the Glory* (1940), *The Heart of the Matter* (1948),

---

[7] It may well be the prominence of violent lawlessness in many of Greene's early novels which has led certain French critics to insist upon the affinity between him and those Existentialist writers who regard the *acte gratuite* as the means whereby one's moral identity is discoverable.

[8] Walter Allen, *op. cit.,* p. 23.

The End of the Affair (1951), and also the interesting entertainment, *The Ministry of Fear*, which appeared in 1943. In the book of 1938 it became clear that the forlorn world of dereliction that he had been portraying in his earlier novels was not simply the squalid arena of futility and meaninglessness that has been so thoroughly explored in modern fiction but was, rather, a world of dimensions, not truly to be understood except *sub specie aeternitatis*. Indeed this book brings to a kind of terrifying conclusion the first phase of his work, and he here gives us an even more sombre description of dereliction than anything that had gone before.

Fred Hale serves his newspaper as its Mysteryman, "Mr. Kolly Kibber": in this role he patrols the Brighton seaside, leaving cards along his route, to be picked up by visitors, and he is prepared to give a reward to the person who identifies him. Hale is the betrayer of Kite, the former leader of some seedy racecourse gangsters, whose present leader is the brutal and sinister seventeen-year-old criminal, Pinkie. For this act of treachery Hale is murdered by Pinkie's henchmen who take his life by cramming down his throat a long piece of the hard candy known as "Brighton Rock."

Shortly before Hale is killed, he is "picked up" by the plump and sensual Ida Arnold, a coarsely amiable tart who, after his death, sets out to track down the murderers. "I'm going to make those people sorry they was ever born. . . . Right and wrong. . . . I believe in right and wrong." When Pinkie discovers the interest she is taking in the affair, he mistakenly dismisses her, saying: "She don't matter . . . she's just a buer." He is, of course, mistaken, for Ida's persistent investigations are to be his undoing. But his miscalculation is inevitable, for Pinkie is incapable of understanding that Ida loves life so deeply that she is "prepared to cause any amount of unhappiness to anyone in order to defend the only thing she believes in." Thus she is a more dangerous adversary than Pinkie realizes, for Fred Hale's murder figures in her imagination as an assault upon that than which there is nothing more sacred—

namely, life itself. "I like fair play," she says. And she feels the necessity for no stronger equipment than this in the realm of fundamental belief: she simply loves the world with a cheery gusto and abandon. The word "stranger" means nothing to her: "there was no place in the world where she felt a stranger. . . . There was nothing with which she didn't feel kinship": for her the "world's all dandy." But for Pinkie the world is like a ". . . jail, it's not knowing where to get some money. Worms and cataract, cancer. You hear 'em shrieking from the upper windows—children being born. It's dying slowly." He says on one occasion to Rose, the little waitress who loves him and who is also a Catholic: "These atheists, they don't know nothing. Of course, there's Hell. Flames and damnation, torments." And when Rose anxiously adds: "And Heaven too," Pinkie replies: "Oh, maybe, maybe."

Now it is in the struggle between Ida and Pinkie that Mr. Greene offers his chief dramatic image of what he believes to be the radical antithesis between the secular and the religious view of the human situation. Ida, it will be remembered, believes that God doesn't mind "a bit of human nature." But Pinkie, despite the desecration of his piety, never forgets that, when he commits murder and takes Rose as his wife in a civil marriage, he has chosen to be damned: it is significant that the words of the petition for peace from the *Agnus Dei* are often on his lips. And though his desperate efforts to evade the machinery of Ida's justice finally culminate in his suicide and hers is the final triumph, she never really gets to Pinkie, nor even to Rose, who says to Pinkie: "I'd rather burn with you than be like her. She's ignorant." As, of course, Ida is, for she knows only Right and Wrong, and nothing of Good and Evil: she is the type of the "natural man," and this is why, within the logic of the novel, her complacent vulgarity and her jolly, good-humored sensuality strike us as being, however robust, something less than human. For, as T. S. Eliot has said in his essay on Baudelaire,

So far as we are human, what we do must be either evil or good; so far as we do evil or good we are human; and it is better, in a paradoxical way, to do evil than to do nothing: at least, we exist. It is true to say that the glory of man is his capacity for salvation; it is also true to say that his glory is his capacity for damnation. The worst that can be said of most of our malefactors, from statesmen to thieves, is that they are not men enough to be damned.[9]

And it is with these—that is, those who "are not men enough to be damned"—that Mr. Greene so richly populates the world of *Brighton Rock*, setting their velleity against Pinkie's energy of will, their abstractedness against the burning reality of him the very purity of whose malevolence discloses, in a paradoxical way, the grace for which he hungers.

But can anything good and gracious come out of the kind of world being described in these early novels? This is, one feels, the great question that Mr. Greene is implicitly raising and answering in the books that appeared during the 'forties— *The Ministry of Fear, The Power and the Glory*, and *The Heart of the Matter*—and in the latter two he created something closely approaching tragedy.

How, though, it will be asked, is it possible for a Christian novelist to manage a rendering of the human story that is at once genuinely tragic and genuinely Christian? Is it not the case that "if God is in fact the Lord of life and history, the deep wound of tragedy is no longer deep?"[10] This is a question that both theologians and literary critics have often posed, by way of denying the possibility in literature of such a thing as "Christian tragedy," it being assumed, on the one hand, that tragic art must be purely tragic, and, on the other, that the Christian drama takes us beyond the dimension of tragedy. But Preston Roberts has reminded us of the error in both

[9] T. S. Eliot, "Baudelaire," in *Selected Essays: 1917–1932* (New York: Harcourt, Brace and Co., 1932), p. 344.

[10] Preston Roberts, "A Christian Theory of Dramatic Tragedy," *The Journal of Religion*, Vol. XXXI, No. 1 (January, 1951), p. 7.

assumptions. For Christian theology, on the one hand, he says,

> does not simply deny or cancel out tragedy. It shifts the locus of tragedy from God, nature, others, or our own essence to an aspect of ourselves and others—an aspect which is rendered sufferable, meaningful, and transformable by virtue of a conjunction between God's freely given grace and our freely received faith. Chance, necessity, and judgment remain. . . . The consequences of sin are not erasable or completely reversible. . . . There is always the generic contrast between what might have happened and did not happen and what may or can still happen. . . . No man falls so far as to be cut off from all possibility of salvation, and no man rises so high as to be beyond all possibility of reversion, stasis or further ascent.[11]

And, on the other hand,

> . . . dramatic tragedy is not simply and purely tragic. The meaning . . . is not all despair and doom. . . . Some of the greatest of dramatic tragedies . . . turn upon the theme of man's idolatry and pretension rather than upon the themes of man's suffering nobility or piteous abnormality. They move from defeat to victory, from doom to grace, and from tragedy to peace.[12]

So it appears that a "Christian tragedy" is possible, since "the events and meanings of which Christian theology consists . . . are not simply and purely 'beyond tragedy,' and literary tragedy 'is not simply and purely tragic.' "[13] It is in the direction of a narrative art which incorporates this kind of complex insight that Mr. Greene has often been moving in his work of the past twenty-five years.

The world into which we are taken by his books of the 'forties at once resembles and differs from that of classical

[11] *Ibid.*
[12] *Ibid.*
[13] *Ibid.*, p. 8.

tragedy, on the one hand, and that of Christian tragedians like Hawthorne and Melville and Dostoievski, on the other. His hero, characteristically, is not the great individual of Greek tragedy: he is, rather, the little man who is, however, very much in the manner of Greek tragedy, immediately placed in a situation that makes him guilty. This situation is simply his membership in the "fallen" world that forms the stage upon which the drama of redemption is to be played out. But the fact that the protagonist is in a situation that makes him guilty at the outset does not predetermine the issue of the action, as in Greek tragedy where whatever the hero does must be wrong (Oedipus must either persist in searching out the cause of the Theban plague or allow the city to be destroyed). For, although not unaffected by the consequences of his own and others' sins, there yet remain vents of freedom through which it is possible for him to transcend the moral ambiguousness of human existence, to the extent of being able to hear and accept the summons to reenact Christ's Passion. And his heroism is defined by his acceptance of this task.

Mr. Greene's hero seems to be endowed with the *hamartia* or tragic flaw laid down by Aristotle as an essential requirement of the tragic man; but this flaw is neither a constituent element of his nature as a finite creature, as in classical tragedy, nor does it issue from an abuse of freedom motivated by pride, as is the case with the Christian tragic hero. He is a man whose dominant emotion is pity, "the terrible promiscuous passion which so few experience" and which is nurtured, says Mr. Greene, by "the conditions of life." It is, indeed, the quality of his compassion, his inability to resist the impulse to bear the griefs and carry the sorrows of his fellow creatures—it is this which makes him a hero: he would have the chastisement of their peace upon himself and, with his own stripes, would have them healed. He is the man whose life is governed by "the horrible and horrifying emotion of pity": for him the great uncanonical sacrament is the sacrament of the brother. But the very imperiousness of his compassion frequently commits him to a position where the felt claim upon him of another's need conflicts with and cannot easily be adjusted to other situations, less immediate and pressing, in which he knows himself to have contrary obligations. Yet so urgent is the immediate and present claim upon the moral imagination that it cannot be resisted, its opposition to other obligations notwithstanding. Thus "the imitation of Christ" becomes a tragic spectacle, insofar as it becomes, ironically, the occasion for the hero's betrayal into sin: yet it is not (as with, say, Brigitte Pian in Mauriac's *La Pharisienne*) the sin of self-righteousness, nor is it (as with Sophocles' Oedipus) the sin of *hybris*: his *hamartia* consists simply in the frailty of the human creature who is unable to be a priest to others without himself being succored by divine grace. But this is not a fact which leaves us feeling angry or desperate, since the pathos of the hero's situation is transcended in the great denouement of the action which consists in the disclosure of a conjunction between human charity and divine charity.

The plot that involves Mr. Greene in the exhibition of this pattern manifests several consistencies as between *The Ministry of Fear, The Power and the Glory,* and *The Heart of the Matter*; and, though each of these books deserves the most careful scrutiny, I must here, for the sake of brevity, concentrate upon *The Heart of the Matter,* which presents its most searching and profound version. Like Arthur Rowe in *The Ministry of Fear* (who kills his disease-ridden wife out of pity) and the fallen whiskey priest in *The Power and the Glory* (who, as he contemplates the uncertain future of his little illegitimate daughter, prays: "O God, give me any kind of death—without contrition, in a state of sin—only save this child"), the hero, Major Scobie, who is a commissioner of police in Sierra Leone, wonders whether, if one knew all the facts, one would not "have to feel pity even for the planets? If one reached what they called the heart of the matter." And, though his vulnerability to suffering is his virtue, it is also his flaw, for by it he is to be brought to the brink of damnation. His story reminds us, in fact, of the priest's description of Péguy in the final pages of *Brighton Rock*, as he tries to comfort Rose after Pinkie's death: "He was a good man, a holy man, and he lived in sin all through his life, because he couldn't bear the idea that any soul could suffer damnation . . . He never took the sacraments, he never married his wife in church. I don't know, my child, but some people think he was, well, a saint."

Scobie is a man of middle age, a convert to the Roman Church, whose life with his nagging, restless wife, Louise, has long since ceased to be an affair of ecstasy and passion. But, though he no longer loves her, he remains bound to her "by the pathos of her unattractiveness." In order to secure the money for her South African holiday, away from the heat and the damp, the ants and the cockroaches of their drab, northwest African coastal settlement, he enters into a financial arrangement with the Syrian usurer, Yusef—an arrangement which he knows his position as a responsible British colonial official ought to forbid.

During Louise's absence the survivors of a torpedoed ship are landed on the Sierra Leone coast, and among them is a nineteen-year-old girl, Helen Rolt, who has been widowed in the shipwreck. Toward this bewildered child-woman (who reminds us of Anthony's Lucia in *England Made Me*) Scobie extends himself in sympathy and compassion, and their friendship soon becomes a secret liaison. Then, Louise returns, and Scobie is faced with the necessity of deciding between his wife's claim upon him and that of Helen, but, since any decision must result in suffering for either, there seems to be no line of action really open. He brings his problem before his priest in the confessional, but, being unprepared to break off the affair with Helen, he cannot be given absolution. Yet, determined to avert his wife's suspicions, he has to pretend that things between them are as usual—which involves his accompanying her to the Communion rail, this being something that Louise, as a strict Catholic, insists upon. He knows, of course, that for him to make his Communion while in a state of mortal sin is for him to risk eternal damnation. But he cannot bring himself to make either Louise unhappy by revealing to her his affair with Helen—or Helen unhappy by breaking things off with her for the sake of Louise. So he goes to the rail with his wife, "watching the priest pour the wine and water into the chalice, his own damnation being prepared like a meal." As he takes God into himself, he prays: "O God, I offer up my damnation to you. Take it. Use it for them." And he is "aware of the pale papery taste of his eternal sentence on the tongue."

But the intolerableness of his situation begins even more strongly to be felt as he realizes that the deception which he is practicing on Louise will require his committing again and again this act of eucharistic blasphemy. One night, as she calls to him to come to bed, a desperate prayer forms itself on his lips: "O God . . . I can't give her pain, or the other pain, and I can't go on giving you pain. O God, if you love me as I know you do, help me to leave you."

His decision has, then, been made: he will destroy himself, for no longer can he shower blows upon the bruised face of Christ by falsely participating in the *missa fidelium*. So he studies the symptoms of angina pectoris and poisons himself with the tablets which his physician prescribes for the illness that he pretends to have.

Here, then, is Mr. Greene's *exemplum* of the Christian hero in a tragic situation: here is the branch that grows out of the "stony rubbish" of our world—the man who, being caught up and possessed by the example of Christ's charity, discovers, as Christ discovered in Gethsemane, that goodness involves suffering, but who does not refuse that suffering, so profound is his compassion for his fellow creatures, his compassion being nurtured by "the conditions of life." The fact that his attempt to reenact our Lord's Passion proves unsuccessful leaves us not with the pity and terror of Greek tragedy but rather with something like the sense of judgment and forgiveness of the Gospels. For, though Scobie betrays God, the last words on his lips, as he falls to the floor after taking the poison, are: "Dear

God, I love. . . ." And the resonances of meaning and implication that have been stirred up within us by the total action persuade us that this man is himself loved and shall be forgiven in some "brave new world."

"Man has places in his heart which do not yet exist, and into them enters suffering, in order that they may have existence." So we are reminded by many of the consistencies of Mr. Greene's fiction, and also by the epigraph (from Léon Bloy) that introduces his novel of 1951, *The End of the Affair*. In this book he put aside the highly charged violence and melodramatic intensity that had been so much a part of his previous work: its scene is neither the agitated underworld of urban gangsters nor some torpid backwater of the tropics but a placid island of London suburbia, Clapham Common, against the background of which is told a tale of middle-class adultery and of a modern woman's submission to an *askésis* highly reminiscent of that *via negativa* of St. John of the Cross.

Between Henry Miles, a middle-aged civil servant, and Sarah, his attractive wife, there grew up during the first months of their marriage one of those curious misunderstandings of the flesh which, when it arises between a husband and wife, if they remain with each other afterwards, often results in their being "kind" to one another for a lifetime. This has for several years been the character of the life that Henry and Sarah have shared; but she, in her robust sensuality, has good-naturedly taken her pleasure wherever it was to be had. And so, when the writer Maurice Bendrix, in gathering material for a story, seeks to study at first hand a senior civil servant, he has little difficulty in getting "copy" from Sarah Miles, who is the wife of such a man: as their relation develops, he falls deeply in love with her and she with him, and this is the beginning of the affair.

But the novel does not begin at the beginning, but somewhere near the end, on a dark, wet January night in 1946, as Bendrix, out for a stroll in spite of the weather, sees Henry "slanting across the wide river of rain" on the Common.

Bendrix overtakes his neighbor who invites him into his study for a drink, and there the worried husband, never suspecting that Bendrix was at one time his wife's lover, confesses his fear that his wife's affections have strayed elsewhere. Many months have now passed since Bendrix and Sarah last met, prior to which they had been lovers for five years, and Bendrix had, throughout this time, been given to periodic outbursts of unjustified suspicion and jealousy: it was simply his nature not to be without fear in love. So now he is curious to discover the identity of the rival who displaced him, and, when he learns that Henry has thought of engaging a detective, he urges this course upon him: indeed, he arranges to engage the operative. But no evidence is found except Sarah's journal, to which the whole of Book III, the central section of the novel is given over.

Now we are taken back—eighteen months before—to that last night on which Bendrix and Sarah made love, during an air raid. We learn that during the raid Bendrix left Sarah and went downstairs, but on the way down a flying bomb exploded. For a few minutes afterwards he lay unconscious beneath a door. When Sarah found him, she thought him dead and refrained from touching his prone figure, lest if she took his hand "it would come away, all by itself, from under the door." Bendrix was only stunned, but Sarah, believing him to be dead, returned to his rooms, knelt down and prayed for the first time in many years to a God in whom she no longer believed: "Dear God. . . . I'll give him up forever, only let him be alive with a chance. . . ." Then Bendrix walked in, and was alive, and Sarah thought "now the agony of being without him starts," and wished that he was safely back dead again under the door.

"Now, of course, I know," Sarah states in her journal, "that this was hysteria." But, whether it was or not, it becomes the occasion for a human being—very modern, very sophisticated, very worldly in her sensibility—to begin to grope her way toward recovery of belief in God. For Sarah, whatever her weakness, is honest, and the vow must be kept, and her problem becomes that of discovering the identity of Him to whom the pledge has been made—together, indeed, with the identity of the one who made the vow.

At first Sarah feels nothing but a terrible loneliness and emptiness—in the apparently irreparable ruin of her soul's joy and happiness, nothing but a "cowardly need . . . of not being alone." Her descent is to sorrow and suffering and solitude. It is an *agonia*, an awful deprivation, a "dark night," and we are reminded of that "frontier" of which Eliot speaks in *The Family Reunion,* "beyond which safety and danger have a different meaning." The word which Sarah uses in her journal is "desert," for this is what she finds round herself, now that her relation with Bendrix has come to an end. She wonders what one can build in the desert, how one can go on living, and whether God, if one could believe in him, would fill the desert. "I have always wanted to be liked or admired," she says.

> I feel a terrible insecurity if a man turns on me, if I lose a friend, I don't even want to lose a husband. I want everything, all the time, everywhere. I'm afraid of the desert. God loves you, they say in the churches; God is everything. People who believe that don't need admiration, they don't need to sleep with a man, they feel safe. But I can't invent a belief.

And she confides to her journal that

> That's asking me to believe too much, that there's anything lovely in me. I want men to admire me, but that's a trick you learn at school—a movement of the eyes, a tone of voice, a touch of the hand on the shoulder or the head. If they think you admire them, they will admire you because of your good taste, and when they admire you, you have an illusion for a moment that there's something to admire. All my life I've tried to live in that illusion—a soothing drug that allows me to forget that I'm a bitch and a fake.

No, she decides, this God who supposedly is able to find something lovable in the bitch and the fake must himself be the sheerest fiction.

But, finally, Sarah is driven, by utter loneliness, to the threshold of faith. For, as she says in her journal, "I want somebody who'll accept the truth about me and doesn't need protection." This is an inclination which she attempts to resist, and she even begins to take instructions from an old-fashioned rationalist who preaches against Trinitarianism and Immortality on London street corners. But he only succeeds in strengthening her growing belief. He argues against the arguments for God, when she had not known there were any—"except this cowardly need . . . of not being alone." So there slowly grows in her, try as she does to smother it out, that delight which Augustine knew, the delight, that is, which is to be had in finding God by failing to find him.

Sarah begins now to sense the possibility of her affair with Bendrix having itself been a figure in the tapestry of the divine purpose. As she looks back and recalls the abandon with which they scattered themselves upon each other, in all the untidiness and disorder of their undeveloped hearts, it occurs to her that perhaps all the time *He* was there, encouraging each to give the other so much love that, when they had finished, there would be nothing left but himself. So the fallen soul embraces fatigue (as Porphyry advised), chooses the despair that has, as Kierkegaard says, "something of the eternal in its dialectic," chooses solitude, in order that it may go to the "desert,"

> to the empty land
> Which is no land, only emptiness, absence,
>   the Void,
> Where those who were men can no longer turn
>   the mind
> To distraction, delusion, escape into dream,
>   pretence,
> Where the soul is no longer deceived, for
>   there are no objects, no tones,

No colours, no forms to distract, to divert
the soul
From seeing itself, foully united forever,
nothing with nothing. . . .[14]

Sarah chooses, in other words, "the secret way," the way of
"the dark night," of which St. John says in *The Ascent of Mt.
Carmel*: "The journey of the soul to the Divine Union is called
night for three reasons: the point of departure is privation of
all desire, and complete detachment from the world: the road
is by faith, which is like night to the intellect; the goal, which
is God, is incomprehensible while we are in this life." This
is the journey that Mr. Greene's heroine undertakes: she
dares "another intensity/For a further union, a deeper communion. . . ."[15] So the end of one affair becomes for her the beginning of another.

Bendrix had, of course, expected to discover that he had
been sexually wronged, but, when he completes his reading of
Sarah's journal, the old bitterness is dispelled. Certain that
they can resume their relation, he telephones her to say that he
is coming to her immediately; but Sarah, though suffering from
acute influenza, goes out into a pouring rain to avoid him
and seeks refuge in a nearby church. Bendrix overtakes her
and persuades her to seek a dissolution of her marriage in
divorce. It turns out, though, that Sarah was not strong enough
to withstand exposure, and she dies a few days later of pneu-
monia, but not before the priest to whom she had been going
for instruction has assured her that her Registry Office marriage is valid and cannot be dissolved: Bendrix learns this from
a letter which, having been misaddressed, reaches him only
after her death.

Again, the affair would seem to be over. But after Sarah's
death Smythe, the rationalist preacher, is cured of a birthmark

[14] T. S. Eliot, *Murder in the Cathedral* (New York: Harcourt, Brace
and Co., 1935), p. 69.
[15] T. S. Eliot, "East Coker," *Four Quartets* (New York: Harcourt,
Brace and Co., 1943), p. 17.

that had disfigured his face; a book which she had owned as a child cures Parkis's little son (Parkis is the detective whom Bendrix had engaged) of appendicitis. And is a miracle wrought upon Bendrix also? There is, but it is not so visible as these more spectacular occurrences. What has happened is that suffering has brought new places into existence in his heart, though at the end of the book the transformation is by no means complete. He, of course—the sensual, agnostic sophisticate—professes to be unconvinced by these "miracles." He talks to Henry about "coincidences," such as having seen over and over again "two cars with the same figures side by side in a traffic block," despite "ten thousand possible numbers and God knows how many combinations." But his very contentiousness makes manifest his deep suspicion that in the life of this woman whom he loved supernature had invaded nature, transcendence immanence, God man. Indeed, the thought that seems most to disturb him is that "if this God exists," and if Sarah, with her lusts and her adulteries and her timid little lies, "can change like this, we could all be saints by leaping," as she leapt, "by shutting the eyes and leaping once and for all. . . . It's something He can demand of any of us." But he resists it: he sits listlessly in his rooms and says to the problematic Person:

> You've taken her but You haven't got me yet. I know Your cunning. It's You who take us up to a high place and offer us the whole universe. You're a devil. . . . But I don't want Your peace and I don't want Your love. I wanted something very simple and very easy: I wanted Sarah for a lifetime, and You took her away. With Your great schemes You ruin our happiness as a harvester ruins a mouse's nest. I hate You, God, I hate You as though You existed.

We imagine that such a one as Augustine might have said to such a man as Bendrix: "Thou couldst not hate the Lord thy God, if thou hadst not already found Him; so rejoice, then, that thou hatest Him, for, in hating Him, thou hast found Him;

and, having found Him, thou mayst, in time, by His grace, discover that thou shouldst love Him, even as He loveth thee."

In the novel of 1955, *The Quiet American,* Mr. Greene appeared to many of his critics to be forsaking the machinery of "Catholic" fiction and to be extending the range of his performance by undertaking for the first time to write within the genre of the political novel, the genre of Malraux and Silone and Koestler and Orwell and Serge. The stresses of the Cold War in the late 'forties and early 'fifties were by way of convincing him, it seemed, that the novel of politics was the form of fiction most appropriate to the contemporary scene, that indeed politics could no longer be relegated to some isolable realm of life, since the characteristic fate of man at the end of the modern age is political. But the interesting difference between Mr. Greene and a Malraux or a Koestler is that his religious radicalism leads him to force into his definition of politics not only the immediate and passing but also some of the more ultimate and permanent exigencies which men face, so that even when, as in *The Quiet American,* his scene is Saigon and war-torn Indo-China in the early 1950's, the real focus of his interest is not so much the politics of contending power-blocs as it is the politics of salvation.

The central and dominant consciousness in *The Quiet American* is that of a middle-aged British journalist, Thomas Fowler, who, having established himself among the Vietnamese and having grown to love the people and the country, has no desire to return to England, despite appeals from his paper to take on larger responsibilities at home. In Saigon, through his opium and his native girl, Phuong, he can escape the embarrassments of an unsuccessful marriage. Here, he can remain uninvolved, unengaged—not, as his fellow journalists call themselves, a correspondent but, as he insists, just a "reporter."

The ethic to which Fowler is committed is the ethic of neutralism; and yet, though his intention is to remain uncom-

mitted and not to take sides, not even with the political position which Europeans know as "neutralism," it is, paradoxically, this very attitude of mind which leads him toward the
anti-Americanism that we have come to expect from European
"neutralists." For the Americans, with their vast power and
their vast programs of good will, are, as Fowler sees them, so
irrevocably—and *innocently*—"committed" to the cause of the
angels, and their faith in the goodness of their own intentions
so induces them to a policy of meddling on a global scale, that
(if he knew it) he would be prepared to find their appropriate
Confiteor in Yeats's couplet:

> We had fed the heart on fantasies,
> The heart's grown brutal from the fare.

This is, indeed, what the American innocence comes to, as
Fowler sees it in Indo-China: it is a monstrous insensibility, a
terrible ignorance of concrete political realities, that makes
every action brutal, despite the humanitarian idealism by
which it is inspired, because it is irrelevant to actual human
need. For all of the vast amount of "commitment" by which it
is complicated, it is an innocence that involves, for him, "a kind
of insanity": thus it is that the violence with which he feels
impelled to reject it leads him, finally, to take sides and, in
effect, to betray his neutralism.

Fowler's animus becomes focused on a bright young
Harvard graduate, Alden Pyle, the "quiet American," who,
with "his gangly legs and his crew cut and his wide campus
gaze," comes over with the Economic Aid Mission, tremen-
dously "absorbed . . . in the dilemma of democracy and the
responsibilities of the West" and "determined . . . to do good,
not to any individual person, but to a country, a continent, a
world." Pyle's desire is to throw the weight of American resources behind the creation of a "Third Force," in which, he
believes, there lies the one hope of saving Indo-China from
both the French colonials and the Communists. The whole
idea is one that he has come by in the books (*The Role of the*

West, The Challenge to Democracy, etc.) of York Harding, an American publicist who once spent a week in Saigon on his way from Bangkok to Tokyo and whose views of the crisis in southeast Asia have had a great influence on Pyle. Indeed, so fully does this young man give his suffrage to Harding's abstractions that he begins to consort with the dissident brigand, General Thé, soon after his arrival, confident that in him the Third Force will have its most effective agent. He will not take the pains to discover how inconsequential, in point of fact, the general is, and in some of the book's most memorable pages Mr. Greene describes the major outcome of Pyle's intrigues— which is a bombing in the public square of Saigon that had been intended to confound a political demonstration but, being badly timed, only succeeds in killing a number of helpless natives, mostly women and children. In an unforgettable passage we are made to look at a legless torso still twitching, "like a chicken which has lost its head," and at a woman who "sat on the ground with what was left of her baby in her lap": "with a kind of modesty," we are told, "she had covered it with her straw peasant hat." As Pyle looks at the ruin, he can only say, "It's awful," and, when he looks at the blood on his shoes, he remarks that he must get a shine before he sees the Minister.

So Fowler has to conclude that "innocence is like a dumb leper who has lost his bell, wandering the world, meaning no harm. . . . You can't blame the innocent, they are always guiltless. All you can do is control them or eliminate them." It is on the latter course that he settles, arranging with Vietminh agents for Pyle's "elimination."

Now, had this novel been written a decade later, in the context of the American adventure in Vietnam under Lyndon Johnson, its anti-American spleen would doubtless be very much less nettling for readers in the United States today than it was in 1956. But, however much the recklessness of American foreign policy in the late 'sixties might lend greater relevance to the novel's polemicism than did the situation in the mid-

'fifties, the book would still represent extreme imbalance, even were it being published today and even were its chronicle of the southeast Asian imbroglio abreast of current events. For at no point does it allow any of the other characters to offer an effective challenge to Fowler: in argument, he is always permitted to push the Americans around, and every significant observation that is made of the American character is clearly pejorative in intent. Pyle, as a Harvard graduate, is said to have taken "a good degree in—well, one of those subjects Americans can take degrees in: perhaps public relations or theatrecraft. . . ." At one point Fowler, as he recalls having entered a lavatory at the American legation, is made to remark: "Even their lavatories were air-conditioned, and presently the temperate tempered air dried my tears as it dries the spit in your mouth and the seed in your body." Or, on another occasion, as one day he idly watches two American girls in a Saigon street, he thinks how impossible it is to imagine them "a prey to untidy passion," and he wonders whether they take deodorants to bed. Mr. Greene was at pains to splatter this kind of nonsense across the entire novel, for he was eager to embrace the absurd picture of American civilization that certain European intellectuals like to cling to, the picture of a civilization whose main supports are air-conditioning and deodorants and food wrapped in cellophane and an inordinate confidence in one's own virtue.

In this connection, perhaps the only response that an American reader can make is to regret that Mr. Greene dislikes us so intensely. But this is the decisive response to be made, for the novelist as novelist ought not to dislike anyone. Yet, in this particular case, that strict disinterestedness which is the seal and proof of the artist's unbroken integrity was undercut by a partisanship whose most basic roots are to be located not in any merely political considerations but, rather, in the religious position that lay behind not only this book but most of its author's most characteristic previous work. For the antithesis between Innocence (Pyle) and Experience (Fowler) that con-

stitutes the basic framework of *The Quiet American* is but an
expression, in the terms of fictional narrative, of the kind of
inverted Calvinism (!) that had previously led this Catholic
novelist—in *England Made Me*, in *Brighton Rock*, in *The
Power and the Glory*, in *The Heart of the Matter*—so frequently to divide the *dramatis personae* of his novels into those
who have been elected to the privilege of damnation and those
who have been cast aside for the reason (in T. S. Eliot's
phrase) that they "are not men enough to be damned." It is, of
course, an attitude easily caricatured, and one that the late
George Orwell was disposed so to treat; but, even allowing for
the extravagance of his lampooning and mockery, one can feel
that he had taken hold of the issue when he said that Graham
Greene seemed to suppose "that there is something rather
distingué in being damned," that "Hell is a sort of high-class
night club, entry to which is reserved for Catholics only, since
the others, the non-Catholics, are too ignorant to be held
guilty, like the beasts that perish."[16]

This dualistic approach to the problem of imagining his
characters did, indeed, over a long time create in many of Mr.
Greene's books two quite different sets of figures. On the one
hand, you have persons such as Minty in *England Made Me*
and Pinkie in *Brighton Rock* and the priest in *The Power and
the Glory* and Scobie in *The Heart of the Matter* who, however many of the reprobated vices they may be guilty of, have
at least the great thing, for their intimacy with Evil gives them
a knowledge of *the difference* between Good and Evil. And
thus they are distinguished from those representatives, on the
other hand, of modern secularity, like Ida of *Brighton Rock*
and Wilson of *The Heart of the Matter*, who merely determine
to do right and wrong. In this strange calculus, for example,
Pyle's ineligibility for damnation is proved by his very innocence, by his well intentioned clumsiness, by his open, smiling,
"unused" face: he knows only Right and Wrong, not Good and

[16] George Orwell, "The Sanctified Sinner," *New Yorker*, Vol. XXIV
(July 17, 1948), p. 61.

Evil: his humanity is too unsoiled to be taken seriously. But Fowler, on the other hand, though not a Catholic as are his predecessors in Greene's fiction, nevertheless has the great thing, for he represents not the authority of virtue and success but, with his opium-smoking and his adultery and his general fatigue, represents rather the authority of evil and failure: and we are expected to find in him a human profundity that is lacking in the young American.

It is in fact this curious rigorism in Mr. Greene that has frequently come perilously near destroying the imaginative cohesion of many of his books, for, as one critic has observed, it has often led him "to treat differently characters who are of equal importance in the structure"[17] of a given novel: he has tended to play favorites with them, falsely romanticizing some and ruthlessly taking advantage of others. Thus, over a long period, he seemed at times a somewhat odd figure—the leading Catholic novelist in the English-speaking world, to be sure, but a writer apparently bent on using his art often as a vehicle for the espousal (unconscious, no doubt) of a romantic diabolism just as perverse and morally problematic as the dandyism of *les décadents* of the late nineteenth century. But, however paradoxical such a development as this may at first seem, something like it may have been the expectable consequence of a Christian writer, for whatever reasons, permitting himself to become *obsessively* preoccupied with his religious position and the differences it establishes between himself and others. For, when this happens, then the religious position itself becomes an unconscionably tyrannical taskmaster, completely dominating the artist and devouring his sensibility: the application of a theological formula is by way of being substituted for the artist's effort to understand and re-create living

[17] Helen Gardner, "François Mauriac: 'A Woman of the Pharisees,'" in *The Penguin New Writing*, No. 31, ed. by John Lehmann (London: Penguin Books Ltd., 1947), p. 102. In this essay which is principally devoted to Mauriac, Miss Gardner also makes some very acute observations about both Graham Greene and Evelyn Waugh.

experience—and, this being the case, some sort of extreme eccentricity is bound to arise.

It is, however, a happy development in Mr. Greene's career over the past decade, that his work has in no great way been flawed by these complications. *The Quiet American* was followed in 1958 by a vivaciously comic book, *Our Man in Havana,* which is very largely given over to a charming spoof of the British Secret Service. It was followed in 1959 by the play, *The Complaisant Lover,* a London drawing-room comedy of adulterous love, in which the tangled relationship between the unpassionate middle-aged husband and his young wife and her lover is resolved, finally, into a *pas de trois* danced to a music without precedent in the world of Mr. Greene's fictions. So, at the close of the 'fifties, there were those who were at the point of concluding that perhaps he was deserting the Catholic themes by which he had been held for twenty years.

But, then, in 1961 there came a brilliant new book, *A Burnt-Out Case,* in which Mr. Greene (in his epistolary Dedication) is careful to announce his purpose as having been that of giving "dramatic expression to various types of belief, half-belief, and non-belief, in the kind of setting, removed from world-politics and household-preoccupations, where such differences are felt acutely and find expression." This setting turns out to be a remote leprosarium in the Belgian Congo. To this cheerless and sequestered place there comes an internationally famous Catholic architect named Querry, who is trying to escape his celebrity and a whole way of life that has lost its savor, not only in the ways of artistic expression but also in the ways of love and even of religious faith. He is a "burnt-out case," like those lepers "who lose everything that can be eaten away before they are cured."

His hope is that, in this distant African settlement, he may once again find a measure of peace. But Rycker, a neighboring *colon,* soon discovers Querry's identity as the world-renowned architect, and conspires with a corrupt English journalist to promote the myth of Querry as a leprophile, a kind of Schweitzer, whose desertion of his European past has been prompted by a missionary ardor. Others in the settlement, for various reasons, endorse this fabrication, so that, much to his distaste, Querry soon finds himself being converted into a legendary figure.

Yet, for all of the annoyances attendant upon his being made the center of a sort of cult, he finds some satisfaction in his new life at the leprosarium, most especially in his friendship with the physician, Dr. Colin, whose religious unbelief and whose unpretentious commitment to the relief of human suffering may put one in mind of Rieux in Camus' *La Peste*. "Sometimes," says Colin, "I think that the search for suffering and the remembrance of suffering are the only means we have to put ourselves in touch with the whole human condition." And such a search, he suggests, such a remembrance, inevitably makes us "become part of the Christian myth."

With this man Querry can have a genuinely honest relationship. But the others are bent on falsifying the reality of his life. Parkinson, the "rag" journalist, finds the prospect of good copy in the notion that Querry is a Great Sinner now doing penance for his past. It titillates Father Thomas to imagine that this distinguished architect has brought the odor of sanctity into the dreary life of his backwoods settlement. And Rycker, the ex-seminarian and spoiled priest, is determined that Querry shall be a sensational figure. None wants to allow him to be his own man, and none escapes bitterness of feeling toward him as a result of his refusal to prance to the piper's tune. Parkinson, being nettled by the mistrust with which he knows himself to be regarded by Querry, persuades Rycker that his young wife and Querry are having an affair, and, when the thing begins to be bruited about, Father Thomas immediately believes it to be true. "This is absurd," murmurs Querry, as he dies of the bullet wound inflicted by the deranged *colon* —"This is absurd or. . . ." And his meaning, presumably, is that both his life and his death are "absurd," *or*, otherwise, they make a kind of figure in the tapestry of such a design as that which is proposed either by Catholic belief or by that agnostic dedication to *la présence humaine* represented by Dr. Colin.

What one is most struck by here is the moral weight and dignity which the novel is thus implicitly proposing to accord a humanism whose inspiration is basically secular. Here, one feels that Mr. Greene is indeed scanning "new styles of architecture" that would have been unthinkable by the author of *Brighton Rock* or *The End of the Affair* or even of such a relatively late work as the play of 1957, *The Potting Shed*. And, similarly, in his most recent novel, *The Comedians* (1966), he appears, again, as one of his critics has remarked, to have "lost his old zest for attacking Pelagians."[18] In this book, for example, there is an American couple, Mr. and Mrs. Smith: Mr. Smith once ran for the Presidency on a vegetarian ticket, and now, in the course of the novel, he and his wife are settling in Haiti, that "shabby land of terror," where they intend to set up a vegetarian center. But at no point does Mr. Greene vent upon these people the kind of ruthlessly destructive irony to which he would most certainly have resorted at an earlier time: they may be small beer, but they are never patronized, and the novel even invites us to acknowledge them as having certain rather estimable qualities.

But though such evidences of a new charity and compassionateness in Mr. Greene are discernible, he has lost none of his old ability—as in his travel books, *Journey Without Maps* (1936) and *The Lawless Roads* (1939), or *The Power and the Glory*—for rendering the seediness and the horror that can be a part of the primitive and violent back-countries of the world; and the spirit of Duvalier's Haiti—its desperate intrigues and rampant savagery—is brilliantly evoked in the book of 1966.

Here, then, is the curve that describes one of the most remarkable bodies of writing in the imaginative literature of our period, a curve which runs from the early studies of mod-

[18] David Lodge, *Graham Greene* (New York: Columbia University Press, 1966), p. 43.

ern dereliction to the later studies of purgation and sanctity which (excepting the comparable work of Bernanos and Mauriac) are without parallel in the fiction of our time; and now at last this curve begins to move into a new phase in which many of the old stridencies are being muted in the interests of a larger generousness and lenience and sympathy. Indeed, the late Morton Zabel's judgment of twenty-five years ago has lost none of its earlier cogency, that Mr. Greene "has found an instrument for probing the temper and tragedy of his age, the perversions and fears that have betrayed it, and the stricken weathers of its soul."[19] Despite his proven capacity to negotiate the hazards of an art that accepts a kerygmatic responsibility, he may not yet have satisfied all our questions, particularly those which concern that rendering of religious reality which is most adequate to the demands of a mimetic fiction. But, nevertheless, he is today one of the most interesting and richly rewarding novelists using the English language: as F. R. Leavis says of Henry James, he has "*added* something as only genius can."[20]

[19] Morton Dauwen Zabel, "Graham Greene," in *Forms of Modern Fiction*, ed. by William Van O'Connor (Minneapolis: University of Minnesota Press, 1948), p. 293. Reprinted from the *Nation*, 1943.

[20] F. R. Leavis, *The Great Tradition* (London: Chatto and Windus, 1948), p. 16.

VII

Sola Gratia—The Principle of Bellow's Fiction

In January of 1956, under the auspices of the Gertrude Clarke Whittall Fund, the late R. P. Blackmur delivered four lectures at the Library of Congress on the literature of the twentieth century. As one reads the printed text of these addresses, it tickles the imagination a little to think of how baffled Mr. Blackmur's audience of housewives and students and government clerks must have been by the flailings and thrashings about of the strange kind of language to which he gave himself in his last years. The little booklet comprising these lectures which the Library published in 1956[1] affords one of many sad examples of how great a hardship the attempt at communication had come to be for this distinguished critic in the late phase of his career: these addresses are all "great general blobs," such as Blackmur claimed to find in much of Whitman's poetry, and an odd sort of vatic delirium in the style makes everything nearly altogether impenetrable. Yet, here and there, the darkness is lit up by flashes of the wit and brilliance of perception that made Blackmur over a long period one of the great princelings of modern criticism: and the

[1] *Vide* R. P. Blackmur, *Anni Mirabiles, 1921–1925: Reason in the Madness of Letters* (Washington, D.C.: Reference Department of the Library of Congress, 1956).

first of these is to be found in the very title itself which he gave to these lectures, *Anni Mirabiles,* for this is what he took the early 'twenties to have been—marvelous years, a time of great harvest in the history of the modern movement. So indeed the period was: it was a time of glory, it was a time of wonders, a time which saw the appearance in 1921 of Pirandello's *Sei personaggi* and some of Pound's most characteristic *Cantos,* in 1922 of Eliot's *The Waste Land* and Joyce's *Ulysses,* in 1923 of Wallace Stevens' *Harmonium* and Rilke's *Duino Elegies,* in 1924 of Mann's *Der Zauberberg,* in 1925 of Valéry's *M. Teste* and Kafka's *Der Prozess.* And so things went throughout the remainder of the decade—which saw, particularly on the American scene, a great efflorescence of remarkable creativity: Dreiser's *An American Tragedy* and Fitzgerald's *The Great Gatsby* in 1925, Hemingway's *The Sun Also Rises* in 1926, Wolfe's *Look Homeward, Angel* and Faulkner's *The Sound and the Fury* in 1929: wonderful years indeed.

Now it has been a habit of American criticism lately to submit the achievement of our writers in this country since World War II to various kinds of stocktaking and fretfully to speculate on the possibility of regarding the years just gone by as having also been *anni mirabiles.* The 'twenties and the early 'thirties are a golden time in American literary life which it is exhilarating to recall: but they are also years that weigh heavily upon us as a challenge, and as a challenge that constantly threatens to become a diminishing reproach, if there cannot be descried in our uncertain present the signs of a stature comparable to that splendid insurgency of forty years ago. So we are all the time taking polls and making tallies, most especially about our fiction; and when the tabulations prove sometimes to be unfavorable, the resulting dejection turns us suddenly into crestfallen obituarists of the novel: but then new polls will be taken and more tallies made, and the hope will revive of finding the present time to be as fruitful as that of Fitzgerald and Hemingway and Faulkner.

Yet, underneath the fervent encomia that are frequently

offered the contemporary scene by the hucksters of *Tendenz,*
there is a certain nettling mistrust, and a nagging intuition
that, certainly in the novel, the postwar period has not aug-
mented, has not *added* anything to the furniture of the imagination in the way that a truly great literature does. It makes
very little sense, however, to launch out into windy pontifica-
tions about the death of the novel, for a national literature only
very rarely finds writers so gifted as the Fitzgerald of *Gatsby*
and the Hemingway of *The Sun Also Rises* and the Faulkner
of *The Sound and the Fury* handling the same genre within a
single generation. Surely it would be silly to postulate the
death of a medium whose most characteristic practitioners
today are people so talented as John Barth, Bernard Malamud,
William Styron, John Hawkes, Norman Mailer, and Thomas
Pynchon. But what counts most heavily against the alarmism
of those who pronounce the novel to be dead is the simple fact
that, at least on the American scene, we have in Ralph Ellison's
novel of 1952, *Invisible Man,* one indubitably great book and
that, in the fiction of Saul Bellow, we have a body of work
whose richness in both form and idea, already while he is only
just in mid-career, promises that his will eventually become
one of the great careers in the international world of our literary life in the second half of the century.

In Mr. Bellow's case, however—and Mr. Ellison's is not
far different—critical assessment has tended frequently to miss
its mark to an astonishing extent. When Maxwell Geismar, for
example, is not searching out the "psychobiological [questions]
. . . at the base of [his] work," he is undertaking to affiliate Mr.
Bellow with "social realism" and is proposing that in such a
book as *The Victim* he is doing, in terms of lower middle-class
Jewish life in New York City, the general sort of thing that
Orwell was doing in relation to the dinginess of the *petit bourgeois* London world of *Keep the Aspidistra Flying*—or Mr.
Geismar is proposing that such a text as *Seize the Day*
presents, in relation to the drab gloom of the upper west-side
of New York, essentially the same *kind* of account that John

O'Hara or a John P. Marquand (!) presents in relation to other areas of American life. Mr. Bellow's métier, we are told, is that of "the social realism school of Dreiser . . . and of such later figures as Ira Wolfert, James T. Farrell, and Nelson Algren."[2] It is an amazing verdict, but not unlike that which has been delivered by other critics less committed in principle than Mr. Geismar to the issues of sociology and "psychobiology." A younger and more perceptive man, Marcus Klein, in a book generally marked by a very fine intelligence, has told us more recently, for example, that the problems faced by all of Mr. Bellow's characters "are reducible to a single problem: to meet with a strong sense of self the sacrifice of self demanded by social circumstance."[3] And it is a similar circle of definition which has been awkwardly flung about his work in much of the critical discussion which it has prompted in the last few years.

What is wrong, of course, in this version of things is not that Mr. Bellow's fiction is uninfluenced by any dialectical sense of the individual's relation to society: on the contrary, his books consistently reveal that the question as to how the individual needs to respond to the requirements levied by "social circumstance" is one of his most absorbing preoccupations as a novelist. Yet social circumstance never defines the ultimate dimension of selfhood in the world of *Augie March* and *Henderson* and *Herzog*: the human individual is in no way shown here to be merely an epiphenomenon of social process: personality is not imagined in ways that suggest it to be wholly immersed in a social continuum and reaching only towards a social destiny. What is in fact one of the more striking features of the fiction is that the central moments in the experience of Mr. Bellow's characters are always, as it were, moments of

[2] *Vide* Maxwell Geismar, "Saul Bellow: Novelist of the Intellectuals," in *American Moderns: From Rebellion to Conformity* (New York: Hill and Wang, 1958), pp. 210–224.

[3] Marcus Klein, *After Alienation: American Novels in Mid-Century* (Cleveland and New York: World Publishing Co., 1964), p. 34.

Existenz in which a man, transcending the immediate pressures of his external environment and the limiting conditions of the social matrix, asks himself some fundamental question about the nature of his own humanity. Thus the contemporary line to which Mr. Bellow belongs is not that tag end of American naturalists—John O'Hara, Nelson Algren, Irwin Shaw—who are committed to a dreary automatism of social reportage and who are, to be sure, convinced that there is some "sacrifice of self demanded by social circumstance." It is, rather, a line reaching from Robert Penn Warren and Faulkner back in the American past towards Mark Twain and Melville and Hawthorne, and towards the European tradition of Dostoievski and Kafka and Svevo and Sartre—the line, in other words, of modern fiction whose principal area of inquiry is the phenomenology of selfhood.

When, in the particular case of Saul Bellow, I speak of his novels as entailing an enterprise of phenomenology, it is not for language then to be too greatly stretched, for his fiction is in fact, one feels, stirred into life, fundamentally, by a certain sort of philosophical endeavor.

There comes a time, it will be recalled, in *The Adventures of Augie March* when, after having just barely managed to escape the nets flung at him by all sorts of people wanting to organize and control his life, Augie finds himself dealing with still another "Machiavellian." Having signed with the Merchant Marine after the outbreak of the War in 1941, he ships out from Boston, two days after his marriage to Stella. But on the fifteenth day out, the *Sam MacManus* is torpedoed, and, following the explosion, Augie scrambles into a lifeboat the other occupant of which is one Basteshaw, the ship's carpenter, who, with a curious pedantry, holds forth in a high-sounding kind of pompous oratory. As the two drift along over the water together, Basteshaw speaks, for example, of a former girl friend who contracted pulmonary phthisis, a condition which, as he informs Augie, "in his lecturer's tone," entails increased temperatures that "often act on the erogenous zones spectacu-

larly." Or, again, this megalomaniac—who has tried all his life
"to be as much of a Renaissance cardinal as one can under
modern conditions"—undertakes to instruct Augie on what he
calls "the reality situation" and describes how his researches in
the physiology of boredom eventuated in his learning how to
create life, to create protoplasm—some of which had been on
the *MacManus,* where he had been continuing his researches:
and, now that it floats somewhere in the ocean, he contemplates the possibility of his having initiated a new chain of
evolution. So it is that this madman's rhetoric moves on, to
ever greater peaks of extravagance and intensity, until Augie at
last thinks weariedly to himself "Why did I always have to fall
among theoreticians!" One cannot help but notice how frequently at many other points Mr. Bellow's fiction wants to express a sense of something ambiguously threatening and bale-
ful in the Idea and in those of its servants whose zeal is
unqualified and absolute. In his monologue called "Address by
Gooley MacDowell to the Hasbeens Club of Chicago,"[4] Gooley
speaks of the "dome of thought" around our heads, "as thick as
atmosphere to breathe. . . . [P]lenty are dying of good ideas.
We have them in the millions. . . . Look at us," he says, "deaf-
ened, hampered, obstructed, impeded, impaired and bowel-
glutted with wise counsel and good precept, and the more
plentiful our ideas the worse our headaches. So we ask, will
some good creature pull out the plug and ease our disgusted
hearts a little?" It is a similar note that is struck in *Seize the
Day, Henderson the Rain King,* and *Herzog.*

Yet, despite his penchant for viewing with alarm the bru-
talizing power of the intellect and the desiccating effects of
modern rationalism, Mr. Bellow is himself perhaps the out-
standing "theoretician" amongst the major novelists of our period, and his books are drenched in speculation. This is not to
say that he conceives the novel to be an essentially expository
medium or that he is a "philosophical novelist," in the usual
sense of that term, for the immediate stuff of his art is not an

[4] In *The Hudson Review,* IV (Summer 1951).

affair of those "pellets of intellection" which are the material of systematic thought: it is, rather, an affair of enormously larky and vital characters and of the interesting relationships into which they are brought with one another and with the world of the American metropolis. But these characters themselves are personages whose most fundamental interest is a "theoretical" interest, and therein, Mr. Bellow seems to feel, is the real wellspring of their humanity.

Joseph, in *Dangling Man,* commits to his journal the reflection that "We are all drawn toward the same craters of the spirit—to know what we are and what we are for, to know our purpose, to seek grace." This is indeed the gravitating passion by which Mr. Bellow's people are moved. Augie March has a great need to ferret out the "axial lines" of life—which is precisely the sovereign aspiration by which Asa Leventhal and Tommy Wilhelm and Eugene Henderson and Moses Herzog are guided. As Joseph says, "if the quest is the same, the differences in our personal histories, which hitherto meant so much to us, become of minor importance." So it makes very little difference at what point the reader enters Mr. Bellow's fiction, since, wherever he makes his way into it, what he encounters are people like the protagonist of *Seize the Day*—who is, we are told, a "visionary sort of animal. Who has to believe that he can know why he exists": what one encounters are "theoreticians" whose most passionate commitment is to a very urgent kind of *Lebensphilosophie,* to the kind of vitally *existential* "theorizing" which is a hallmark of many of the central personages in twentieth-century fiction, of Musil's Ulrich and Joyce's Stephen Dedalus, of Lawrence's Birkin and Mann's Hans Castorp, of Malraux's Hernandez and Vincent Berger, of Camus' Rieux and Penn Warren's Jack Burden.

It deserves to be stressed that the inquiry into the meaning of human existence which is carried forward by Mr. Bellow's protagonists is not, experientially, a bootless thing of abstract dialectic: it is, instead, a search which they are plunged into by the pressure of concrete circumstance, by the

wreckage of hope and the bitter taste in their own lives of in-
authenticity. One among them tells himself, on a certain crucial day of awakening, that he must undertake a great new
effort, that otherwise it is likely that his life will simply wither
away, with nothing remaining—"nothing left but junk." It is
indeed the character of rubble, of mess, of disarray, that defines
a part of what is initially problematic in the situation of Mr.
Bellow's people: they have stumbled into one or another dark
and airless pocket of the world—where confidence is broken
by piles of little disappointments, where nerves are rubbed
raw by the cheats and condescension that are suffered at the
hands of duplicitous friends and relatives, and where the spirit
is smothered by all the pledges and promises it has made and
found impossible to fulfill. "The world is too much with us, and
there has never been so much world," Mr. Bellow remarked a
few years ago in a review of Philip Roth's *Good-bye, Columbus*; and this is very much the sort of complaint one imagines
his own characters wanting weariedly to express, as they face
the human bustle and density of their drab little space amid
the great noisy, sprawling urban wilderness—which, whether
it is encountered in Chicago by an Augie March or in New York
by a Tommy Wilhelm, requires to be thought of as a "somber
city." "Hot, stony odors" rise up from subways, and traffic
seems to "come down . . . out of the sky": everything is draped
with soot, and nowhere does one hear any happy "epithala-
mium of gentle lovers." The scene or site of the novels is, in
short, where it is in Joyce's *Ulysses*, in Canetti's *Auto da Fé*, in
Dos Passos's *The Big Money*, in Graham Greene's *It's a Battlefield*—"a populous and smoky city," where one would not have
thought "death had undone so many."

The stars are capricious, and the burdens that people must
bear exact, therefore, a great expense of spirit: as a consequence, their fingernails are bitten and their eyes red-rimmed,
and they often do not feel well, suffering a sense of "conges-
tion" or extremes of fatigue, an obscure pain in the side or a
raging headache—signs that they have not done well in their

isolateness. Joseph, the young man whose diary (composed in the months during which he awaits his call-up into the army) forms Mr. Bellow's first book—the novel of 1944, *Dangling Man*—no longer takes any real delight in his devoted wife Iva: he explodes at the members of his family and picks quarrels with his friends, "storing bitterness and spite which eat like acids at [his] endowment of generosity and good will"; and, gripped by a strange "narcotic dullness," he is growing fat and slovenly, as more and more—like Beckett's Murphy—he becomes "rooted to [his] chair." Or, again, Asa Leventhal, the unheroic hero of Mr. Bellow's second novel, *The Victim* (1947), has slipped into early middle age as one who has just barely missed failure in the world of the city's job-market: he edits a small New York trade paper, but his competence at the job does not altogether allay his intermittent anxiousness about the security of his tenure. He is attentive to his brother's wife and children in the brother's absence, but grudgingly so: like the young protagonist of *Dangling Man*, he turns a dour peevishness and spleen upon his friends and is given to nursing imagined slights and insults, for he is a "bitter and suspicious" man: he often does not even trouble to answer the friendly greeting of a waitress in a restaurant, though he tells himself that he ought to be more responsive: his burly, disheveled figure presents an appearance which is "unaccommodating, impassive," and, in the oppressive heat of a New York summer, he sweats profusely and suffers headache and heart tremor and a sense of his very head being filled with the pungent odors of the city. But even more blistered by experience is Tommy Wilhelm, the protagonist of the brilliant *novella* of 1956, *Seize the Day*—a man without work and very nearly penniless; badgered for money by the wife from whom he is separated and scorned by his smug, unfeeling father; ruined in physique and going to seed in every way, yet desperately scrounging about New York for some merest foothold—a man whose throat is nearly bursting with a "great knot of ill and grief" as his "day of reckoning" approaches. And that great Tarzan of a man whom we meet in *Henderson the Rain King* (1959), for all of his millions and for all of his rude health and energy, knows how onerous it is to "lie buried in yourself" and is filled with an aching need to "burst the spirit's sleep." Indeed, not even the irrepressible little *picaro* of *The Adventures of Augie March* (1953) is untouched by the generalized *malaise* of Mr. Bellow's world, for, at every turn, he finds himself surrounded by "destiny moulders . . . and wizard evildoers, big-wheels and imposers-upon," and the city against the background of which most of his drama is played out is a place of crime and violence and suffering. The world that this fiction takes us into is of a sort to put us in mind of the old monition, "Though he believe it, no man is strong."

Yet the effect of these books is never depressive and enervating, and their *personae* are not felt, in the end, to be denizens of the Underground: indeed, I first spoke of their great vitality and—using a piece of Mr. Bellow's favorite slang—of their "larkiness": and this, curiously, is the final impression they make upon us, of being, most of them, very larky people. The sense of animation and exuberance that we are given comes, of course, in part from the buoyant language of which Mr. Bellow is so brilliantly vivacious an impresario. In many of the marvelously subtle and perspicacious essays making up his book of 1962, *The Barbarian Within*, Fr. Walter Ong, in a very profound way, is reminding us of a truism which seems frequently to have been forgotten by a generation whose most characteristic mentors in criticism have taught us to believe "that it is neither the potter who made it nor the people, real or fictional, to whose lives it is tangent, but the well wrought urn itself which counts. . . ."[5] The great preoccupation of contemporary criticism has been with *the text*, with the work of art *as such*, for it has been supposed that only by squinting at the poem or the novel as an *object* could criticism locate norms by which its discourse might become

[5] Walter J. Ong, S.J., *The Barbarian Within* (New York: Macmillan Co., 1962), p. 15.

really corrigible. But, this line of thought having long since been driven more than ragged, it is good that such a theorist as Fr. Ong should now be reminding us again of what ought never to have gone unremembered, that a work of literary art, in its most primitive reality, is something "said"—not simply an object clearly and distinctly framed in space, but a "word" spoken *by one man,* "a moment in a dialogue."[6] The "voice" of the artist is conveyed, of course—as Father Ong fully understands—through the "objective" structures of poetry and fiction and drama: which is to say that its invocations and evocations are accomplished through the artist's various "masks." But the writer's mask is not itself vocal: it is an instrument (whether of plot or scene or "point of view") whereby the voice is enabled to register interesting variations in tone and pitch and rhythm and stress, but it does not itself modify the authorial voice in the way that a mute modifies the sound of a violin[7]: so, given the primitively vocal and aural character of literary experience, it is the *voice* which is heard in a work of art that remains one of the principal realities inviting the disciplined attention of that uncommon reader whom Virginia Woolf generously called "the common reader." And it is, I want now to say, the voice that one constantly hears, and overhears, in Mr. Bellow's fiction which does in part give us so great a sense of the lively suppleness of the human reality being portrayed.

Here, for example, are the opening lines of *The Adventures of Augie March*:

> I am an American, Chicago born . . . and go at things as I have taught myself, free-style, and will make the record in my own way: first to knock, first admitted; sometimes an innocent knock, sometimes a not so innocent. But a man's character is his fate, says Heraclitus, and in the end there isn't any way to disguise the nature of the knocks by acoustical work on the door or gloving the knuckles.

[6] *Ibid.,* p. 36.
[7] The analogy is Father Ong's, though his use of it differs somewhat from mine: *ibid.,* p. 60.

These sentences, in their cascading bounce and friskiness and wit, could, by no stretch of the imagination, be thought to have come from the pen of a Hemingway or a Faulkner or a Penn Warren, or indeed from that of anyone other than Saul Bellow: the voice (though "masked" by the *persona* of the novel's hero) is unmistakably his—a voice that says, "Gee, what a funny, mysterious, surprising bloke man is, even when he's on his uppers! What shrewdness it takes to keep up with his craft and enterprise! How inspiriting it is to think that, maybe, things finally will give way—before intelligence and good humor and *esprit*: but how necessary it is that we not tell ourselves lies and that we not lose our sense of how wonderful is the gift of life!" This is the voice that one hears throughout these books, even when it is speaking of suffering and humiliation and despair; and it is, I say, this voice that makes even an Asa Leventhal or a Tommy Wilhelm somehow larky.

But what is most decisive in the shaping of character in Mr. Bellow's fiction is the resoluteness with which he refuses to allow his people merely to wriggle in their despondency and dispeace. The texture of their lives is banal and gritty, because, one imagines, this is what Mr. Bellow takes to be the general quality of life in our great metropolitan communities, and his people do therefore bear upon themselves the characteristic stigmata of the age—its *anomie*, its nostalgia, its alienation. But he will not permit them to *rest* in their distress: they carry great burdens, but Mr. Bellow's way of plotting the human story requires that they be brought to the point of attempting *dis*burdenment: though they are nagged by the "feeling of alienation," a way is prepared by which they may come to understand, as the young protagonist of *Dangling Man* says, that "we should not make a doctrine of our feeling." So the old journalist Schlossberg, in *The Victim*, says: "Choose dignity." And there comes a time when Henderson feels called upon to say sternly to himself: "Henderson, put forth effort." And Moses Herzog, for all of his "schooling in grief" and weighed down as he is by trouble, is finally brought, like Asa Leventhal,

to "a kind of recognition," that he owes the powers that created him "a human life." It is a similar *anagnorisis* towards
which the human drama tends generally to move throughout
Mr. Bellow's work.

This drama becomes explicitly a drama of reconciliation,
however, only in the late books, in *Seize the Day, Henderson
the Rain King*, and *Herzog*: in the early books grace is more a
hope than a reality. It is in *Dangling Man* that we get the most
tenuous and the most muted expression of this hope. Here, the
central figure is, of course, Joseph, a young "apprentice in
suffering and humiliation," who, at the outbreak of World War
II, gives up his job in a Chicago travel bureau to await his
draft-call. In the months that follow, he retires to the little cell
that he and his wife occupy in a rooming-house, there to become an "earnest huntsman of himself," as he anticipates "the
minor crises of the day" (". . . the maid's knock, the appearance of the postman, programs on the radio. . . .") and contemplates what may be involved in the vocation of a good
man. But he soon falters in his "retreat," and, far from becoming a happy experience of deepened self-recognition, it does
instead prove to be a sterile *cul-de-sac* in which Joseph finds
himself. increasingly defenseless before a strangely disabling
inertia that settles down upon him: his predicament begins,
paradoxically, to be that of a man *trapped*—in his freedom.
And he is quite free: Iva, his wife, earns their living: so he is
free of any formal daily appointments; and, keeping his distance from friends and family (except for an occasional encounter), he is free of virtually all human involvements. But
his solitude is not a rich and fecund thing, but something arid
and debilitating: as he admits in his diary, "I have begun to
notice that the more active the rest of the world becomes, the
more slowly I move. . . . I grow rooted to my chair." Though,
as he says, "I am unwilling to admit that I do not know how to
use my freedom," the fact is, nevertheless, that, day after day,
as he sits in his room, rooted to his chair and anticipating the
minor crises of the day, his freedom becomes a cheerless void

—in which this descendant of Dostoievski's Underground Man and Goncharov's Oblomov and Svevo's Zeno simply dangles. He is jailed in the prison of his own ego, and, thus doubled back upon himself, it is no wonder that "bitterness and spite" corrode his "endowment of generosity and good will." He thinks that the end of all our striving, that the goal towards which man perennially has to struggle, is "pure freedom." But, at last, soured as his life is in the acedia of its isolation, he cannot put aside the realization that, if indeed it is freedom which is the proper goal of man, this must surely be a freedom *from* precisely that into which he has too deeply entered— namely, one's own private selfhood. The self needs somehow to escape its own cage, to avoid being "humped protectively" over its own life. He is forced, in short, to admit: "I had not done well alone." Thus, in its stress on the need for self-tran-scendence, the book takes a step towards what were to be the principal emphases of Mr. Bellow's later fiction. But it is only the merest step, for Joseph's illumination issues in nothing more than a hastily written note to his draft board requesting that he be called up "at the earliest possible moment." On his last civilian day, as Iva is packing his things, he inwardly exults at being now "in other hands": "Hurray for regular hours! And for the supervision of the spirit! Long live regimentation!" But not even the manifest irony with which these final lines are carefully fringed can quite obscure the paltriness of the Army as a redemptive principle, in the kind of spiritual context which Mr. Bellow's narrative so brilliantly establishes. So his book of 1944 strikes us as making a testimony which is, finally, too provisional, and as thus lacking an ultimate cogency. But, in the degree to which it finds its center in a "theoretician" whose great hope is for a new "colony of the spirit," it can now be seen to have been presaging the main course of Mr. Bellow's later fiction.

His second novel, *The Victim* (1947), is no less provi-sional and indecisive, in its embrace of a cathartic principle, than *Dangling Man*. But Mr. Bellow here implicates his protagonist, Asa Leventhal—like Joseph, a "theoretician" who hovers over "craters of the spirit"—in a complex structure of human actions and relationships which requires him to do something more than merely engage in a continuous self-interrogation. But he is by no means exempted from the embarrassments of self-arraignment. For one hot summer evening, in a little neighborhood park near his New York apartment-building, he is suddenly approached by a shabby bystander whom, with some exertion of memory, he recognizes as a man he had known very slightly a few years earlier, Kirby Allbee. Allbee was then working on the staff of a trade magazine, and he had arranged for Leventhal, who was unemployed at the time, to be interviewed by his editor. The interview went badly, with Asa responding irately to the provocative boorishness of Rudiger, and the anger of these exchanges did in fact lead the editor not only to throw Leventhal out of his office but even to fire Allbee for having proposed the meeting. Now Allbee, meeting Leventhal for the first time in several years, accuses him of bearing the real responsibility not only for his dismissal from *Dill's Weekly* but also for his subsequent decline, irreversibly, into failure and hand-to-mouth impoverishment. Indeed, Allbee charges Leventhal—to Asa's utter astonishment —with having deliberately undertaken, on the day of that interview, to ruin him, in retaliation for some outburst of anti-Semitism that he had delivered himself of at a party a few nights earlier and that he knows Leventhal to have overheard. It is a strange indictment in response to which Leventhal can only splutter out confusedly: "I haven't thought about you in years, frankly. . . . What, are we related?" And, laughing surlily, Allbee answers, "By blood? No, no . . . heavens!"

But how, then, are they related? This is the issue which the novel wants to explore. Here is a New York Jew—an obscure functionary in the great machine of the city's business— living a careful, conventional, apparently irreproachable life. Then, all of a sudden—like the abrupt appearance of Joseph K.'s accuser at the beginning of Kafka's *Der Prozess*—a paranoiac anti-Semite accosts him and bitterly complains of the injury that he has suffered at Leventhal's hands. Nor do matters end there. For in his wife's absence—Mary is helping her recently widowed mother move from Baltimore to Charleston—his self-declared victim, claiming no longer to have shelter, invades his flat, soiling it with his personal filth, upsetting the normal routines of Leventhal's tidy life, secretly ransacking personal papers to take possession even of the intimacies of Asa's marriage, and finally taking over his very bed to couple with a woman whom he brings in from the streets. Strangely, Leventhal acquiesces in all this outrageous plunderage. For the force of Allbee's reiterated accusations unsettles him to the point of compelling him to look back into the past. As he inquires into his own motives and solicits the judgments of friends who were privy to the circumstances of a few years ago which Allbee has now called up, he does indeed begin to feel that perhaps this man is not, as he first claims, solely responsible for his own misfortune, that perhaps he, Asa, has himself in some measure contributed to it: this uncouth paranoiac is not wholly right in all his furious allegations, but then he may not be wholly wrong—and, once he begins inwardly to make this admission, Leventhal's defenses against his adversary are effectively broken, and he is entrained towards discovering the true meaning of his own humanity.

In what ways are we really members one of another? If we shoot a bird, do we wound ourselves? How is a man related to his neighbor? What is the full meaning of responsibility? These are the questions that bristle before this perplexed defendant. At first he wants simply to say: "Why pick on me? I didn't set this up any more than you did. Admittedly there was a wrong, a general wrong." But Allbee will not let him off the hook and persists in saying *You! . . . You! . . . You!*

One Sunday afternoon, as Leventhal sits in a restaurant with a group of friends, he listens to the wise old journalist, Schlossberg, reflecting on the difficult equilibrium that man's nature requires him to seek. "It's bad to be less than human and it's bad to be more than human." And there comes a time when Leventhal's conscience begins to enforce upon him the hard truth that to be "human" is indeed to be "accountable in spite of many weaknesses," is to be in fact one's brother's keeper. But is there, then, a point beyond which the keeping of one's brother becomes more than human? So it would seem. For on a certain night Leventhal wakens to find gas pouring out of his kitchen oven: in an attempt at suicide Allbee would have murdered him as well, so he throws him out; further to temporize with this unhappy creature would be both more *and* less than human.

Then, a few years later, Leventhal (now solidly success-ful) and his wife are in a theatre one evening where, after the second curtain, by chance they meet Allbee in the lobby. This final episode is curiously tentative and indistinct. Though Allbee, having apparently made some sort of recovery, is ele-gantly dressed and squiring about a once famous actress, Leventhal, as he faces him, is given a sense of decay. Although Allbee, as he recalls that earlier period in his life, faces Leven-thal shamefacedly and with self-mockery, he yet manages to say, as he presses Asa's hand, "I know I owe you something." And so he does: but each is in the other's debt. For it was through Allbee's demoniac agency that Leventhal was brought to a "kind of recognition"—that we cannot choose whom to love, that we are required to love all homeless men who re-quire to be sheltered under our care, lest

> . . . we make a scarecrow of the day,
> Loose ends and jumble of our common world,
> And stuff and nonsense of our own free will. . . .

So the initial phase of Mr. Bellow's fiction may be consid-ered to form a movement from the stiflingly solipsistic atmos-phere of a first novel, marked by the modish isolationism of the modern *avant-garde*, towards a substantially greater positivity of affirmation—that "No man is an Iland, intire of it selfe. . . ."

Thus the way had already been prepared, really, for the

magnificent book which he published in 1953, *The Adventures of Augie March.* In his *New Republic* review of *Augie,* Robert Penn Warren remarked the extent to which Mr. Bellow's essay in "the apparent formlessness of the autobiographical-picaresque novel" in the book of 1953 represented a radical departure from "the Flaubert-James tradition" which he had turned to such brilliant account in his first two novels. This turning did, undoubtedly, at the time, give the public an astonished sense of a certain melodramatism in Mr. Bellow's career as a writer, for the tightness of structure and muteness of style characteristic of his early work seemed in no way to have presaged the pyrotechnical extravagance of language and narrative procedure marking *The Adventures of Augie March*: in 1953, it appeared to be the most surprising development in the literary life of the period. But, startling as the changes were that Mr. Bellow was negotiating in the basic style of his artistry, it may be that they would not have been quite so startling had *The Victim* been read more closely, for the moral meaning of that book might well have been taken, logically, to entail an inevitable turning towards a more open form.

Unlike the Joseph of *Dangling Man,* who is drawn into himself and who, as a consequence, is hard and inflexible, Augie is a tractable and resilient young man endowed not with "singleness of purpose" but with an unquenchable hospitality toward experience. Thus he "circles"—uncommittedly, and believing that "gods [may] turn up anywhere"—from managing a sport-goods shop in Evanston to training an eagle for iguana-hunting in Mexico, from running a Chicago coalyard to consorting with Trotsky's lieutenants in Mexico City, from vagabondage in Detroit to black-market operations in Paris, from Depression poverty to post-World War II affluence. He is an ebullient *picaro* in search of a fate which he can regard as worthy of his natural endowments, and it is his insatiable appetite for adventure which gives the novel its huge expansiveness, causing it to span continents and generations and to make room for nearly a hundred personages, altogether re-

markable in their vital eccentricity and vividness of presence.
Many years ago, in discussing Theodore Dreiser, Mr. Bellow
expressed admiration for Dreiser's great "lifting power," for his
ability to make his fiction "lift up" great masses of human
actuality, of American experience, of social fact. It is a similar
"lifting power" that helps to make *The Adventures of Augie
March* so impressive a feat of the novelistic imagination: it
notices and names and evokes and gathers in so rich an
abundance of material that its teeming world seems barely
once removed from the existential reality of the modern world
itself. Mr. Bellow says: "The great pleasure of the book was
that it came easily. All I had to do was be there with buckets
to catch it." This is indeed the impression that the novel makes
upon us—this sense of a beautifully easy improvisation being,
however (as Penn Warren reminded us in his review of the
book), "a dramatic illusion . . . [which is] the last sophistication of the writer. . . ."

But, though Augie never finds that which he can confi-
dently accept as "a worthwhile fate," he keeps the "opposition"
that old Einhorn in Chicago discovered in him as a boy. For all
of the pliancy which permits him to play the games of so many
different people (the young book-thief, Padilla; the trade-
unionist, Grammick; the unbalanced millionaire and research-
ist on the "history of human happiness," Robey; the Trotskyite
Frazer; the Armenian lawyer and black-marketeer, Mintou-
chian), there comes a point when he must always "offer resistance and . . . say 'No!'" to those who want to manage and
manipulate his life—whether it be to his brother Simon, who
wants him to make money and become a big wheel; or to the
Renlings, who want him to be their adopted son and heir; or to
Thea Fenchel, who asks a self-dedication to her special sort of
underworld; or to the various others under whose influence he
is brought by the adventures of life. Thus it is that the persistent rhythm of the book is (as the English critic Tony Tanner
has acutely observed) "a drifting into things finally stopped by
a sudden digging in of the heels or a sudden flight from at-

tachment,"[8] for Augie does not want, as he says, to be "sucked into . . . [any] of those . . . currents where I can't be myself." It is as Einhorn says: 'You've got *opposition* in you. You don't slide through everything. You just make it look so." Clem Tambow tells Augie that he "can't adjust to the reality situation," and to this he is not inclined to offer any rebuttal, for he knows himself to be one who wants "to have a charge counter to the central magnetic one and dance his own dance on the periphery."

So Augie always has "trouble being still" and never has "any place of rest"—and this is why, I suspect, the novel over which he presides lacks any true conclusion. Yet this young "American, Chicago born," wants always very much to find a way of being still, since his great hope, as he says, "is based upon getting to be still so that the axial lines can be found." This, to be sure, is his most basic passion (as it is of all those "theoreticians" whom Mr. Bellow elects to a pivotal position in his books), finding the "axial lines" of life. But though, by the end, there is no evidence of Augie's having ever really found this lambent center of gravity, he persists, nevertheless, in his refusal to "live a disappointed life": as he says on the final page of the novel, with his characteristic insouciance, "I may well be a flop at this line of endeavor. Columbus too thought he was a flop, probably, when they sent him back in chains. Which didn't prove there was no America." Yet, finally, Augie has at least won through to the crucial insight that leads directly into the remarkable novels of Mr. Bellow's maturity— that, as he says, "When striving stops, there they are [i.e., the "axial lines"] as a gift."

Now it is just here that we are brought to what begins indeed to seem *the* axial line of Mr. Bellow's whole vision of the world, most particularly as it is expressed in the late books, in *Seize the Day* (1956), *Henderson the Rain King* (1959), and *Herzog* (1964)—that, when striving stops, there it is, the

[8] Tony Tanner, *Saul Bellow* (Edinburgh: Oliver and Boyd, 1965), p. 48.

infinitely poignant fullness and beauty of the very miracle of life itself. It begins to appear, in other words, that·what we confront in this whole body of fiction is a radically religious perspective on the human reality. For though Mr. Bellow's protagonist is, characteristically, like Joseph in *Dangling Man,* a "creature of plans" and projects, the recognition that he has ultimately to achieve, particularly in the late novels, is that his plans and projects must at last yield before those tidal rhythms of life which ordain (as it is put in one of the Anglican Prayer-book's most famous Collects) that "in returning and rest we shall be saved, in quietness and in confidence shall be our strength," and that we shall be brought by the Spirit to that Presence "where we may be still. . . ."

"Damn braces, bless relaxes," says a wise half-truth of William Blake's ("half," because, in certain areas of experience, it may be equally important to make the converse testimony). And it is a similar thing that, increasingly, Saul Bellow is also wanting to say, that there is a certain ultimate dimension in the life of the human spirit in which strenuousness is of no real avail; that true sanity of mind and heart is not won by grabbing at life, by jamming our barns full and packing our banks tight;[9] that moving about the world "with clenched fists even though we keep them in our pockets"[10] does not lead to abundance of life; that *fullness* of life cannot be accumulated "like bank notes or garments"[11]; that the kleptomania which prompts us to fill "our little backyards with all kinds of things"[12] which strenuousness can lay hands on only makes our last state worse than the first; and that, therefore, we must not "force the saw, flail the wind, beat the waves, uproot the

[9] *Vide* Samuel H. Miller, *The Great Realities* (New York: Harper & Bros., 1955), p. 162. The quotations from this book which are cited in the four footnotes immediately following acknowledge my indebtedness to the language of one of the most beautifully written and brilliantly original essays in ascetical theology of our time.

[10] *Ibid.,* p. 160.

[11] *Ibid.,* p. 164.

[12] *Ibid.,* p. 162.

seed"[13]: for, when striving stops, there it all is, as a gift—of Grace.

In my citation of the Anglican Collect for Quiet Confidence and in my use of Martin Luther's famous formula—*sola gratia*—in the title of this essay, I will perhaps appear to be wanting to bring the design of Mr. Bellow's thought into the ambiance of things that are distinctively Christian. But to attempt this would surely be an error in tact and in definition, for the ethos of his fiction is, of course, manifestly drenched in the life and lore of Jewish experience. And one suspects, indeed, that Bellow's great sympathy for something like a doctrine of *sola gratia* is a consequence of his having been influenced at some very deep level of his mind and sensibility, by the Hasidic strain of Jewish spirituality. But the essential thrust that I am here remarking need not be given any "denominational" tag at all, really. For it can be taken to be a "natural law" governing the life-world of the *homo religiosus*, that (as Simone Weil phrased it) "by pulling at the bunch, we make all the grapes fall to the ground,"[14] and that the way into Truth and Felicity is therefore (to change the metaphor) the way of "letting oneself fall"—like "the first flight of a baby eagle, pushed out of the nest by its parents, and then discovering to its amazement that the invisible ocean of light in which it is dropping is capable of bearing it up."[15] In the life that is lived at the Center of life there is no straining, no muscular effort, but only a certain kind of strict attentiveness and (as Gabriel Marcel terms it) *invocation*: there, at the Center, we consent to take our hands off our lives and simply to wait—for the stroke of Grace: it is something like this which is said in the *Bhagavad-Gita* and by Lao-Tse, in the Hasidism of the Baal-Shem-Tov and by Meister Eckhart. "Damn braces, bless

---

[13] *Ibid.*, pp. 164–165.

[14] Simone Weil, *Gravity and Grace*, trans. Arthur Wills (New York: G. P. Putnam's Sons, 1952), p. 171.

[15] Karl Heim, *The Transformation of the Scientific World View* (London: S.C.M. Press, 1951), p. 167.

relaxes." And it is also a kind of *falling*-into Peace which seems to be the essential reality being dramatized in the late work of Saul Bellow.

It is perhaps in *Henderson the Rain King* that this salient principle of Mr. Bellow's fiction finds its clearest rendering, though it is their inattentiveness to its presence in *Seize the Day* which has, I suspect, led many of his critics to be so baffled, finally, by that brilliant *novella*. Mr. Bellow tells us that "shoulders are from God and burdens too," and the harried protagonist of *Seize the Day*, Tommy Wilhelm, seems to have received more than his share of God's largesse. This ex-actor and ex-salesman is unemployed and, having fallen behind in the world's rat-race, at forty-seven years of age is without any hopeful prospect at all: he is down to his last seven hundred dollars, and the wife from whom he is separated is brutally pressing in her insistence upon absolute promptness in his rendering of the support-payments: nor will the cold little Philistine who is his father—a formerly distinguished physician now living in comfortable retirement—assist him in any way at all, not even with the cheap help of words of encouragement. In addition to all the external disarray in Tommy's life, he is himself, despite desperate attempts to keep up appearances, fast going to seed, his body spoiled with fat and broken-windedness, with neurotic over-eating and phenobarbital.

Indeed, the day which is recorded in Mr. Bellow's narrative is the "day of reckoning" that has rapidly been drawing near: "a huge trouble long presaged but till now formless was due." "I'm so choked up and congested . . . I can't see straight," Tommy moans, as he contemplates the wreckage of his foundered life and grows terrified by the thought that he may even have thrown away his last seven hundred dollars, in permitting the self-declared psychologist, Dr. Tamkin, to manage his money in stock-market speculations. Nor does this surmise prove to be amiss, for, when he goes in search of the wily little confidence-man ("full of high sentence" about "seizing the day"), he finds that he has absconded. It is as he is chasing

by religious scruples from removing the frogs, though they believe the frogs are contaminating the water: they think they are suffering a plague sent by the gods. So Henderson determines to come to their assistance—but, in attempting to explode the frogs out of the water, he blows up the cistern as well. Having visited this disaster upon the Arnewi, he must then, of course, leave. But, before his short stay among them is thus concluded, he has an interview with Willatale, the old lady who with an impressive dignity presides over these people as their Queen. This interview brings him a great solacing comfort, because of what he feels to be the sensitive penetration with which the Queen perceives his heart's deepest aspiration, when she says to him, "Grun-tu-molani"—which means "Man want to live."

Henderson's most crucial encounter, though, is with the Wariri—who are, as his guide Romilayu tells him, "chillen dahkness," and indeed their rites and manners are cruder, are very much more savage and violent, than those of the Arnewi. But their King, Dahfu, is a man of great gentleness and sophistication who makes Henderson feel immediately "that we could approach ultimates together." And so they do. For, after Henderson survives certain initial tests, Dahfu, with great patience, undertakes his education in the things of the spirit. "Granted, grun-tu-molani is much," says Dahfu, "but it is not alone sufficient. Mr. Henderson, more is required." And it is the additional virtues which he wants his American friend to have. So he prescribes a most exigent discipline. It involves a daily descent into the den of a lion which Dahfu has himself trapped and tamed and which he keeps in an underground vault beneath his palace. Henderson is "all limitation . . . contracted and cramped"—"self-recoiled"—and Dahfu perceives that this man who has all his life inwardly cried, "I want, I want, I want," must be taught how to relax. His way of doing this involves his requiring Henderson each day to draw nearer and nearer to the lion, and finally to romp about the den on all fours, roaring and snarling as loudly as his lungs will permit.

Thus it is that Dahfu takes Henderson to "the bottom of things," being certain that if his American visitor can learn, like the lion, "not [to] take issue with the inherent" and to relax, his fear will be overcome and his "consciousness [will be made] to shine": his excessive "ego-emphasis" will be mitigated, will be "loosened up"—and then he can move into the profound peace that comes when a man is no longer glued to his own finitude but when, having learned to submit to Being-itself, he can be claimed by a waft of Grace and delivered into perfect felicity. "Damn braces, bless relaxes": this is what Dahfu wants to say to his pupil. And, indeed, Henderson's last state is better than the first, for the importunate voice within —"I want, I want, I want"—has been stilled: at the end, when the plane on which he is bound for New York stops at Newfoundland for fuel and he gets out to leap about "over the pure white lining of the gray Arctic silence," he is a man whose spirit's sleep has been pierced; no longer does he need to *rush* through the world in the old way, for he has broken out of the cycle of *becoming* and into the realm of *being*—because, back there, with Dahfu, he became (in Rilke's phrase) a "deeply kneeling man."

Here, of course, one feels that Mr. Bellow's eagerness to enunciate a principle of redemption released an allegorical passion so rampant as very nearly to have overwhelmed altogether his commitment to the novel as a form; and, in retrospect, it seems that the exuberant sportiveness of the language in which the book is written and the rich inventiveness with which scene and incident are created may have produced the illusion of novelistic structures which in fact have been virtually suspended. Yet, if Henderson—with his size-22 collar and his enormous bulk and his aching teeth and his pig farm and his two wives and all his millions—is more a presence than a man, he is certainly the most memorable comic presence in recent fiction. And though his outrageous shenanigans and buffoonery sometimes come close to parodying Mr. Bellow's deeper meanings, this writer's *deepest* meaning may well be that the kind of nonchalance about itself which is expressed in self-parody can easily be afforded by a humanity whose "ego-emphasis" has been "loosened up" by the realization that the gift of life is to be had only "when striving stops."

Mr. Bellow's brilliant book of 1964, *Herzog*, carries forward the basic design of his thought, morally and religiously—though, here, it is expressed far more with the extremely subtle indirection characteristic of *Seize the Day* than with the allegorical simplicity of *Henderson*. Moses Herzog is a forty-three-year-old Canadian Jew whose life has largely been spent (sometimes) in the midst of and (sometimes) on the fringes of academic circles in Chicago and New York. He is an intellectual historian specializing in the Romantic movement, and his book, *Romanticism and Christianity*, though it never made a great splash, had, at the time of its appearance, established him as a young scholar of considerable originality and promise. But Herzog, bearing as he does a "great bone-breaking burden of selfhood," lacks some necessary gift for success. As the novel opens, his life appears very nearly to have collapsed into utter failure: he is without any academic portfolio; he has squandered a patrimony of twenty thousand dollars on the unredeemable dilapidation of an isolated country house in the Berkshires; he has been cuckolded by his best friend and deserted by Madeleine, the beautiful and malevolent bitch whom he forsook his first wife Daisy to marry; and his scholarly researches on Romanticism have reached an impasse, so that he has virtually given up his work on the book in progress. Indeed, the pressures of life have taken so heavy a toll that "some people thought he was cracked and for a time he himself had doubted that he was all there."

But then, at what seems to be the end of his tether, he begins to write letters—which are never posted—to his former mistresses and to General Eisenhower, to professional rivals and to his dead mother, to Adlai Stevenson and Martin Heidegger, to his first wife and to Friedrich Nietzsche, to contemporary British physicists and to Russian intellectuals of the nineteenth century, and "to everyone under the sun," even to God himself. Through this discipline of letter-writing—and through the recollection of the past and the sorting out of his experience that this discipline entails—Herzog undertakes to gather up and re-order the scattered fragments of his life. The novel very largely consists of these letters—marvelously en-grafted to the basic dramatic design—and of a plethora of flashbacks which gradually unfold the entire history of this man, by means of a *montage* whose execution is a beautifully dazzling feat of narration.

Now what is so engaging about this erratic and charming scapegrace, this representative mid-century "anti-hero," who takes a vain satisfaction in his slightly faded handsomeness and who is so unadept at fending for himself in the rough and tumble of the world—what is so engaging about him is that, as he stands amidst the debris of his imprudent life, though he has constantly to resist the invading pressures of madness, he steadfastly refuses the "foolish dreariness" of "the Wasteland outlook." He has had his "schooling in grief," but he will not "tout" the Void; and he knows enough about the whole Ro-mantic experiment to understand that the modern fascination with the "'florid extremism" of Crisis and Alienation leads nowhere but into what is only another blind alley. For all of his failures as scholar and lover and husband and father, he has no desire to contract out of history: so the "transcendence" that beckons for him is that which he finds the philosopher Jean Wahl to be calling "transcendence downwards": our job, in other words, is not to get outside of life but to find within the human situation itself a redemptive center and a healing grace.

It is after his final confrontation with Madeleine that Moses begins to find a new steadiness and serenity. He is suddenly one day stirred by his love for his little daughter, and he takes a plane from New York to Chicago, in order to pay her a visit. A friend arranges with Madeleine for him to spend an afternoon with the child. All goes well until, as he is return-

ing June to her mother in a rented car, he becomes involved
with another motorist in a minor collision. Since—for reasons
which are fully explained—he happens to have an unregistered
revolver on his person, the policemen who come to the scene
are required to "book" him: so June has to accompany him to
the precinct station. After she has come for the child, as he
faces his wife's motiveless malignity and rage, he slowly begins
really to see that the brutal violence of this destructive woman
has about it "a fringe of insanity." Yet the very fire of her
pointless malevolence has a certain purgative effect, for it
elicits from him an inward act of rejection. He knows that he
owes the powers that created him "a human life," and he
makes us feel the dawning realization in himself that living "a
human life" involves, however quietly and unobtrusively, the
making of a sort of testimony—not to apocalypse and crisis
and alienation, but in behalf of the "ordinary middling human
considerations." So he goes back to his house in the Berkshires,
there at last to bring his letter-writing to an end and, like
Candide, to begin to cultivate his garden, with the beautiful
Castilian Ramona Donsell, a successful New York business-
woman, who adores him and for whose robust sensuality and
delicious Shrimp Arnaud he has a fine appetite.

But, though Bellow's story is a story of salvation and of
Paradise Regained and though Herzog's letters are dense with
a very sophisticated kind of commentary on the lore and ideology of modern intellectual life (recalling in this respect the
Mann of *Der Zauberberg* and *Doktor Faustus*), the novel is in
no way a solemn morality. It is drenched in a fun and light-
heartedness and wit which have that very Jewish sort of
bounce and rhythm by which *The Adventures of Augie March*
is so noticeably marked. The gaiety and playfulness that give
raciness to Mr. Bellow's language and *élan* to his deployment
of character and situation are a part of what is substantive in
his message: he wants to convey a most stringent judgment of
that *Angst*-ridden mentality which has for so long been our
fashionable mode of seriousness, and he wants to suggest that

there is healing in laughter. Indeed, the comedy of *Herzog* is a comedy of redemption, and of a redemption whose catalyst is of the same sort as that which initiates the process of restoration in Mr. Bellow's earlier books—namely, the quitting of anxiety, of stress, of struggle. For Moses begins to hear "indefinite music within" and to be on his way towards blessedness once he decides "to surrender the hyperactivity of this hyperactive face. . . . just to put it out instead to the radiance of the sun." Then it is that a new peace settles over the novel, as he, in the final chapter—now back at his property in the Berkshires —begins to paint a piano for little June and walks quietly in the woods and makes arrangements with a local cleaning woman to put his house in order. "Whatever had come over him during these last months, the spell really seemed to be passing, really going." Indeed, the time even comes when he gives up his letter-writing. "Yes, that was what was coming, in fact. The knowledge that he was done with those letters." For, now "feeling that he was easily contained by everything about him," he has "no messages for anyone else. . . . Not a single word." By returning and rest and quietness, he is brought—by Grace—into a new domain of the spirit, where it is good to be, since here (as St. Bernard says) a man

> . . . . vivit purius,
> Cadit rarius, surgit velocius, incedit cautius,
> Quiescit securius, moritur felicius,
> Purgatur citius, proemiatur copiosius.

Perhaps as a result in part of influences exerted on the English scene by F. R. Leavis and on the American scene by Lionel Trilling, there is a strange and clumsy usage that contemporary criticism has fallen into, of naming the writer a "moralist" who handles the art of fiction in such a way as to advance a serious comment on the meaning of human existence. So much has this designation come to be a part of our critical lexicon that I am almost now at the point of so denominating Saul Bellow. But *Webster's New International Dictionary of the English Language* tells us that a moralist is "one who moralizes; a teacher or student of morals; a writer seeking to inculcate moral duties." This is the exact meaning of the term, and so it should be used, if it is to be used scrupulously. But though the novelist is no doubt in some sense a "student of morals"—in the sense, however, not of "ideals" but of the actualities of human behavior—neither Mr. Bellow nor indeed any serious artist in fiction undertakes to "moralize" or "to inculcate moral duties." Such may be in part the job of a priest or a spiritual director, but it is not the job of the novelist. In fact—in the passage that I quoted earlier on from his monologue called "Address by Gooley MacDowell to the Hasbeens Club of Chicago"—Mr. Bellow has already recorded his belief that today we suffer from a surfeit of "wise counsel and good precept"; and thereby he has very clearly forsworn for himself the role of "moralist."

So it is not by any such term as this that we shall properly express our sense of the weight and dignity of his achievement. What needs rather to be said, I think, is that that weight and dignity reside not in his enactment of the role of moralist but in the profundity with which his fiction negotiates (in Kierkegaard's phrase) a "teleological suspension of the ethical." What is substantive in his art is not, in other words, primarily to be located in the dimension of morality at all: it is, rather, to be found in the more ultimate dimension in which we search for what ought to be the fundamental orientation or posture of the human spirit towards reality. Here, in this dimension of things, Bellow's deepest engagement, as I have been attempting to suggest, appears to be with the mystery of what in Christian theology is called *Justification* (*through*-faith, *by*-Grace-alone), or of what Hebraic spirituality comprehends in its concept of *teshubah* (the "turning" of the self, in quietness and humility, away from self-sufficient "striving" towards the mysterious reality of Grace). The daily *Tahanun* of the Jew's morning prayer says: "Our Father, our King, be gracious unto us and answer

us, for we have no works. . . . Save us according to thy grace."
And, despite its independence of any explicitly theistic position, it is, nevertheless, in some such direction as this that Mr.
Bellow's fiction moves. His novels do not exhibit, to be sure,
the kind of manifest indebtedness to a special dogmatic tradition that marks the fiction of a Bernanos or a Graham Greene;
but they are not thereby prevented from forming, as they do,
one of the most profoundly religious renderings of experience
in the literature of our time.

VIII

Flannery O'Connor's Testimony:
The Pressure of Glory

In many of his books of recent years, the historian of religion, Mircea Eliade, has been contending (as he says at one point in *Birth and Rebirth*[1]) that "modern man's originality, his new-ness in comparison with traditional societies, lies precisely . . . in his wish to live in a basically desacralized cosmos." For Professor Eliade, the *désacralisé* represents that style which human life takes on, when a decision is made to situate all value and aspiration within the dimension of the *profane* and when Transcendence is conceived to be a chimerical superstition of the pre-scientific imagination. Desacralization, in other words, as a kind of mutation in cultural history, entails something vastly more profound than the mere collapse of formal theistic religion. For the *désacralisé* cuts deeper than anything that might be said to be an affair of "ideology," and it involves that total secularization of consciousness which is distinguished by an inability to descry any reality in the world that evokes a sense of ultimacy or of radical significance.

The man whose sense of reality has been formed by the "advanced" culture of a profane society has lost, or is by way of losing, God: but, more basically, he is a man whose life is

[1] Mircea Eliade, *Birth and Rebirth,* tr. by Willard R. Trask (New York: Harper & Row, 1958), p. 9.

267

lived at a great distance from the Sacred. Indeed, like the hero of Hemingway's *A Farewell to Arms,* his first impulse is to be even a little embarrassed "by the [very] words sacred, glorious. . . ." For his experience is without any numinous "thresholds": he does not live on "the borderland of a something more."[2] His time is not intersected by any dimension of Eternity. Nature is untouched by Supernature; the threshold of the Holy is gone—and maybe (if we are to believe the sociology of what is called "depersonalization") even the "thresholds" that we are given by our relations with other persons, maybe even these are lost.

The English philosopher Ernest Gellner, in a brilliantly crotchety critique of Linguistic Analysis, says that, though this is a philosophic movement which "often considers the pursuit of world-views to be *the* cardinal sin of thought,"[3] it yet does itself in fact have a view of the world—a view of the world which is statable in such a proposition as "The world is what it is" or "Things are as they are," or, as it was put in the proposition by Bishop Butler which G. E. Moore took over as a kind of motto of his own philosophy: "Everything is what it is and not another thing." It is precisely such a banalization of reality as this that is the end-result of radical profanization: the world is experienced as silent and is conceived to be merely what it is, and not another thing. *All* the numinous thresholds of experience are lost: everything is *leveled* and (as a consequence) "platitudinized," so that man himself loses his substantial reality and becomes a creature filled with the kind of porousness that characterizes so many of the images of contemporary sculpture—"full of holes and gaps, faceless, riddled with doubts and negations, starkly finite."[4]

Nor should it be supposed that reflection upon the pe-

[2] Philip Wheelwright, *The Burning Fountain: A Study in the Language of Symbolism* (Bloomington: Indiana University Press, 1954), p. 8.

[3] Ernest Gellner, *Words and Things: A Critical Account of Linguistic Philosophy* (London: Victor Gollancz, 1959), p. 99.

[4] William Barrett, *Irrational Man: A Study in Existential Philosophy* (Garden City: Doubleday, Anchor Books, 1958), p. 57.

culiar kind of spiritual tragedy involved in "desacralization" entails merely a shuffling and reshuffling of fictive counters invented by the Christian apologist for the sake of bullying his secular brethren into submission. This would, of course, be a misapprehension that has long since been undermined by the psychologists who deal in "the crisis of identity" and the sociologists who specialize in "alienation" and the "mass-man." But, to say nothing of these dreary reports, we have only to recall some of the representative heroes and anti-heroes in the literature of the last forty or fifty years—Eliot's Prufrock, Kafka's Gregor Samsa (*Metamorphosis*), Graham Greene's Minty (*England Made Me*), Sartre's Roquentin (*Nausea*), Arthur Miller's Willy Loman (*Death of a Salesman*), Camus' Meursault (*The Stranger*)—we have only to recall such modern personages as these to be put in mind of a certain denudation and a certain death that the human spirit itself seems to have suffered as a result of having ousted itself from the precincts of sacral reality.

But however much the desacralized universe of modern secularity may be a universe without thresholds, the world that is at man's disposal is not in truth merely

> A heap of broken images, where the sun beats
> And the dead tree gives no shelter, the cricket no relief,
> And the dry stone no sound of water. . . .[5]

It is, rather, a universe that asks us to be "radically amazed" at "the silent allusion of [all] things to a meaning greater than themselves."[6] For the world is not simply *what it is*; on the contrary, it is filled with "the miracles which are daily with us," and these are not matters of the sensational and the magnificent—like volcanic eruptions or uncommon psychic phenomena—but of the ordinary and the

[5] T. S. Eliot, *The Waste Land*, in *Collected Poems of T. S. Eliot: 1909–1935* (New York: Harcourt, Brace, 1936), pp. 69–70.

[6] Abraham J. Heschel, *Between God and Man*, edited by Fritz A. Rothschild (New York: Harper & Row, 1959), p. 38.

commonplace, in that dimension of their depth which forever eludes all our categories and *withstands* exhaustive analysis. A modern philosopher may smugly say, in effect, "The world is what it is," but the more truly human attitude is surely that of astonishment that there is a world at all and that its processes and functioning are governed by the regularities which science studies. Indeed, scientific research itself, as Abraham Heschel reminds us, is only "an entry into the endless, not a blind alley. . . . One answer breeds a multitude of new questions. . . . Everything hints at something that transcends it. . . . What appears to be a center is but a point on the periphery of another center."[7] The ineffable dwells not merely in the grandiose and the remarkable but in every nook and cranny of our experience—in the rain's satisfying the desolation of the earth and the mysteries of vegetation, in the beauty of holiness and the radiance of true sagacity, in all the bounties of nature and civilization and in all the blessings and defeats of life.

Nor is the essential dignity of the world fully honored apart from the attitude of "radical amazement" before its amplitude and mystery and sublimity. Indeed, perhaps the surest sign of what Professor Eliade calls "desacralization" is the habit of *taking things for granted,* the habit of indifference to what is most primitively marvelous in man himself and in the world which constitutes the theatre of his living. True wonder is not an indolent complacency or state of content with ignorance: it is not an indifference toward creative research and rational analysis, nor is it a reverencing of the *unknown.* For *mystery* is not the unknown but, rather, that surplusage of meaning in what is known, that inexhaustible Ground of reality by which we are moved when we perform an act of true attention before the creatures of the earth. Thus it is not something that arises out of the perceptual process itself; *mystery* is not, in other words, a name for a merely subjective reality. It is, rather, an ontological category, for it speaks not of anything foisted upon the world by the human imagination but of "a most powerful

[7] *Ibid.,* p. 46.

presence beyond the mind" which makes for "a fundamental norm of human consciousness."[8] It is not something which we infer from a psychological reaction but rather that to which the *sense* of mystery, of wonder, of amazement, is a response.

> We do not come upon it only at the climax of thinking or in observing strange, extraordinary facts, but in the startling fact that there are facts at all. . . . We may face it at every turn, in a grain of seed, in an atom, as well as in the stellar space. Everything holds the great secret. For it is the inescapable situation of all being to be involved in the infinite mystery. We may continue to disregard the mystery, but we can neither deny nor escape it. The world is something *we apprehend but cannot comprehend.*[9]

As Paul Tillich said in one of his finest sermons, ". . . you cannot think or say: Life has no depth! Life is shallow. Being itself is surface only."[10] And the human reality cannot legitimately be either thought or said to be merely an affair of surface and without depth, because it is never anything, if profoundly experienced, that can, as it were, be "seen through." The deep things of self-knowledge and love, of suffering and joy and holiness do always, finally, resist exhaustive analysis, and thus they offer a kind of attestation to the environing Mystery which is ineradicably a part of our human life-world.

So, insofar as it is the distinctive privilege and vocation of humankind to retain a sense of wonder before the "miracles which are daily with us"—insofar is man indeed a creature "trailing clouds of glory," for he is "isled" in an atmosphere effulgent of mystery and wonder, and glory. For him to have lost any lively awareness of this fact is for him to have "fallen" into the profane: for this is what "desacralization" most deeply entails—not merely the deadening ossification of the creedal

[8] *Ibid.,* p. 54.
[9] *Ibid.,* p. 45.
[10] Paul Tillich, *The Shaking of the Foundations* (New York: Charles Scribner's Sons, 1948), p. 57.

formularies of the great received traditions of religious orthodoxy but the death of all awareness of any animating power or
presence amid and within the familiar realities of nature and
history, the loss of any radical amazement before the rich
complexity and plentitude of the world. Thus it is that perhaps
the extremest heresy which the human spirit can embrace is
that which has, as it were, been codified by modern positivism,
of supposing that man's only transaction is with those things
which can be weighed and measured and handled in a calcu-
lating and deliberate way.

Indeed, it is just the inclination of the men and women of
our age toward this most impertinent of all heresies that has
sometimes awakened in the modern writer a kind of rage and
led him to make his writing itself an act of violence. And in
Léon Bloy, Charles Péguy and the early T. S. Eliot, in Georges
Bernanos and Graham Greene (to mention only a few), we
encounter a line of artists who confront the profanization of
life in the modern world by saying in one way or another, and
with a violent kind of urgency and harshness, *"J'accuse!"*

Now it is as a part of this tradition that we ought, I
believe, to understand the legacy of that remarkably valiant
and gifted young American, Flannery O'Connor, who departed
this life at her home in Milledgeville, Georgia, in the summer
of 1964, after a long and painful illness. The cruel fate which
struck her down before her fortieth birthday kept her, unfortunately, from producing a large body of work. But in her two
novels—*Wise Blood* (1952) and *The Violent Bear It Away*
(1960)—and her two collections of stories, *A Good Man Is
Hard to Find* (1955) and *Everything That Rises Must Con-
verge* (1965), she leaves a body of work which is to be
counted among the finest fiction produced anywhere by her
literary generation. What makes it in part so notable are the
radical kinds of moral judgment into the service of which she
was so intent on putting her art. It was indeed always an art
that very much wanted to wake the spirit's sleep, to break that
somnolence into which we flee from the exactions of the moral

life; and it consistently expresses a fierce kind of rage at the feckless, lack-lustre slum to which the human world is reduced when, through indolence of spirit or failure of imagination, men have lost all sense of the pressure of glory upon the mundane realities of experience and have thus "fallen" into the profane. It was, one feels, in just such a velleity as this that Flannery O'Connor found what she took to be most characteristically defective in the life of our time: for her, the major sickness of the age was something like what medieval doctors of the soul called *acedia*, and it is to this condition that her art is principally responding.

This is a response, however, which is not merely negative in its thrust. It has, of course, its negative side, and a part of what is most vivacious and cogent in Miss O'Connor's fiction is an affair of her genius for polemical engagement and for a stinging critique of the sterile banality of life-style that is bred by modern secularity. But there is also another side of her response to the modern scene, and one which I am helped to identify by a remark of the late C. S. Lewis about the English fantasist, George Macdonald. Recalling the impact that Macdonald's *Plantastes* had had upon him, when he first chanced to read it in his youth, he said: "It did nothing to my intellect nor (at that time) to my conscience. Their turn came far later and with the help of many other books and men. . . . What it actually did to me was to convert, even to baptize . . . my imagination."[11] Something like this may also be what Miss O'Connor was aiming at in part. She had, in other words, a constructive purpose as well as a negative purpose: she wanted not only to exhibit what is banal and trivializing in the desacralized world of modern unbelief but also to portray its vacuity in such a way as to stir the imagination into some fresh

[11] C. S. Lewis, *George Macdonald: An Anthology* (New York: Macmillan, 1947), p. 21. My attention has been called to this passage by my student, Gunnar Urang, who, in a dissertation-in-progress at the University of Chicago, finds C. S. Lewis' fiction to represent an attempt to "baptize" the modern imagination.

awareness of what has been lost—and thus to "baptize" it, to render it open and responsive once more to the dimension of the Sacred and the pressure of glory.

The negative and critical side of this stratagem is everywhere a part of Miss O'Connor's writing, but perhaps at no point can it be felt with such force as in her novel of 1960, *The Violent Bear It Away*. Francis Marion Tarwater is a fourteen-year-old boy who has been reared in the backwoods of Georgia by a great-uncle, Mason Tarwater, whose violent bibliolatry has determined him to raise up the boy "to justify his Redemption." The two lessons which the old man has year-in and year-out enjoined upon his nephew are the necessity of giving him a decent burial when he dies and his obligation somehow to do what he himself has never been able to manage, the baptizing of the idiot child of young Tarwater's uncle, Rayber, who lives in a neighboring city where he practices his profession of psychologist as a school official. At last, one morning the old man does die: as he sits down to his breakfast, "red ropes appear in his face," a tremor passes over him, his mouth twists down sharply on one side, and he is dead, but remaining "perfectly balanced, his back a good six inches from the chair back and his stomach caught just under the edge of the table, . . . [h]is eyes, dead silver, . . . focussed on the boy across from him!"

But young Tarwater does not now proceed properly to inter the body: the morning heat is oppressive, and, after taking a few too many swigs of the old man's liquor, instead of digging a grave, he simply sets fire to the shack, with the body still inside. Then he leaves the little isolated strip of corn patch where they have lived together for so long and goes off to the city to look up Rayber. But the old man cannot so easily be gotten away from, and the central *agon* of the novel grows out of the fierce competition between Old Tarwater (or his spiritual legacy) and Rayber for the boy's suffrage to their respective views of reality.

The boy himself had at first been a ward of Rayber's, but

had been kidnapped by Old Tarwater, lest the child become simply "a piece of information inside . . . [Rayber's] head." For at a still earlier time, many years before, the old man, while living with Rayber, had discovered that the schoolteacher's apparent interest in his vocation as a prophet of the Lord was something all faked and dishonest. At first Rayber had asked the old man "numerous questions, the answers to which he had sometimes scratched down on a pad, his little eyes lighting every now and then as if in some discovery." And Old Tarwater was by way of thinking that he was on the verge of converting his nephew—until he discovered that Rayber was making him the subject of magazine articles in which it was asserted that "[h]is fixation of being called by the Lord had its origin in insecurity." Then it was that the old man realized that "every living thing that passed through . . . [Rayber's] eyes into his head was turned by his brain into a book or a paper or a chart." "Where he wanted me was inside that schoolteacher magazine. He thought once he got me in there, I'd be as good as inside his head and done for and that would be that, that would be the end of it." It was, he felt, a blasphemy that was being committed against his person, and so he left Rayber's house. When, some years later, after young Tarwater's orphanage had necessitated his being taken over by his uncle, his great-uncle kidnapped him, bringing him to his little corn patch out in the country and thus rescuing him from what had very nearly been his own fate, of being simply a piece of information inside Rayber's head. "I saved you to be free, your own self!" he likes to shout at the boy—" . . . not a piece of information inside his head!" *And* Old Tarwater saves the boy in order that he might know that "Jesus is the bread of life."

The old man, having been "schooled in the evils that befall prophets"—"in those that come from the world, which are trifling, and those that come from the Lord and burn the prophet clean"—having been "schooled" in calamity and having been "called in his early youth," the old man is possessed by "a rage of vision," and his nerves have been made taut by his sense of the pressure of Glory: he is a man consecrated by his overpowering conviction that the true country of the soul is the Sacred. So, for all of his grotesque fantastications—his belief that the sun will one day "burst in blood and fire" and that "a finger of fire" will destroy the sinful human city—he has in himself the dignity of an absolute spiritual heroism.

But on Rayber the novel is merciless in venting a spleen whose malice is reserved for those who inhabit a world that is utterly desacralized. With all the heartless inhumanity of his psychological gadgetry—his charts and graphs and I.Q. tests—his is a "headpiece filled with straw." "He's full of nothing," says Old Tarwater—"taking secret tests on me . . . crawling into my soul through the back door and then . . . [saying] to me, 'Uncle, you're a type that's almost extinct!' " He is a hollow man, a man full of nothing because, as Old Tarwater says,

> He don't know it's anything he can't know, . . . That's his trouble. He thinks if it's something he can't know then some-body smarter than him can tell him about it and he can know it just the same. And if you were to go there, the first thing he would do would be to test your head and tell you what you were thinking and howcome you were thinking it and what you ought to be thinking instead. And before long you wouldn't belong to your self no more, you would belong to him.

A man full of nothing—who cannot look intently at anything, not even at "a stick or a stone, the line of a shadow, the absurd old man's walk of a starling crossing the sidewalk," for to permit himself fully to encounter any aspect of the world is for him to run the risk of being cross-questioned out of the unreality in which he lives. So he is frightened of love—not of "love in general," for he "knew the value of it and how it could be used," but of the kind that was "without reason, love for something futureless, love that appeared to exist only to be itself, imperious and all demanding, the kind that would cause him to make a fool of himself in an instant."

Old Tarwater had regarded Rayber's idiot son as "precious in the sight of the Lord," despite his incompetence—but, to the child's father, he is simply "a mistake of nature." And suspecting what is true, that, despite young Tarwater's asserted unbelief, the old man's "seed" has fallen into him and that he intends to try to baptize the child (as Old Tarwater himself had tried on several occasions to do, until finally he was run away from Rayber's house by the police), Rayber says to him, "You want to avoid extremes. They are for violent people . . ."

But Rayber's intuition about his nephew does indeed in the end prove to be right. For the old man's seed has fallen into young Tarwater, and he is quick to seize the first real chance that comes along to perform the duty laid upon him by his fanatical great-uncle. Rayber has taken the two, his little son and young Tarwater, out of the city to a lodge, a kind of motel, for a brief holiday, hoping that it will afford him some way of reaching his nephew and winning his confidence. But there it is that young Tarwater, after rowing the little boy out onto the bordering lake one afternoon, baptizes the child— and, in doing so, drowns him. From this point on, of course, he is a criminal and an outlaw, hunted and pursued; but it is in this extremity that he comes to realize that he does in truth belong to "that violent country where the silence is never broken except to shout the truth." He realizes, in other words, that the fire which encircles him is that which "had encircled Daniel, that had raised Elijah from the earth, that had spoken to Moses." He knows himself to bear an inescapable vocation to "WARN THE CHILDREN OF GOD OF THE TERRI-BLE SPEED OF MERCY": so he moves "steadily on, his face set toward the dark city, where the children of God lay sleeping."

Thus it is that we are put in mind of what St. Matthew's Gospel tells us, that "from the days of John the Baptist, the kingdom of heaven suffereth violence and the violent bear it away" (11:12). They, of course, by reason of their very violence, represent deformity and are misshapen: yet it is a humanly comprehensible deformity, and its passionateness in the things of the spirit can be, even if obliquely, a means of grace. But, as Dante says, those "paltry, who never were alive," who spend their substance "without infamy and without praise," are "of a truth . . . odious to God and to his enemies"; these are they who, having forsaken all the numinous "thresholds" of experience, are simply "full of nothing."

Of these *isolés* Rayber is an extreme instance in Flannery O'Connor's fiction. But there are many other acidulous portraits—particularly in the stories collected in *A Good Man Is Hard to Find*—of the reduction in human stature, of the sterility and dessication, that are brought by the disease of positivism, of supposing that life can simply be brought to heel and made to submit to management. This sterile rationalism is often, by some stroke of irony, doubled back upon its own essential incompetence (as in the Mrs. McIntyre of "The Displaced Person," or the Hulga Hopewell of "Good Country People," or the Sheppard of "The Lame Shall Enter First"). Indeed, wherever the poison of secularity attacks the mind, a terrible neutrality of spirit and dreariness of life sets in—as in the Ruby Hill of "A Stroke of Good Fortune," disgustedly fighting off knowledge of her own pregnancy with disgusted recollections from childhood of her mother's various pregnancies; or the drunken and neglectful parents of the hapless little boy of "The River" (in *A Good Man Is Hard to Find*) who live in a dreary little subway of the world and who provide an environment for their child's nurture in which there is the very stench of the profane, the very odor of damnation itself.

But, then, Miss O'Connor's art finds its poise not merely in horrified rejection of the dehumanizing wilderness that is created by radical secularity. For it is also a part of its purpose to "baptize" the modern imagination, to render the human story in such a way as to stretch the secular memory to the extremest possible limits, so that some awareness will be reawakened of how deep the deep places of human life really are, and of how insistently a transcendent dimension presses in upon the horizontal plane of existential reality. Her procedure here, however, does not involve any sort of direct presentation of the Christian evangel; it is, rather, something very subtly circuitous and dialectical. As she herself said, "When you can assume that your audience holds the same beliefs you do, you can relax a little and use more normal ways of talking to it; when you have to assume that it does not, then you have to make your vision apparent by shock—to the hard of hearing you shout, and for the almost blind you draw large and startling figures."[12]

But her "figures" are never of faith and sanctity, or at least they are so only rarely. For she felt that "writers who see by the light of their Christian faith will have, in these times," to run the risk of working with "the grotesque, . . . the perverse, and . . . the unacceptable": they "will find in modern life distortions which are repugnant to [them], and [their] problem will be to make these appear as distortions to an audience which is used to seeing them as natural; and [they] may well be forced to take ever more violent means to get [their] vision across to this hostile audience."[13]

This was in fact frequently the course that Miss O'Connor did herself take, and thus the figures that her fiction draws are not only large and startling, but, very often, they are figures of murderers and mountebanks, of rapists and gangsters and neurotic religious zealots, of the hopeless young and the desperate old. It might even be said that cheating and callousness and violence and the harming of the innocent and moral squalor are the bone and marrow of her art. Yet such a characterization of it would be acceptable, or partially so, only if it were also informed by the recognition that the ultimate law governing Flannery O'Connor's fiction is that of the *coincidentia op-*

[12] Flannery O'Connor, "The Fiction Writer and His Country," in *The Living Novel, a Symposium,* edited by Granville Hicks (New York: Collier Books, 1962—originally published by Macmillan in 1957), p. 163.
[13] *Ibid.,* pp. 162–63.

positorum. For what she seems to have felt is that, since the great pieties of Christian belief are not normally characteristic of our culture, they cannot therefore become the subject matter of an authentic contemporary art. But, if the human material of a truly contemporary literature has to be secular, then let it be radically secular, since negation, if it be profound enough, may itself, by reason of its very radicalism, begin to evoke sensibilities capable of a religious perception of reality—and thus the opposites will coincide, at the heart of darkness.

So it was, one suspects, the hope of achieving something like a *coincidentia oppositorum* that led Miss O'Connor to people her books with so many monsters of nihilism and blasphemy: it is by such a dialectical route as this, she seems to have felt, that the Christian writer stands his best chance of baptizing the secular imagination of our time.

Of this whole stratagem, it is undoubtedly her first novel, *Wise Blood* (1952), that affords the finest example. Its protagonist, Hazel Motes, is a young self-ordained evangelist of an hysterical nihilism, who comes out of the backwoods of Tennessee, proclaiming the gospel of "no truth behind all truths," that "nothing matters but that Jesus was a liar": his church is the "Church Without Christ." Hazel's home, originally, was a little Tennessee hamlet called Eastrod, and there it was, as a boy of twelve (the age at which Jesus announced that he had to be about his Father's business), that he first felt a vocation to preach, partly no doubt as a result of the impact upon him of his grandfather who was an itinerant evangelist—"a waspish old man who had ridden over three counties with Jesus hidden in his head like a stinger." But then came the Second World War and the requirement for Haze of military service, which he took to be simply a "trick to lead him into temptation"; and so, in a way, it was, for it was amid the dislocations of army life that "he had all the time he could want to study his soul in"—and, studying it, he found "it was not there," that fornication and blasphemy and sin "ain't nothing but words," that

"Jesus is a trick on niggers," and that "there was no Fall because there was nothing to fall from and no Redemption because there was no Fall and no Judgment because there wasn't the first two."

After he is mustered out of the army, Haze returns to Eastrod, but there had originally been no more than about twenty-five inhabitants of the place, and, now, all are gone, his family house deserted, with weeds growing through the porch floor. He decides not to stay, but to go on to the city of Taulkinham, which is to be the scene and site of his curiously inverted evangelism in behalf of what is now for him the great truth, that there is no truth behind all truths. There, in the downtown streets, he mounts his old rat-colored Essex car to preach the Church Without Christ: "I'm member and preacher to that church where the blind don't see and the lame don't walk and what's dead stays that way. . . . it's the church that the blood of Jesus don't foul with redemption." But, despite its passionateness, his preaching elicits little more than a hunch of the shoulder from his bemused and perfunctory auditors: "He's a preacher," says a woman one night to her companions. "Let's go."

Nor is the response that comes from the one person in whom he does strike a spark the sort that brings him any satisfaction. Little Enoch Emery encounters Haze soon after the young preacher comes to Taulkinham. He once attended, as he says, "thisyer Rodemill Boys' Bible Academy that a woman sent me to. If it's anything you want to know about Jesus, just ast me." But, formed as he has been by the fossilized banalities of a bankrupt fundamentalism, he is really unprepared to reckon with what is genuinely radical in Haze's testimony. So when he hears Haze inviting his streetcorner congregation one night to show him a "new jesus," in order that this "jesus" might be set up in the Church Without Christ and that they might thereby be given proof that they haven't been redeemed—when Enoch hears this, his wise blood "confers with itself," and he decides to steal (and does steal) from the municipal museum a little shrunken mummy that has long fascinated him, offering it to Haze as a "new jesus." But Haze had been speaking ironically that night, and his nihilism does not in literal truth have any use at all for a "new jesus," for he wants nothing to shield him, or others, from the blank emptiness that he has seen beyond the world's horizon. As he says, "There's no such thing as any new jesus. That ain't anything but a way to say something."

Indeed, Haze wants nothing that will adjust him "O.K. to the modern world," neither any orthodoxy of belief nor any new codification of heterodoxy. Nor does he allow himself to be distracted by the claims of sensuality. He has, it is true, affairs with two women, first with the blowzy prostitute, Mrs. Leora Watts, and then with Sabbath Lily Hawks, the serpentine daughter of a street-preacher. But, in each case, he makes us feel that he takes the woman "not for the sake of the pleasure in her, but to prove that he didn't believe in sin since he practiced what was called it."

Sensuality, in other words, were it to be enjoyed and reveled in for its own sake, would mock the truth—the truth that there is no truth behind all truths, that there is nothing in reality that can be depended upon either to sanction or to comfort the human spirit. And just as surely would that truth be mocked, Haze feels, were its proclamation in any way to be commercialized. So he is infuriated when Hoover Shoats, an oily confidence man who calls himself Onnie Jay Holy, proposes that they form a business alliance. Shoats used to be on the radio, with a program of "Mood, Melody, and Mentality" called "Souls-ease" that gave "real religious experiences to the whole family." He has a great gift for salesmanship and knows a good racket when he finds one: so when he happens on Haze preaching one night and hears the talk about a "new jesus," he is immediately thrilled by his sense of the possibilities: "I never heard a idear before that had more in it than that one. All it would need," he tells Haze, "is a little promotion." But Haze is repelled by the sliminess of the little grafter and will have nothing to do with him—whereupon Shoats promises to run him "out of business." The next night he appears on Haze's corner, with a man strikingly like Haze in appearance who wears the same "glare-blue" suit and white hat, a consumptive named Solace Layfield. Shoats gathers the crowd around and takes up a collection after Layfield concludes the same sort of harangue Haze has been nightly delivering, from atop a high rat-colored car identical with Haze's old machine. Haze watches the whole episode, and, afterwards, follows Layfield on his way home and runs him down with his automobile (which is in truth, as Caroline Gordon reminds us, his pulpit[14]). And the judgment he flings at the dying man is short and blunt—"You ain't true."

But Layfield's untruth is of a piece with what Haze everywhere encounters, whether it be that of Enoch or Hoover Shoats or Asa Hawks (who, though an unbeliever, preaches Christ, simply as a small business operation), or the indifferent strangers who glare at him atop his Essex and dismiss him with the epithet "wise guy" or "rabble rouser." All these may be instanced finally in the policeman who, in an act of gratuitous malevolence, pushes his Essex over an embankment and thereby destroys his "pulpit."

Once his car is gone, Haze is, it seems, utterly undone, and, having faced the agnosticism and unconcern and mendacity of the world, there is nothing left for him to do but to destroy his capacity to see anything more. So he does what Asa Hawks had years before only pretended to do: he blinds himself with quicklime. Thereafter—to the bafflement of his landlady, Mrs. Flood, who, carefully remarking his harmless oddity and his government pension, had decided to marry him—he submits himself to the sternest mortifications, lining his shoes with rocks and broken glass, wearing barbed wire underneath his shirt, eating only enough just barely to prevent starvation. At last, after wandering one night for hours in a driving icy

[14] Caroline Gordon. "Flannery O'Connor's *Wise Blood*," *Critique,* II (Fall, 1958), 6.

rain, he is discovered two days later by two young policemen cruising in a squad car who find him "lying in a drainage ditch near an abandoned construction project." "I want to go on where I'm going," he tells them in a hoarse whisper. And one of the officers—saying, "We don't want to have no trouble with him"—hits him over the head with his new billy. Haze dies a few minutes later in the squad car.

So, first his automobile—or his pulpit—being destroyed and then his very life being taken by deputies of the World, the last state of the Enemy of God, in being itself a kind of crucifixion, puts us in mind of what we may all along have neglected to notice, namely, of how much the forms of his denial have had to be precisely those whose unreality he has wanted so strongly to assert. Thus there begins to come into view what may be the possibility of an ultimate *coincidentia oppositorum*. (In this connection, it is significant that, at the very last, as Mrs. Flood looks down upon Haze's dead body, it occurs to her, in a moment of sudden clarity, that this man who had moved so far and so deep into darkness had himself become a "pin point of light.")

"It is all very neatly worked out," says Jonathan Baumbach in his essay on the novel, and he finds "this very neatness . . . [to be] the besetting limitation of Miss O'Connor's fictional world."[15] But neatness is surely a most shockingly incongruous term to use for the description of these brilliantly outrageous fables. For their special sort of bounce and rhythm is in large part an affair of the remarkable autonomy which Miss O'Connor allowed the creatures of her imagination and which is always by way of enabling these freaks and grotesques very nearly to get out of hand altogether and to slip outside the framing structures of the fictions. But the stability of the structures is finally maintained, and it is just the resistance that her characters offer to these structures which provides something

[15] Jonathan Baumbach, *The Landscape of Nightmare: Studies in the Contemporary American Novel* (New York: New York University Press, 1965), p. 99.

of a measure of how superbly gifted was Flannery O'Connor's controlling hand. Her stories are often *almost* at the point of becoming a ghastly kind of comic strip, but they never quite become so, and the audacious funambulism with which this tightrope is negotiated is a fascinating thing to watch.

Hers was, to be sure, an art that found its chief materials in the eccentric and the deformed, and in the remote backwaters of the Southern Bible Belt. But, like the Hardy of the Wessex novels and the Faulkner of the Yoknapatawpha country, she knew how to turn the very remoteness of her scene to advantage: and, however *outré* may be the crankiness of her *dramatis personae*, if we look hard enough, we can find in the very crookedness of their aberrancy what she called "the lines that create spiritual motion."

Finally, I cannot resist remarking, however irrelevantly, the charming bit of testimony which comes from one of her friends, that it was her habit invariably to end her letters with the word "Cheers"—which may just remind us that what is not least remarkable, in this late and difficult time, is that hers is a body of fiction made rich and radiant by a Christian presence whose wit and brilliance and (notwithstanding all the Gothic furniture) whose cheerfulness we are only now at last beginning to discern.

Bibliographical Notes and Acknowledgments

"Dostoievski: The Costs of Unbelief in the Major Fiction" was first published (as "Dostoievski—Tragedian of the Modern Excursion into Unbelief") in *The Tragic Vision and the Christian Faith*, ed. by Nathan A. Scott, Jr. (New York: Association Press, 1957). Its first published form has here been somewhat revised.

"Hardy and the Victorian *Malaise*" was first published (as "The Literary Imagination and the Victorian Crisis of Faith: The Example of Thomas Hardy") in *The Journal of Religion* (Vol. XL, No. 4: October, 1960). The original essay has here been altered in small ways.

"Kafka's Anguish" was first published in *Forms of Extremity in the Modern Novel*, ed. by Nathan A. Scott, Jr. (Richmond: John Knox Press, 1965).

"The Modest Optimism of Albert Camus" entails the major part of a small book, *Albert Camus*, published in England in 1962 by Bowes & Bowes Ltd. (London) and imported to the United States by Hillary House of New York; and this book was based on an essay bearing the title of this present version which first appeared in *The Christian Scholar* (Vol. XLII, No. 4: December, 1959).

"Beckett's Journey into the Zone of Zero" was first published (as "The Recent Journey into the Zone of Zero: The Example of Beckett and His Despair of Literature") in *The Centennial Review*

(Vol. VI, No. 2: Spring, 1962). The original version has here been somewhat revised.

"Graham Greene: Christian Tragedian" first appeared in *The Volusia Review* (Vol. I, No. 1: 1954), a journal published at Bethune-Cookman College in Florida whose first number was its last. The original essay was published, in revised form, in *Graham Greene: Some Critical Considerations*, ed. by Robert O. Evans (Lexington: University of Kentucky Press, 1963). And the present version, now revised again and substantially enlarged, incorporates materials from a review of Mr. Greene's *The Quiet American* which appeared in *The Christian Century* (Vol. LXXIII, No. 31: 1 August 1956).

"*Sola Gratia*—The Principle of Bellow's Fiction" was first prepared for publication in *Adversity and Grace: Studies in Recent American Literature*, ed. by Nathan A. Scott, Jr. (Chicago: University of Chicago Press, 1968).

"Flannery O'Connor's Testimony: The Pressure of Glory" was first published in *The Added Dimension: The Art and Mind of Flannery O'Connor*, ed. by Melvin J. Friedman and Lewis A. Lawson (New York: Fordham University Press, 1966).

Harcourt, Brace has generously permitted me to quote from T. S. Eliot's *Murder in the Cathedral*; and Random House has kindly permitted me to quote from Robert Penn Warren's *Brother to Dragons* and W. H. Auden's *New Year Letter*.

My thanks are herewith tendered to these editors and publishers for their original hospitality and for the permissions which they have kindly given for the republication of these materials in this book.

I am also grateful to my typist, Mrs. Sonya Illianova, for the cheerfulness and great care with which she prepared the manuscript.